European Yearbook of International Economic Law

EYIEL Monographs - Studies in European and International Economic Law

Volume 48

The European Yearbook of International Economic Law (EYIEL) is a Springer-publication in the field of International Economic Law (IEL), a field increasingly emancipating itself from Public International Law scholarship and evolving into a fully-fledged academic discipline in its own right. With the yearbook, editors and publisher make a significant contribution to the development of this "new" discipline and provide an international source of reference of the highest possible quality.

The EYIEL covers all areas of IEL, in particular WTO Law, External Trade Law of major trading countries, important Regional Economic Integration agreements, International Competition Law, International Investment Regulation, International Monetary Law, International Intellectual Property Protection and International Tax Law.

EYIEL publishes articles following a substantive review by the editors and external experts as appropriate.

The editors have published extensively in the field of IEL and European Law alike. They are supported by an international Advisory Board consisting of established scholars of the highest reputation.

EYIEL Monographs is a subseries of the European Yearbook of International Economic Law (EYIEL). It contains scholarly works in the fields of European and international economic law, in particular WTO law, international investment law, international monetary law, law of regional economic integration, external trade law of the EU and EU internal market law. The series does not include edited volumes. EYIEL Monographs are peer-reviewed by the series editors and external reviewers.

Foster Maluleke

Compliance with Decent Work Standards by Multinational Enterprises

Springer

Foster Maluleke
CCMA National Office
Commission for Conciliation, Mediation and Arbitration (CCMA)
Johannesburg, South Africa

ISSN 2364-8392 ISSN 2364-8406 (electronic)
European Yearbook of International Economic Law
ISSN 2524-6658 ISSN 2524-6666 (electronic)
EYIEL Monographs - Studies in European and International Economic Law
ISBN 978-3-032-21260-3 ISBN 978-3-032-21261-0 (eBook)
https://doi.org/10.1007/978-3-032-21261-0

This Springer imprint is published by the registered company Springer Nature Switzerland AG
The registered company address is: Gewerbestrasse 11, 6330 Cham, Switzerland

Acknowledgements

This monograph focuses on finding ways to ensure that multinational enterprises comply with internationally recognised human and labour rights throughout their global supply chains. It is based on research conducted during my doctoral studies at the University of Pretoria from 2021 to 2024. My initial motivation for this research arose from my concern about the poor working conditions faced by employees involved in the production of goods for powerful multinational enterprises. My supervisor, Professor Stefan van Eck, is dedicated to improving the situation of precarious workers and provided valuable insights into the connection between human and labour rights, decent work, and sustainable development.

I extend my heartfelt gratitude to Professor Emeritus Manfred Weiss from Goethe University in Frankfurt for the constructive discussions that shaped my approach to this study. I am especially indebted to Professor Beryl ter Haar, the Director of the Centre for International and European Labour Law Studies, for our insightful conversations. Additionally, I am grateful to my colleagues at the Commission for Conciliation, Mediation and Arbitration for their support.

The unwavering support of my family has been essential in my efforts to complete this monograph. I am deeply grateful to my mother, Mrs. Florah Maluleke, and my wife, Thandeka Maluleke; their constant love and encouragement sustained me throughout my four years of research. I also sincerely appreciate the support of my daughters, Ntsumi and Ntsako.

Competing Interests The author has no competing interests to declare that are relevant to the content of this manuscript.

Contents

List of Abbreviations

AJLP	Australian Journal of Legal Philosophy
AU	African Union
AUILR	American University International Law Review
BJIL	Brazilian Journal of International Law
BJIL	Brooklyn Journal of International Law
BJWA	Brown Journal of World Affairs
CAS	Committee on the Application of Standards
CEACR	Committee of Experts on the Application of Conventions and Recommendations
CGD	Center for Global Development
CHRLR	Columbia Human Rights Law Review
CJE	Cambridge Journal of Economics
CULR	Capital University Law Review
DLR	Deakin Law Review
ECCJ	European Coalition for Corporate Justice
ECHR	European Convention on Human Rights
ECHR	European Court of Human Rights
ELLJ	European Labour Law Journal
ELR	Erasmus Law Review
EREPJ	Employee Rights and Employment Policy Journal
ESU	European Scientific Journal
EU	European Union
FDI	Foreign Direct Investment
GJIL	Georgetown Journal of International Law
HRJ	Human Rights Journal
HHRJ	Harvard Human Rights Journal
HRPLJ	Hastings Race and Poverty Law Journal
ICCPR	International Covenant on Civil and Political Rights
ICESCR	International Covenant on Economic, Social and Cultural Rights
IHRLR	Intercultural Human Rights Law Review
IJGLS	Indian Journal of Global Legal Studies

IJLR	International Journal of Labour Research
IJPAI	International Journal of Policy, Administration and Institutions
ILC	International Labour Conference
ILO	International Labour Organization
ILR	International Labour Review
JHD	Journal for Human Development
JWR	Journal of Workplace Rights
JWTO&C	Journal of World Trade Organisation and China
LCLR	Lewis & Clark Law Review
LLJ	Law Library Journal
MDGs	Millennium Development Goals
MJIL	Miskolc Journal of International Law
MNE	Multinational enterprise
NPC	National Contact Point
NPO	Non-profit organisation
OECD	Organisation for Economic Co-operation and Development
PELJ/PER	Potchefstroom Electronic Law – Journal/Potchefstroomse Elektroniese Regsblad
R&J	Regulation & Governance
RFTA	Regional Free Trade Agreement
SADC	Southern African Development Community
SDGs	Sustainable Development Goals
UCILR	University of California Irvine Law Review
UCLAJIL	University of California Los Angeles Journal of International Law
UDHR	Universal Declaration of Human Rights
UDMLR	University of Detroit Mercy Law Review
UMICR	University of Miami International and Comparative Law Review
UN	United Nations
USA	United States of America
WCGS	Wittenberg Centre for Global Studies
WTO	World Trade Organization
YHDLJ	Yale Human Rights & Development Law Journal

Chapter 1
Introduction and Background

1.1 Introduction

In recent decades, the conventional framework of labour regulation, once primarily based on strict government enforcement, has undergone a profound transformation. This evolution has given rise to a dynamic global labour governance system that reflects the complexities of today's world.[1] Historically, international labour law concentrated on the responsibilities outlined by the International Labour Organisation (ILO) for its member states, effectively confining discussions about labour standards violations to the actions of individual governments.[2]

However, the landscape has shifted dramatically with the increasing prevalence of cross-border transactions involving a diverse array of non-state actors, including international organisations, non-governmental organisations (NGOs), and multinational enterprises (MNEs).[3] As a result of globalisation, MNEs have grown in both number and complexity. Added to this, they have moved production to countries with less regulatory burdens and low wages to lower their labour costs and gain a comparative advantage over their competitors.[4] This creates a race to the bottom for labour conditions, where poor countries try to attract MNEs by providing the weakest labour protections and the least amount of regulation and oversight.[5]

Lyutov argues that 'because of their immense scale and the financial resources at their disposal, MNEs have been able to confront governments ... and such created a

[1] Hassel (2008), p. 231.

[2] Son (2013), p. 23.

[3] Son (2013), p. 23.

[4] Payne (2017), p. 597.

[5] Payne (2017), p. 597. Collingsworth (2002), p. 183, states that human and labour rights have been purposefully ignored to make it easier for MNEs to maximise profits.

F. Maluleke, *Compliance with Decent Work Standards by Multinational Enterprises*, European Yearbook of International Economic Law 48,
https://doi.org/10.1007/978-3-032-21261-0_1

governance gap'.[6] Additionally, MNEs cannot attain membership in the ILO, and therefore, they are not subject to international scrutiny.[7] In this context, Ruggie summarised the challenge by stating that 'MNEs barely exist under international law'.[8] He argues that there is currently no central regulatory body at the global level, and the national laws in the countries where MNEs operate may be weak, poorly enforced, or even non-existent.[9] The international community has responded to the challenges posed by MNEs by adopting MNE codes of conduct that outline human and labour rights, as well as procedures for addressing complaints in cases of violations.

This contribution argues that, despite significant progress in promoting human and labour rights through various multistakeholder initiatives, substantial challenges remain in providing remedies for employees who experience human and labour rights violations by MNEs. This study contends that, without a credible dispute resolution institution offering binding procedures and remedies for victims, these codes of conduct risk becoming little more than hollow statements. This book advocates for the establishment of an effective dispute resolution mechanism under the supervision of the ILO.

1.2 Research Questions and Aims

Considering the challenges outlined above, this book seeks to answer the following research questions:

This book will explore whether labour rights should be categorised as human rights and how such a classification could impact the precarious circumstances of workers employed in the global supply chains of MNEs. The study will assess the role of the ILO in ensuring that MNEs contribute to the pursuit of decent work. It will also evaluate the effectiveness of the ILO's complaint-handling mechanisms regarding violations of human and labour rights by MNEs.

---

[6] Lyutov (2017), p. 32. See also Ratner (2001), p. 463, who argues that as companies have become more international, they have also become increasingly independent of government oversight. Sharma (2018), p. 20, suggests that 'human rights treaties and instruments, along with local legal systems, should be enough to regulate business activity'. But the real situation is that MNEs can effectively escape from both international and national legislation. That is so because international human rights treaties were created to be applied mainly to states and, consequently, the subsequent legal development of those instruments was mainly made neglecting MNEs as legal actors.

[7] Kamminga (2005), p. 2. Paper presented at the 71st Conference of the International Law Association, plenary session on Corporate Social Responsibility and International Law, Berlin, 17 August 2004. Ruggie (2013), p. 320, argues that 'MNEs barely exist under international law'.

[8] Ruggie (2013), p. 320.

[9] Ruggie (2013), p. 317. See also Amao (2011), p. 35, who states that 'MNEs operate in a vacuum between ineffective national laws and non-existent or unenforceable international law'. Maryanov (2000), p. 401, argues that the rapid growth of the global marketplace has outpaced the instruments of governance, allowing corporations to profit in the interim from unregulated and cheap labour.

Additionally, this study will examine the effectiveness of the dispute resolution mechanisms provided by the Organisation for Economic Co-operation and Development (OECD) and NGOs related to complaints of human and labour rights violations against MNEs. Furthermore, it will explore the role of International Framework Agreements (IFAs) in holding MNEs accountable for human rights and labour rights violations within their global supply chains.

1.3 Significance of the Study

Employees who believe that their human and labour rights have been infringed by MNEs, their suppliers, or subcontractors have several options to enforce their rights and seek remedies. They can utilise dispute resolution procedures available in their own country's legal system, file civil claims in local courts, or consider the procedures offered in the home country of the MNE. Additionally, they may also rely on soft law instruments to address their concerns. The sections below discuss the said dispute resolution procedures.

1.3.1 Dispute Resolution Procedures Within Host States of MNEs

It is submitted that employees whose human and labour rights are being violated by MNEs should, in the first instance, explore remedies catered for in their national jurisdictions.[10] Such procedures are usually designed to provide expeditious and less costly dispute resolution mechanisms.[11] Newaj argues that modern labour relations no longer envisage procedures that imitate criminal trials, which are technical and complex.[12] She argues that the labour relations procedures should not be bound by the same strict rules as criminal and civil cases.

Commenting on the right of parties to have legal representation at the Commission for Conciliation Mediation and Arbitration (CCMA) in South Africa, Van Eck and Kuhn argue that since the inception of the CCMA in 1995, 'the architects of the LRA, have adopted the policy decision to limit the role of legal practitioners during conciliation and arbitration proceedings'. They share that:

---

[10] In South Africa, the employees may approach the Commission for Conciliation, Mediation and Arbitration. Their dispute will be conciliated and if unresolved, they may request for arbitration. www.ccma.org.za.

[11] Grogan (2017), p. 7. See also Section 138(1) of the Labour Relations Act 66 of 1995 which provides that 'the labour relations disputes must be determined fairly and quickly, and the substantial merits of the dispute must be dealt with, with the minimum of legal formalities and mainly without legal representation'.

[12] Newaj (2019), p. 641.

> Lawyers make the process legalistic and expensive. They are also often responsible for delaying the proceedings due to their unavailability and the approach they adopt. Allowing legal representation places individual employees and small businesses at a disadvantage because of the cost.[13]

However, this system has largely failed to ensure that MNEs adhere to internationally recognised human and labour rights. This is primarily because MNEs operate in multiple jurisdictions and are only obligated to follow the national laws of the countries in which they operate. In other words, MNEs cannot be held accountable for not complying with international standards unless those standards have been ratified by the respective state where they conduct their business.[14]

Apart from lodging cases in tailor-made labour tribunals and courts, employees also have the option of litigation in a country's civil courts. In South Africa, however, litigation against MNEs in civil courts is rarely pursued due to the high costs and complexities involved in the court procedures. It is argued that the civil court system is unsuitable for resolving labour disputes. A notable example is the case of *Nkala and Others v Harmony Gold Mining Company Limited and Others*[15] in which the South Gauteng High Court was asked to determine whether workers, including former employees, had the right to file a class action seeking damages against the defendant mining MNEs for alleged negligence resulting from exposure to dust, which resulted in tuberculosis and silicosis.[16]

The defendants were, amongst others, large MNEs from around the globe: MNEs such as Anglo American, Anglo Gold, Gold Fields, and African Rainbow Minerals were involved. In an apparent victory, the High Court ruled that the employees were entitled to lodge such an application.[17] The next enquiry was for the court to determine the main issue, namely, whether the defendants were liable for the damages due to negligence. To complicate the matter further, the defendant MNEs appealed against the finding of the High Court but later withdrew it. The parties thereafter reached a settlement agreement, which resulted in a R5 billion compensation fund award for gold miners afflicted with Silicosis and TB.

The resolution ultimately favoured the employees. Nonetheless, the case highlights the difficulties that employees face due to the technical delays of the procedures. In addition to the above, the employees were fortunate to have legal representation, made possible only through 'pro bono' services. It is imperative to

---

[13] Van Eck and Kuhn (2019), p. 721.

[14] For example, the South African government only promulgated the National Minimum Wage Act in 2019. Prior to its promulgation, MNEs would pay salaries that they themselves deemed fit, despite being aware that international laws required employees to be paid minimum wages. Even after the minimum wage was set, the MNEs will only be held to be in violation if they fail to pay the bare minimum.

[15] 2016 (7) *BCLR* 881 (GJ).

[16] The applicants in the proceedings represented up to 500 000 workers (including former mine workers) and their dependents. Some of the applicants were silicosis patients and some were TB patients.

[17] At para 15.

establish expedited and cost-effective procedures to aid employees lacking financial resources. Such procedures should allow employees to lodge complaints of violation of human and labour rights against MNEs.

1.3.2 Dispute Resolution Procedures at the Home State of the MNE

Employees who experience violations of human and labour rights by MNEs have the option to pursue legal claims in the courts of the MNEs' home countries. However, these legal avenues are seldom pursued in practice, often due to the complexities associated with the issues at hand. In some cases, such legal action may be necessary when certain claim procedures or remedies are not accessible in the host countries where the MNEs operate. Additionally, employees who wish to sue MNEs in their home countries may need to demonstrate that they have referred their case to a more appropriate forum. Failure to provide this evidence could lead to the dismissal of their claims.

The case of *Lubbe v Cape plc*[18] is a good example of employees instituting a claim against a MNE at the home state courts. In this case, the employee (Lubbe) and thousands of other similarly situated employees (referred to as the plaintiffs) sued Cape PLC (the defendant). The defendant was incorporated in England under the name Cape Asbestos Company Limited, principally to mine and process asbestos. The employees sued the company for personal injuries arising from asbestos exposure received while working at Cape SA's subsidiary.[19]

At the commencement of the proceedings, the defendant made an application to stay the case on the basis that the case should be determined in South Africa and not in England.[20] The employees argued that substantial justice would not be done in SA because legal aid was not available and there was no reasonable likelihood that lawyers would accept a contingency fee for such a complex case.[21] The trial court held that South Africa was the country with jurisdiction to hear the matter. The plaintiffs were aggrieved and appealed. On appeal, the House of Lords held unanimously that South Africa was indeed a more appropriate forum for hearing the claim. However, they held that it was highly likely that legal representation for the claimants would be unavailable.[22]

Further, the expert evidence suggested a denial of justice would result, exacerbated by the lack of procedures in South Africa to accommodate multi-party

[18] W.L.R. 1545 (2000).

[19] At para 15.

[20] *Lubbe* at para 16.

[21] *Lubbe* at para 17.

[22] At para 32.

actions.[23] This meant that lifting the stay was appropriate, and the action continued in the English courts.[24] Regarding the merits of the case, the court had to answer two questions: the first one concerned whether a parent company is responsible for ensuring compliance with health and safety by its overseas subsidiaries.[25] If the above question is answered in the affirmative, the court should proceed to determine whether the employees suffered personal injury. Such a task entailed that the issues relevant to each employee included the following: diagnosis, prognosis, causation, and special damage.[26] The court held that whether the MNE was responsible for the well-being of employees of its subsidiary would be determined through ordinary principles of law of negligence.[27] In an apparent victory of the employees, the matter was resolved. This settlement agreement has, however, prevented the development of the law in this area.[28]

Further, in the earlier decision in *Chandler v Cape Plc*,[29] an employee was employed by Cape Products, the then subsidiary of Cape Plc (an English MNE). Cape Products was dissolved, and its employer liability insurance policy contained an exclusion clause on asbestosis claims. The employee lodged a negligence claim against Cape Plc (parent company) of his employer, wherein he alleged that the parent company had a legal duty of the well-being of the employees of the subsidiary.

In *Chandler*, the issue to be decided was whether the parent company was legally liable for the failure of its subsidiary to care for its workers. The court developed four requirements under which such a duty might be held to apply to the parent company.[30] First, the business activities of both the parent company and subsidiary company should be closely related; second, the parent company should possess advanced knowledge of relevant aspects of health and safety of the specific industry.

Third, the working system of the subsidiary company should be considered unsafe, and the parent company should have known or anticipated that the subsidiary and its employees would depend on its advanced knowledge for their protection.[31] According to the court, there was no need to demonstrate that the parent company regularly interfered in the health and safety protocols of the subsidiary. The court held that businesses operated by the two companies were essentially identical.[32]

---

[23] *Chandler* at para 29.

[24] As above.

[25] *Chandler* at para 20.

[26] *Chandler* at para 21.

[27] Ahmed (2022), p. 62.

[28] See Schoeman (2019), p. 457 who argues that resolutions of disputes only after the courts decided to hear the case have significant impact on the development of the law in this area of cross-border torts/delicts.

[29] [2012] EWCA Civ 525.

[30] At para 61.

[31] *Chandler* at para 80.

[32] *Chandler* at para 89.

In conclusion, the court held that the parent company was aware of its subsidiary's health and safety procedures. It knew that the subsidiary's work system was unsafe. As such, it ought to have ensured that the subsidiary took measures to ensure that employees are safe.[33] The court held further that the parent company had assumed a duty to advise the subsidiary on measures it should implement to ensure that employees are safe whilst at work. Having applied the above test, the court found that the parent company breached its obligations by failing to ensure that an employee of its subsidiary was safe.[34]

It is argued that the above cases illustrate that litigation against MNEs has the potential to become complex and extremely costly in some circumstances. As Schoeman stated, 'litigating about where to litigate diverts the focus from the substantive issues that need to be decided'.[35] The tests developed by the courts are extremely sophisticated and technical. It is submitted that only employees with financial means may be able to defend their rights using such procedures. It is submitted that most employees will likely be unable to invoke such procedures. Therefore, a simplified, cost-efficient, and effective procedure for employees employed by MNEs is needed.

1.3.3 Dispute Resolution Procedures Under Soft Law Mechanisms

In response to the failures of national governments to hold MNEs accountable for human and labour rights violations, the international community has developed various international instruments to promote compliance with decent work standards and respect for human and labour rights by MNEs. These international instruments include the following: the UN Guiding Principles on Business and Human Rights, adopted in 2012; the OECD Guidelines; the ILO MNE Declaration; the UN Global Compact, published in 2000; and the EU Supply Chain Due Diligence Directive. In addition to the above regulatory instruments, a new regime of private governance of labour standards for MNEs has emerged. Such mechanisms take the form of codes of conduct adopted by MNEs and NGOs. This form of regulation holds MNEs to their obligations in two ways.

First and foremost, this initiative is designed to apply pressure on MNEs to uphold internationally recognised human and labour rights. Moreover, this initiative seeks to hold MNEs accountable for not complying with their commitments as outlined in corporate social responsibility (CSR) instruments, such as codes of conduct.[36] Gutterman defines CSR as:

---

[33] *Chandler* at para 62.

[34] *Chandler* at para 81.

[35] Schoeman (2019), p. 457.

[36] See Chap. 5 para 5.1 for discussion on enforcement of MNE codes of conduct.

> the continuing commitment by business to behave ethically and contribute to economic development while improving the quality of life of the workforce and their families as well as of the local community and society at large.[37]

Under this regime, the regulatory mechanisms have moved away from rule-setting towards problem-solving.[38] This approach is premised on the principle that powerful economic actors have obligations that extend beyond the boundaries of their own organisations.[39] At the core of this conception of the global supply chain system is a recognition by some MNEs that they have ethical obligations regarding the practices of their suppliers and sub-contractors.[40] Kun states that 'such an approach makes actors other than the direct or primary employer co-responsible or liable for ensuring respect of some human and labour rights in their supply chains'.[41] Given the challenges mentioned, there is a significant need for research in this area of law.

1.4 Methodology

This book comprises the following two main research methods, namely a doctrinal analysis and one based on law reform theory. The core elements of doctrinal scholarship encompass a rigorous conceptual examination of pertinent legislation and case law to elucidate a statement of the law pertinent to the subject matter being investigated.[42] This methodology encompasses the identification and analysis of legal precedents and legislative interpretation.[43]

This method is relevant to the topic at hand as there are several existing sources of law regulating the conduct of MNEs, which date back to the 1970s UN Code, the ILO MNE Declaration, and the OECD Guidelines. As such, a study of the current regulatory mechanisms is required. The study will involve an analysis of international standards, labour legislation, case law, books, articles, and other related sources.

It is submitted that this theoretical analysis, which combines descriptive and analytical approaches based on the available primary and secondary sources, is best suited for this study. The data was collected through an extensive literature survey, library research and internet searches. While emphasising the overall efforts of actors in preventing human rights and environmental impacts, the author used comparative legal analysis to recommend the effective implementation of CSR standards as a mandatory requirement. To this end, the author relied on soft laws,

[37] Gutterman (2023), p. 5.
[38] Ter Haar (2013), p. 94.
[39] Bair and Palpacuer (2015), p. 182.
[40] Arnold and Hartman (2006), p. 685.
[41] Kun (2015), p. 53.
[42] Hutchinson and Watson (2015), p. 579.
[43] Hutchinson (2015), p. 130.

investment treaties between countries, statutes, reports, databases, and various government and non-government documents.

The law reform theory is concerned with bringing the law in line with current conditions, ensuring that it meets current needs and removing defects in the law. It also adopts new or more effective methods for administering the law and dispensing justice, and the hope is expressed that the recommendations of the study will provide a viable theoretical basis that may lead to improved access to justice.[44] Based on the fact that this study aims to develop a new model to regulate MNEs at the international level, theory development defines one of the research methods to be employed in this study.

1.5 Structure of the Book

Chapter 1 provides a basic introduction to the study, briefly outlining the contextual background and explaining the research question. It also discusses the significance of the study. The chapter then introduces the concepts of MNE and human rights due diligence, providing statistics on several significant violations of internationally recognised human and labour rights. Additionally, it explains the historical context and background regarding the use of soft law instruments to promote compliance with human and labour rights by MNEs.

Chapter 2 will address the notions of decent work in the context of human and labour rights. An assessment will be conducted to establish whether labour rights constitute human rights. This chapter will focus on decent work standards and human rights in global supply chains. The study will adopt the approach that all labour rights are human rights and that the two can hardly be divorced.

Chapter 3 will evaluate the structure of the ILO in norm-setting and monitoring mechanisms concerning MNEs. This chapter will further analyse the efficacy of the enforcement mechanisms of the ILO in relation to MNEs, particularly the ILO MNE Declaration.

Chapter 4 will assess the role of the OECD and its functions. The OECD Guidelines and OECD enforcement mechanisms will be analysed. This chapter will analyse the efficacy of the enforcement mechanisms of the OECD, particularly the OECD Guidelines. Chapter 5 will appraise the extent to which NGOs can be considered effective in guaranteeing compliance with labour standards. These include evaluating codes of conduct developed by NGOs, the effectiveness of auditing, and the certification processes in ensuring compliance with decent work standards by MNEs.

Chapter 6 will analyse the scope of International Framework Agreements and how they are to be utilised to enhance compliance with decent work standards in global supply chains. This chapter will analyse the efficacy of collective bargaining

[44] Hutchinson (2015), p. 130.

processes at the international labour law level. Chapter 7 will explore the provisions of the Directive of the European Parliament and the Council on Corporate Sustainability Due Diligence. A theoretical assessment will be conducted since the Directive has recently been adopted and has yet to be implemented, meaning its effectiveness has not yet been tested.

Chapter 8 covers the conclusion and recommendations. The chapter will highlight the main findings with respect of the research question. A conclusion will be made on whether the existing regulatory mechanisms are adequate to regulate MNEs. Conclusions will further be drawn on what reforms should be introduced to eliminate various problems that have been encountered. Issues such as introducing a new dispute resolution forum at international or regional levels will be addressed. Ultimately, the chapter will discuss the model formulated to address the legal problem.

The sections below introduce and discuss key concepts, namely, MNE and human rights due diligence.

1.6 What Is a Multinational Enterprise?

It is submitted that it is necessary that a precise and concise definition of the term 'MNE' should be established. Such a definition will ensure that the regulatory instruments adopted by international bodies apply to relevant companies capable of human and labour rights violations. It should be stated that the primary instruments that were adopted to regulate MNEs, namely, the Tripartite Declaration of Principles concerning Multinational Enterprises and Social Policy published in 1977 (the ILO MNE Declaration)[45] and the OECD Guidelines for Multinational Enterprises on Responsible Business Conduct published in 1976 (OECD Guidelines),[46] contain no precise definition of an MNE.

The ILO MNE Declaration describes a MNE to 'include enterprises – whether fully or partially state-owned or privately owned – which own or control production, distribution, services or other facilities outside the country in which they are based'.[47] The OECD Guidelines follow a similar wide approach by describing MNE as 'companies or other entities established in more than one country and so linked that they may coordinate their operations in various ways'.[48]

The definitions above appear to have set the tone for future efforts to define the notion of MNE.[49] It is submitted that the above definitions are too broad and are not

[45] See the discussion in Chap. 2 para 2.2.

[46] See Chap. 4 para 4.2.

[47] Para 6 of the ILO MNE Declaration.

[48] See para 4 of the OECD Guidelines. See also the detailed discussion in Chap. 4 para 4.1–4.2 below.

[49] See also Baez (2000), p. 191 who defines 'MNE' as 'a parent company that directly engages in foreign production in one or more countries besides the country in which the parent company is located'.

appropriate for the promotion of the effective regulation of MNEs. The mentioned definitions classify companies as MNEs irrespective of their size and revenue. Under such an approach, a small business with fewer employees may also be classified as a MNE if it has more than one branch in two or more countries. This would be the case even if the business has an annual turnover of not more than $40 million which is the minimum annual revenue required of a business to be regulated under the European Union Supply Chain Mandatory Due Diligence Directive.[50]

It is argued that a business with such qualities poses no threat to human and labour rights on a global scale, as such companies can be regulated under the national laws of their host country. Therefore, it is argued that a precise definition which considers the factors covered in the ILO and the OECD definitions but also includes the size and annual revenue of the business, would be more appropriate.

This view is in harmony with that of the European Union Supply Chain Mandatory Due Diligence Directive,[51] which requires businesses to meet certain revenue thresholds to comply with due diligence requirements.[52] To this extent, the Directive provides that it applies to two types of companies, namely: EU registered companies with over 500 employees with a net annual turnover of $150 million. The Directive is also applicable to companies not meeting the above requirements but identified to operate in a high-impact sector and have more than 250 employees with a net turnover of $40 million.[53]

1.7 Human Rights Due Diligence

The argument posited by Kun is that modern MNEs lack vertical integration; instead, they operate within intricate networks of subcontracting chains for both production and labour.[54] This perspective is reinforced by scholars like Ruggie, who emphasises that MNEs are complex entities due to their transnational production networks, supply chains, and global value chains.[55] It is crucial to recognise that holding MNEs legally accountable for human and labour rights violations in facto-

[50] See Chap. 7 para 7.1–7. 4.

[51] As above.

[52] As above.

[53] Article 2 of the EU Supply Chain Due Diligence Directive.

[54] Kun (2015), p. 54.

[55] See Ruggie (2013), p. 19 effectively illustrates this issue through the example of the Apple iPhone 6, which exemplifies a producer-led production network. The device's components are sourced from an astonishing 785 suppliers across 31 countries. While the product is designed in the United States, it is primarily assembled in China, where a majority of suppliers totaling 349 are based. Furthermore, approximately 60 suppliers are located in the U.S., many of which are themselves MNEs or headquartered abroad. This complexity underscores the significant challenges in regulating MNEs and highlights the need for more nuanced approaches to ensure accountability in global supply chains.

ries situated in other countries is neither practical nor reasonable, given their limited control over these third-party operations.[56]

At the heart of the existing regulatory mechanism, it is a requirement for MNEs to conduct human rights due diligence as a method to ensure compliance with human and labour rights.[57] Due diligence is a process through which 'MNEs should identify, prevent, mitigate, and account for how they address their actual and potential adverse impact on human rights.'[58]

The definition above entails that MNEs should develop policies along their supply chain to improve compliance with human and labour rights.[59] This study endorses the approach of Ter Haar, who agrees with this view. She understands human rights due diligence as a problem-solving mechanism, which seeks to identify the problems and supports MNEs to find solutions to prevent situations of non-compliance with regulations.[60] Such understanding implies that MNEs do not incur legal liability for failure to meet the expectations contained in the codes of conduct.

Weiss agrees and describes codes of conduct as 'light touch or soft law regulations', and he continues that there is only a moral obligation on MNEs to adhere to them.[61] Under this approach, codes of conduct are not meant to enforce human and labour rights in a similar way to courts, but instead they seek to minimise the risk of non-compliance with human and labour rights by MNEs. As Ter Haar states, 'the codes of conduct do not formulate new labour standards nor intend to do so, but they recognise the ILO as the competent body to set international labour standards'.[62]

The understanding presented above is supported by this study. However, this book aims to explore ways to make the obligations outlined in these instruments less voluntary. It is argued that, in their current form, these voluntary instruments are unlikely to bring about any meaningful change in workers' lives, as evidenced by the results in the section below.

1.8 Statistics on Human and Labour Rights Compliance by MNEs

There are several recognised tools which are used to assess the level of compliance with due diligence requirements by MNEs. One such tool is the Corporate Human Rights Benchmark (CHRB). According to Cirlig:

[56] As above.

[57] Alhambra et al. (2020), p. 237.

[58] Alhambra et al. (2020), p. 328. See also OECD Guidelines para 4 which describes due diligence as 'a risk-based due diligence to identify, prevent, mitigate and account for how they address actual and potential adverse impacts on matters covered by the OECD Guidelines'.

[59] Alhambra et al. (2020), p. 328.

[60] Ter Haar (2013), p. 84.

[61] Weiss (2013), p. 16.

[62] Ter Haar (2013), p. 84.

> the CHRB provides a comparative snapshot of the largest MNEs on the planet, looking at the policies, processes, and practices they have in place to systematise their human rights approach and how they respond to serious allegations.[63]

The first pilot ranking was published in 2016 and ranked the top 100 MNEs in the agricultural products, apparel, and extractive industries.[64] The ranking assessed MNEs across six themes: firstly, governance and policies; secondly, adherence to human and labour rights; thirdly, complaints mechanisms capable of providing remedies; fourthly, the MNEs' human rights practices; fifthly, the MNEs' approach to allegations of human and labour rights violations; and sixthly, transparency of human and labour rights approach.[65]

The CHRB measures how companies perform across 100 indicators based on the UNGPs.[66] It uses publicly available information on issues such as forced labour, protecting human rights activists and the living wage to give companies a maximum possible score of up to 100%. It is submitted that the results were skewed towards the lower bands, which was a reflection that many MNEs failed to implement the UNGPs and other internationally recognised human rights and industry standards.

According to the 2022 CHRB insights report, 127 MNEs in the apparel sector, automotive manufacturing sector, extractives sector, food and agricultural products sector, and the ICT manufacturing sector were assessed to determine their level of compliance with human and labour rights obligations.[67] The key findings were that MNEs do not regulate human and labour rights in their supply chains. It is disappointing that only one-third of MNEs were found to have created obligations from the companies involved in their supply chains to adhere to human and labour rights. Further, only 11% of the assessed MNEs were found to have created obligations for third party companies to comply with internationally recognised human and labour standards.[68]

Further, only 2% of the assessed MNEs were found to have adopted processes to track the number of workers that are affected by these issues in their supply chains and disclose progress.[69] For example, on the issue of forced labour, the assessment showed that while 63% of the food and agriculture MNEs include a supplier requirement that prohibits restrictions to workers' freedom of association, only 9% were found to have worked with their suppliers to address the issue, and only 2% reported progress on it.[70]

Similarly, of all ICT MNEs assessed, only 33% were found to have processes to support their suppliers, and 9% monitored and reported progress on the issue. The

---

[63] Cirlig (2016), p. 234.

[64] Cirlig (2016), p. 234.

[65] Cirlig (2016), p. 234.

[66] CHRB Insights Report (2022) 4.

[67] CHRB Insights Report (2022) 5.

[68] CHRB Insights Report (2022) 12.

[69] CHRB Insights Report (2022) 12.

[70] As above.

most concerning finding was that over 50% of the allegations of serious human and labour rights infringements occurred in MNEs' supply chains. These findings suggest that MNEs' failure to enforce human and labour rights in their supply chains could result in worker rights abuses.[71] The findings in the automotive sector were also discouraging. It was found that 16 MNEs (55%) scored zero on all indicators across human and labour rights compliance with due diligence requirements, whilst 7 MNEs (24%) scored zero on all indicators across remedy and grievance mechanisms.[72]

The results in the above study are consistent with other similar studies. The study commissioned by the Director-General for Justice and Consumers of the EU found that only 37% of the 16 MNEs interviewed conducted due diligence related to human and labour rights.[73] Further, of those MNEs, it was only 16% that conducted due diligence for their suppliers.[74] In another related study conducted by the German Federal Foreign Office, which assessed the level of compliance by larger German MNEs, it was found that only 22% of them monitored compliance with human and labour rights by their foreign subsidiaries and contractors.[75]

Based on the above results, it is argued that the voluntary corporate instruments that require MNEs to implement due diligence have not been successful at securing respect for human and labour rights. This study agrees with other scholars, such as Anner, who states that 'violation of human and labour rights continues notwithstanding the existence of international norms and procedures established at the international level by organisations such as the ILO, several trade unions and other social movements'.[76]

The next section focuses on the historical background of legal instruments promoting compliance with human and labour rights by MNEs.

1.9 The Evolution of Legal Frameworks Regulating MNEs

According to Weiss, there are two approaches to legal instruments that are used to promote compliance with human and labour rights by MNEs.[77] These approaches are classified either as soft law or hard law or at times a combination of the two (also referred to as a 'hybrid approach').[78] The term hard law is understood to refer to

[71] CHRB Insights Report (2022) 13.

[72] CHRB Insights Report (2022) 19.

[73] https://op.europa.eu/en/publication-detail/-/publication/8ba0a8fd-4c83-11ea-b8b7-01aa75ed71a1/language-en. Date visited 13 September 2025.

[74] As above.

[75] Smit (2020), p. 48.

[76] Anner (2017), p. 56.

[77] Weiss (2013), p. 19.

[78] Weiss (2013), p. 19.

binding legal instruments.[79] The most common example of hard law at the international level is treaties and Directives.[80] The benefits associated with hard law instruments are well documented. According to Shaffer and Pollack, hard law instruments usually contain sanctions for non-compliance and as such, there is a cost of reneging, which is an incentive for compliance.[81] The sanctions may take the form of fines or withdrawal of licenses where the MNE is found to have violated its legal commitments. As such, hard law instruments allow the parties to commit themselves more credibly to the adopted legal documents.

Furthermore, hard law instruments usually require member states to ratify them which allows for direct application. According to Shaffer and Pollack, such instruments have additional benefits related to compliance.[82] To this, they add that: where treaty obligations are implemented through domestic legislation, they create new tools that mobilise domestic actors, increasing the costs of a violation and thus making their commitments more credible.[83] Scholars in favour of a hard law approach argue that hard law instruments better allow member states to monitor and enforce their commitments, including through dispute settlement bodies such as courts.[84] Their view finds support in this study.

Regrettably, the UN member countries have taken an unreasonable long period to conclude and adopt a hard law instrument to enforce compliance with human and labour rights by MNEs.[85] The UN has been at this process for approximately 50 years, starting with the 1970s when developing countries pushed for a Code on Transnational Corporations (TNCs).[86]

The said failures led to the emergence of soft law instruments to regulate MNEs. Ter Haar states:

> Whether desirable or not from a legal perspective, one of the reasons for using soft law instruments to regulate social matters is the failure of public actors, such as governments and international organisations, to adopt legally binding rules on social matters at transnational level.[87]

Soft law refers to 'co-operation based on instruments that are not legally binding, or whose binding force is somewhat weaker than that of traditional law, such as codes of conduct, guidelines, roadmaps, peer reviews'.[88] It is argued that despite the wide

---

[79] Druzin (2017), p. 361.

[80] Senden (2004), p. 1.

[81] Shaffer and Pollack (2010), p. 717.

[82] Shaffer and Pollack (2010), p. 717.

[83] Shaffer and Pollack (2010), p. 718.

[84] Shaffer and Pollack (2010), p. 719.

[85] Mares (2022), p. 1523.

[86] Mares (2022), p. 1523.

[87] Ter Haar et al. (2011), p. 338.

[88] See the official website of the OECD. https://www.oecd.org/content/dam/oecd/en/publications/reports/2013/04/international-regulatory-co-operation_g1g2ebb3/9789264200463-en.pdf. Date visited 13 September 2025.

adoption of soft law instruments to promote compliance with human and labour rights obligations by MNEs, there is, however, no concise definition for the term 'soft law'.[89] Furthermore, it is argued that its benefits are minimal. Guzman, for instance, states that 'soft law is not law at all, strictly speaking'.[90] Referring to CSR instruments, he argues that 'the obligations they create are neither soft law nor hard law: they are simply not law at all'.[91]

Despite the wide adoption of soft law instruments, there is evidence that shows serious human and labour rights infringements in the global supply chains of many well-known MNEs. The failures of soft law to reduce violations prompted some governments to seek ways to translate some aspects of the soft law approach into binding legal standards.[92] For instance, in 2021, the German government passed the Corporate Due Diligence in Supply Chains Act on corporate due diligence in supply chains. This marked the first time that German-based MNEs were legally obliged to respect human and labour rights in their entire supply chain.[93] The Act created obligations to comply with human and labour rights by MNEs which, amongst others, include the establishment of a risk management system. It is encouraging that the EU parliament has recently adopted the Supply Chains Due Diligence Directive, which prescribes obligations for MNEs and imposes penalties for non-compliance.[94]

Scholars such as Weiss and Ter Haar believe that neither hard law nor soft law on its own is sufficient to regulate working conditions for workers of MNEs. They instead support a hybrid approach. Ter Haar explains the theory of hybrid structures as 'sources that operate at the same time and contribute to a common goal, act in a multi-fold interplay of public and private actors in the processes of norm-building and norm-implementing'.[95] She warns that rivalry can exist when the traditional form of regulation creates unacceptable standards that could be avoided by a governance process.[96]

---

[89] Choudhury (2018), p. 963. According to Choudhury, soft law refers to 'principles, norms, standards or other statements of expected behaviour that do not create enforceable rights and duties'.

[90] Guzman and Meyer (2010), p. 172.

[91] Guzman and Meyer (2010), p. 172.

[92] Guruparan and Zerk (2021), p. 10. See also para 1.2 above for evidence of human and labour rights violations.

[93] Article 3 of the Corporate Due Diligence in Supply Chains Act of 2021. The government of France also passed the Corporate Duty of Vigilance Act, which create a legal obligation for French based MNEs which employs more than 5000 employees in France and over 10 000 elsewhere in the world to conduct due diligence in respect of all companies involved in their supply chains. The failure by MNEs to conduct due diligence obligations would result in them being liable to penalties. However, after assessment by the French government of the application of the law, it was found that whereas some MNEs have made real progress, others did not implement the due diligence obligations which resulted in the Act being discontinued. See Zamfir (2020) EU 5.

[94] See Chap. 7 para 7.1.

[95] Ter Haar (2013), p. 74.

[96] Ter Haar (2013), p. 75.

The author argues that neither the exclusive application of hard law nor soft law instruments will increase compliance with human and labour rights by MNEs. This study supports the view that a partnership of both soft law and hard law approaches will provide a solution to the identified gap. The next chapter focuses on the notion of decent work and whether labour rights should be classified as human rights.

References

Ahmed M (2022) Private international law and substantive liability issues in tort litigation against multinational companies in the English courts: recent UK Supreme Court decisions and post-Brexit implications. J Priv Int Law

Alhambra A, Ter Haar B, Kun A (2020) Harnessing public institutions for labour law enforcement embedding a transnational labour inspectorate within the ILO. Int Organ Law Rev

Amao O (2011) Corporate social responsibility, human rights and the law. Routledge

Anner M (2017) Monitoring workers' rights: the limits of voluntary social compliance initiatives in labour repressive regimes. Global Policy Volume

Arnold G, Hartman P (2006) Worker rights and low wage industrialization: how to avoid sweatshops. Johns Hopkins University Press

Baez C, Michele D, Margaret D, Christine D (2000) Multinational enterprises and human rights. Univ Miami Int Comp Law Rev

Bair J, Palpacuer F (2015) CSR beyond the corporation: contested governance in global value chains. J Transnatl Aff

Choudhury B (2018) Balancing soft and hard law for business and human rights. Int Comp Law Q

Cirlig R (2016) Business and human rights: from soft law to hard law. Juridical Tribune

Collingsworth T (2002) The key human rights challenge: developing enforcement mechanisms. Harv Hum Rights J

Druzin B (2017) Why does soft law have any power anyway? Asian J Int Law

Grogan J (2017) Workplace law. Juta South Africa

Guruparan K, Zerk J (2021) Influence of soft law grows in international governance. Int Aff J

Gutterman S (2023) Corporate social responsibility: definitions and theories. Springer

Guzman A, Meyer T (2010) International soft law. J Leg Anal

Hassel A (2008) The evolution of a global labour governance regime'. Int J Policy Adm Inst

Hutchinson T (2015) The doctrinal method: incorporating interdisciplinary methods in reforming the law. Erasmus Law Rev

Hutchinson T, Watson B (2015) Law librarians, law libraries, and legal research in the post-internet era. Law Libr J

Kamminga M (2005) The evolving status of NGOs under international law: a threat to the inter state system? In: Alston P (ed) Non-state actors and human rights. Oxford University Press

Kun A (2015) From transnational soft law to national hard law - regulating supply chains. Pecsi Munkajogi Kozlemenyek

Lyutov N (2017) Traditional international labour law and the new global kind: is there a way to make them work together. ZBORNIK PFZ

Mares R (2022) Regulating transnational corporations at the United Nations – the negotiations of a treaty on business and human rights. Int J Hum Rights

Maryanov D (2000) Sweatshop liability: corporate codes of conduct and the governance of labour standards in the international supply chain. Lewis Clark Law Rev

Newaj K (2019) Does the incorrect classification of misconduct charges constitute substantive unfairness? EOH Abantu v CCMA (2019) 40 ILJ 2477 (LAC)' (2020) 41(3). Nelson Mandela University

Payne T (2017) Retooling the ILO: How a new enforcement wing can help the ILO reach its goal through regional free trade agreements. Indian Journal of Global Legal Studies
Ratner S (2001) Corporations and human rights: a theory of legal responsibility. Yale Law J
Ruggie J (2013) Multinationals as global institution: power, authority and relative autonomy. Regul Gov
Schoeman E (2019) Litigating about where to litigate: Vendenta Resources Plc v Lungwe [2019] UKSC 20' (2019). Comp Int Law J South Afr
Senden L (2004) Soft law in European community law. Oxford Press
Shaffer G, Pollack A (2010) Hard law vs soft law, complements, and antagonists in international governance. Minn Law Rev
Sharma S (2018) Corporate social responsibility: from the lens of human rights. Int Res J Manag Sociol Humanity
Smit L, Bright C, McCorquodale R, Bauer M, Deringer H, Baeza- Breinbauer D et al. (2020) Study on due diligence requirements through the supply chain: Final report [Country Reports were authored by Lia Heasman (Denmark, Finland and Sweden)]. European Union, 571 p. https://doi.org/10.2838/39830
Son C (2013) Extending corporate liability to human rights violations in Asia. J Int Area Stud
Ter Haar B (2013) Love, Flirt or Repel: hybrid global governance of the ILO core labour standards. Eur J Soc Law
Ter Haar B, Alhambra A, Kun A (2011) Soft on the inside, hard on the outside: an analysis of the legal nature of new forms of international labour law. Int J Comp Labour Law
Van Eck S and Kuhn R (2019) Amendments to the CCMA Rules: Thoughts on the good, bad and the curious. Industrial Law Journal
Weiss M (2013) International labour standards: a complex public-private policy mix. Int J Comp Labour Law Ind Relat
Zamfir L (2020) Towards a mandatory EU system of due diligence for supply chains. European Union

Chapter 2
Decent Work, Labour Rights and Human Rights in the Context of MNEs

2.1 Introduction

This chapter has three purposes: Firstly, to analyse the notion of a decent work agenda in the context of MNEs; secondly, to establish whether labour rights constitute human rights; and thirdly, to evaluate the relationship between decent work and human rights. Cohen and Moodley note that the main goal of the International Labour Organisation (ILO)[1] is 'the achievement of decent and productive work for both women and men in conditions of freedom, equity, security and human dignity'.[2] Since the launch of the decent work agenda by the ILO in 1999, this concept has evolved into a worldwide goal and has been endorsed in prominent human rights proclamations and United Nations (UN) resolutions.[3] The ILO defines the term decent work as:

> Decent work sums up the aspirations of people in their working lives. It involves opportunities for work that is productive and delivers a fair income, security in the workplace and social protection for all… and equality of opportunity and treatment.[4]

It is submitted that the ILO's definition comprises several human and labour rights already catered for in other ILO legal instruments. Such rights include the right to freedom of association, equal treatment, and social protection that are provided in

---

[1] See Chap. 3 para 3.1.

[2] Cohen and Moodley (2012), p. 319.

[3] Piasna and Bruchell (2020), p. 1. The UN aims to eliminate poverty in all its forms and dimensions, including extreme poverty through 17 sustainable development goals (SDGs). Sustainable development goal 8 is of particular interest in this book and it seeks 'to promote sustained, inclusive and sustainable economic growth, full and productive employment and decent work for all.'

[4] ILO 1999. https://www.ilo.org/topics-and-sectors/decent-work. Date visited 13 September 2025.

F. Maluleke, *Compliance with Decent Work Standards by Multinational Enterprises*, European Yearbook of International Economic Law 48,
https://doi.org/10.1007/978-3-032-21261-0_2

the Fundamental Rights Declaration of 1998.[5] However, this is not a negative aspect. The decent work agenda brings these fundamental rights together and strengthens existing rights.

Bellace argues that the nature of rights contained in the definition of decent work is important as it has the potential to influence how decent work efforts are prioritised to the labour market.[6] This study supports the view that the inclusion of important human and labour rights in the definition urges the labour market role players to pay special attention to decent work, and that the decent work agenda should be handled with extreme urgency.[7]

The elements covered in the said definition are also essential when it comes to the measurement of progress made with respect to the attainment of decent work. Clearly, decent work is not only limited to the income derived from any job. In this regard, the ILO states that:

> Work has a social value and purpose. In addition to being a source of income, work is a source of personal dignity, family stability and peace in a community. It is not just an economic activity.[8]

In other words, the ILO advocates for an approach that enables the attainment of employment, income and social protection without undermining workers' rights and established international standards. To this, Rombouts and Zekic add that decent work should prioritise the preservation of the fundamental human and labour rights and ensure that workers are provided with safe working conditions and fair compensation. Additionally, it should guarantee a sufficient income for workers to sustain themselves and their families.[9]

The significance of the last-mentioned statement is that it covers a wide scope and, most importantly, elevates the right to decent work to the level of fundamental human and labour rights. Bellace argues that there is an obvious nexus between the right to decent work and fundamental human rights.[10] She states that 'the right to

---

[5] See para 5 below.

[6] Bellace (2011), p. 7.

[7] Bellace (2011), p. 7. She mentions that to some extent, there may be a lack of understanding as to what exactly is meant by decent work. Moreover, in some countries such as the US, the term seems analogous to fair labour standards, and as a rallying cry to action, it does not possess the same urgency as fundamental principles and rights at work.

[8] Cohen and Moodley (2012), p. 320.

[9] Rombouts and Zekic (2020), p. 346.

[10] These include the ILO's fundamental rights conventions which are:

a. C029 - Forced Labour Convention, 1930.
b. C087 - Freedom of Association and Protection of the Right to Organise Convention, 1948.
c. C098 - Right to Organise and Collective Bargaining Convention, 1949 (No. 98), C100 - Equal Remuneration Convention, 1951.
d. C105 - Abolition of Forced Labour Convention, 1957.
e. C111 - Discrimination (Employment and Occupation) Convention, 1958.
f. C138 - Minimum Age Convention, 1973 (No. 138) and
g. C182 - Worst Forms of Child labour Convention, 1999 (No. 182).

decent work is inextricably connected to the fundamental principles outlined in the 1998 declaration'.[11]

Commenting on the decent work agenda, Van Eck shares the same sentiment as Bellace on the view that there is a link between decent work and fundamental human rights.[12] He, however, adds that the aim of the decent work agenda is 'to balance the realisation of fundamental rights at work; the promotion of job creation; the promotion of effective social protection for all; and the encouragement of tripartism and social dialogue'.[13] He argues that the decent work agenda has led to a shift in the attention of the ILO from an agenda rights-focused to one which includes policies with the capacity to create jobs and reduce poverty.[14]

This study supports the view that decent work should not be viewed merely as an objective, but as a means of achieving targets of sustainable development and an overall aim to eradicate poverty in all its forms.[15]

2.2 The Decent Work Agenda

The then president of the Republic of Costa Rica, Oscar Arias, at the ILO's conference in 2006, described the decent work agenda as 'an agenda for development that provides a sustainable route out of poverty'.[16] The ILO considers the decent work agenda as a vital approach for achieving the goals of full and productive employment, as well as ensuring decent work for all.[17]

The decent work agenda is based on four pillars which are as follows: firstly, promotion of employment; secondly, enhancement of social protection and social security; thirdly, promotion of social dialogue and tripartism; and fourthly, respect of the fundamental rights at work'.[18]

In the following section, each of the pillars is discussed in more detail.

---

[11] Bellace (2011), p. 7.

[12] Van Eck (2013), p. 602.

[13] Van Eck (2013), p. 602.

[14] Van Eck (2013), p. 602.

[15] The UN's 2030 Agenda for Sustainable Development is a comprehensive plan outlining measures to abolish poverty and transform the world into a peaceful, sustainable environment for all.

[16] https://www.ilo.org/publications/decent-work-agenda-looking-back-looking-forward-growing-consensus. Date visited 13 September 2025.

[17] https://www.ilo.org/topics-and-sectors/decent-work. Date visited 13 September 2025.

[18] ILO (1999) 2.

2.2.1 *The Promotion of Employment*

The right to work is contained in several international instruments. For instance, in 1948, the UN adopted the Universal Declaration of Human Rights (Universal Declaration) which provides that 'everyone has the right to work, to free choice of employment, to just and favourable conditions of work and to protection against unemployment'.[19] The Committee on Economic, Social, and Cultural Rights (CESCR) gives meaning to the right to work and states that 'a right to work must mean a right to decent work'.[20] The right to decent work is also recognised in other important regional legal instruments, which include the African Charter on Human and Peoples' Rights.[21]

The ILO estimates that over 207 million of the world were unemployed in 2022 compared to 186 million in 2019.[22] This study submits that it is difficult to perceive how the right to decent work can be made practical against the background of such high rates of unemployment.[23] Nevertheless, the right to decent work is considered by many people as a vital element of social protection since the effective enjoyment of other human rights will be difficult to achieve without the right to work being guaranteed first.[24]

This study agrees that the right to decent work is not possible without people being employed. Therefore, a core element of decent work is the proportionality of the employment levels in a specific country.[25] After all, a significant number of people do not have other sources of income. Therefore, merely recognising that people have the right to work does not effectively address the economic and social rights.

---

[19] Article 23:1 of the Universal Declaration of Human Rights.

[20] UN Committee on Economic, Social and Cultural Rights (CESCR), General Comment No. 18: The Right to Work. Against the background of the ILO's quest to create jobs, the argument in favour of MNEs may seem attractive as they are perceived to create jobs. However, this study submits that jobs should not be created at all costs. Yes, new jobs are supported, but aspects like child labour and unsafe working conditions are of paramount importance.

[21] Article 15 of the African Charter on Human and Peoples' Rights provides that 'every individual shall have the right to work under equitable and satisfactory conditions, and shall receive equal pay for equal work'.

[22] World Employment and Social Outlook: Trends 2022. Geneva: International Labour Office, 2022. Accessible at https://www.ilo.org/publications/flagship-reports/world-employment-and-social-outlook-trends-2022. Date visited 13 September 2025.

[23] Rombouts and Zekic (2020), p. 341. Nonetheless, it is important to note that the right to work does not guarantee employment as an enforceable right. It merely places a positive obligation on governments to promote job creation. This is what the first pillar of the ILO's decent work agenda seeks to achieve.

[24] See article 6 of UN Committee on Economic, Social and Cultural Rights (CESCR), General Comment No. 18: 'The Right to Work' which states that the right to work is essential for realising other human rights and forms an inseparable and inherent part of human dignity.

[25] Anker et al. (2003), p. 155.

In the context of this study, it is important to note that MNEs do create jobs. As discussed in Chap. 1, this is an important factor. However, it is just as important that these jobs should be sustainable and should not impair human dignity.[26]

2.2.2 *Enhancing Social Protection*

The second pillar of the decent work agenda promotes the importance of social security protection. There is no commonly accepted definition of the term social security. However, the ILO defines social security as 'a human right which responds to the universal need for protection against certain life risks and social needs'.[27] This definition elevates social security to the level of a fundamental human right.

Notwithstanding the importance of social security, the percentage of the world population with social security coverage remains very low. According to the ILO, only 20% of the world population has adequate social security coverage. In developing countries, less than 10 per cent of the working population is covered by social security.[28]

At the international level, the ILO Social Security (Minimum Standards) Convention, 1952 (No. 102) is the only instrument that provides a list of minimum standards relating to social security. The list includes: 'medical care; sickness benefits; unemployment benefits; old-age benefits; occupational injury benefits; family benefits; maternity benefits; and survivors' benefits'.[29] It is concerning that the convention only requires each member state to provide three of the said protections.[30] Further, the convention prescribes very low percentages to indicate that the member states should at least provide social security.[31]

However, Van Eck and Vettori warn that the unrealistic and unaffordable levels of higher social security may negatively impact developing countries. They state

---

[26] See Chap. 1 para 1.1.

[27] https://www.social-protection.org/gimi/C102Gateway.action?lang=EN#:~:text=The%20human%20right%20to%20social%20security%20means%20that,in%20other%20words%20when%20they%20are%20in%20need. Date visited 13 September 2025.

[28] ILO (2007) 5.

[29] https://www.ilo.org/secsoc/areas-of-work/legal-advice/WCMS_205340/lang%2D%2Den/index.htm#:~:text=The%20Social%20Security%20%28Minimum%20Standards%29%20Convention%2C%201952%20%28No.,standards%20for%20all%20nine%20branches%20of%20social%20security. Date visited 13 September 2025.

[30] Article 2 of C102 - Social Security (Minimum Standards) Convention, 1952 (No. 102).

[31] In terms of Article 9 of C102 - Social Security Convention, 1952 (No. 102). The following prescriptions apply: '(a) prescribed classes of employees, constituting not less than 50% of all employees, and also their wives and children; or (b) prescribed classes of economically active population, constituting not less than 20% of all residents, and also their wives and children; or (c) prescribed classes of residents, constituting not less than 50% of all residents; or (d) prescribed classes of employees constituting not less than 50% of employees in industrial workplaces employing 20persons or more, and also their wives and children'.

that 'since unemployment insurance provides unemployed persons with a means to survive, the quest of some of them to find a job is not as urgent as it would otherwise have been, and they may consequently take more time looking for a job'.[32]

The higher the benefits, the longer the time involved in finding a job and the higher the impact on the economy.[33] Okpaluba echoed the same view and states that the assistance provided to beneficiaries of social security should advocate a departure from the assistance-based exercise towards promotion of employment and make unemployment less attractive.[34]

It is submitted that these opinions that cast doubt on the expansion of social security measures should be treated with caution. The reasons are two-fold. First, especially in developing countries, there is limited social security protection in place. Second, such opinions may have an eroding effect on the laudable goals of the decent work agenda. The more burning question in the context of this study is how to ensure that MNEs comply with their social security law obligations. Are soft law provisions sufficient or should hard law measures be introduced more extensively? It is argued that if social security rights are generally accepted as human rights, it can contribute significantly to improving the position of persons employed by MNEs.

The current Minimum Standards Convention does not prescribe how the member states should extend social coverage to their citizens. Further, social security measures are mostly available to former employees who worked in the formal sector. As such, employees in the informal sector, which is proportionally larger in poor nations than in developed nations, are not enjoying social coverage. It is argued that the standards in the convention were deliberately set at a lower percentage to ensure that the ILO member countries easily achieve compliance.

It is submitted that unless social security is expanded to the informal sector, decent work for all will remain aspirational.

2.2.3 *Enhancing Social Dialogue*

The third pillar promotes social dialogue. Generally, 'social dialogue between different social and economic groups … is an essential attribute of a democratic society and a means of resolving inevitable conflicts'.[35] Within the employment context, social dialogue occurs at three levels:

> between employers and employees in relation to terms and conditions of employment; between the management and workers over the functioning of an enterprise; and between social partners and public authorities on social and economic policy.[36]

---

[32] Van Eck and Vettori (2001), p. 422.

[33] Van Eck and Vettori (2001), p. 422.

[34] Okpaluba (2012), p. 205.

[35] Ghai (2003), p. 132.

[36] As above.

The ILO declares on its official website that the right to freedom of association is closely linked to social dialogue. It usually takes the form of collective bargaining between trade unions and employers' organisations.[37] In the South African context, Grogan states that 'the central objective of modern industrial relations is to promote collective bargaining to reach agreements by which relations between management and employees will be regulated'.[38] South Africa is in the fortunate position to have the right to collective bargaining being recognised in its Constitution.[39]

There is, however, a challenge in as far as MNEs are problematic to regulate and there is no legal requirement to engage in collective bargaining at international level. As such, trade unions cannot legally negotiate with MNEs despite the fact that the latter make important decisions which materially affect the terms and conditions of employment in companies involved in their supply chains.[40] Despite the problems experienced in the area of International Framework Agreements, such instruments serve to bridge a gap, and they should be promoted.

2.2.4 Rights at Work

The fourth pillar of the decent work agenda is rights at work. Globalisation and the operations of MNEs present tremendous challenges to decent work.[41] Due to a desire for labour market flexibility, MNEs utilise independent suppliers to

---

[37] https://www.ilo.org/public/english/dialogue/download/brochure.pdf. Date visited 13 September 2025.

[38] Grogan (2017), p. 404.

[39] Section 23 of the Constitution provides as follows:

1. Everyone has the right to fair labour practices.
2. Every worker has the right
   a. to form and join a trade union;
   b. to participate in the activities and programmes of a trade union; and
   c. to strike.
3. Every employer has the right
   a. to form and join an employers' organisation; and
   b. to participate in the activities and programmes of an employers' organisation.
4. Every trade union and every employers' organisation has the right
   a. to determine its own administration, programmes and activities;
   b. to organise; and
   c. to form and join a federation.

[40] See Chap. 6 para 6.1 for a detailed discussion on collective bargaining with MNEs.

[41] Frey and MacNaughton (2016), p. 442.

manufacture their products.[42] MacNaughton & Frey argue that such processes encourage deregulation, privatisation, and the increase of informal employment.[43] According to the authors, this contributed significantly to decline in respect for labour rights and core elements of decent work, and a sharp increase on job insecurity.[44]

The promotion of labour rights has been a major concern to the ILO since its inception, and it has developed several international standards which defines these rights.[45] This study is particularly interested in the rights contained in the ILO Declaration on Fundamental Principles and Rights at Work, adopted in 1998 which are: freedom of association, the eradication of forced labour, the elimination of child labour and unfair discrimination at work. Freedom of association and the right to collective bargaining have been discussed in detail under social dialogue and social protection above. The remaining rights are discussed below.

The characterisation of work as decent presupposes that the work concerned respects the international human and labour standards of those performing the work.[46] It follows that not all jobs are good and acceptable. Two forms of work that are particularly unacceptable are: forced labour and child labour. Such work must be identified and eliminated.[47]

It is hereby submitted that the right to decent work should not be considered in isolation from human and labour rights conventions. In particular, the ILO Declaration on Fundamental Rights at work of 1998. In parts that follow, the question of whether labour rights constitute human rights will be answered.

2.3 Do Labour Rights Constitute Human Rights?

As stated in Chap. 1, the challenges posed by MNEs have outpaced the regulatory capacity of individual ILO member countries.[48] Such a phenomenon brought increased attention to the impact of corporate practice on human and labour rights.[49] The question whether labour rights constitute human rights has attracted much interest amongst lawyers, judges, researchers, trade unionists, and other activists and at times sparking intense discussions.[50] In human rights law and labour law

---

[42] See Chap. 1 para 1.2.

[43] Frey and MacNaughton (2016), p. 12.

[44] Frey and MacNaughton (2016), p. 305.

[45] Van Eck et al. (2020), p. 111.

[46] Article 8 of the UN Committee on Economic, Social, and Cultural Rights (CESCR), *General Comment No. 18: The Right to Work.*

[47] Okuwa (2020), p. 1760.

[48] See Chap. 1 para 1.2.

[49] Dawkins (2022), p. 2.

[50] Sychenko (2017), p. 268.

scholarship, some believe in unequivocally recognising labour rights as human rights, while others approach this with scepticism and suspicion.

Hepple defines human rights as 'rights that are inherent to all human beings, regardless of race, sex, nationality, ethnicity, language, religion, or any other status. These rights include the right to life and liberty, freedom from slavery and torture, freedom of opinion and expression, the right to work and education'.[51] In South Africa, these rights are enshrined in the Constitution.[52]

The degree to which worker' rights are realised in a country serves as an indicator of the overall status of human rights. Repressive governments prohibit independent trade unions and resort to arresting members of trade unions.[53] Hepple makes a valid point that NGOs and trade union movements play a critical role in determining and shaping labour rights into human rights.[54] Historically, trade unions and NGOs focused on different approaches to labour rights. Kolben states that the traditional focus of trade unions has been workplace social justice, and on the other hand, NGOs generally chose to focus on political and civil rights issues such as arrest of political activists, freedom of speech and press issues.[55]

Trade union movements usually organise the workers in the formal sector to address workplace concerns.[56] However, due to an increased informal sector associated with the operations of MNEs, the traditional methods of mobilisation are no longer well-suited to such environments and circumstances. In order to adapt to the changing circumstances, trade unions and other labour movements have strategically utilised advocacy methods that are more traditionally associated with human rights NGOs.[57]

According to Hepple, such methods include: labelling of employee exploitation as human rights abuses to gain sympathy and exert pressure against MNEs and all companies involved in their supply chains.[58] MNEs also contribute to shaping labour rights as human rights. They respond to the activism of labour rights NGOs and global trade union campaigns by adopting private regulatory mechanisms declaring that they adhere to human and labour rights.[59] As discussed in Chap. 1, these mechanisms include self-regulation and partnerships with third-party monitors or associations.[60]

[51] Hepple (2003), p. 15.

[52] See para 6.1.4 below.

[53] As above.

[54] Hepple (2003), p. 450.

[55] Kolben (2010), p. 450.

[56] Hepple (2003), p. 450.

[57] As above.

[58] As above.

[59] See Chap. 5 para 5.1–5.2.

[60] See Chap. 1 para 1.2.

The conclusion that labour rights, or at least certain labour rights, are human rights has a series of implications for MNEs. It is suggested that should labour rights be recognised as human rights, this will have the effect that arguments in favour of economic efficiency over the realisation of human rights would fall away.[61]

2.4 Arguments in Favour of the Classification of Labour Rights as Human Rights

Scholars in favour of the classification of labour rights as human rights include Hepple, Collins, Stefano, and Antonio. They argue that managerial prerogatives and their impact on workers necessitate the need for labour rights to be framed as human rights.[62] Collins shares the same sentiment and states that 'the very existence of an employment relationship places the human rights of a worker at risk'.[63] Collins further argues that employers can, and frequently do, exercise their managerial and disciplinary powers in a manner that interferes with the most fundamental rights of the individual worker.[64]

Therefore, adequate safeguards against human rights infringements are necessary if workers are to receive full protection of their rights.[65] Mantouvalou shares the sentiment that managerial prerogatives cannot be effectively balanced by a contract of employment only. In this regard, she argues that 'the employment contract may contain terms that are unfair, to which the employee would not have agreed had it not been for the power imbalance and the economic dependency'.[66]

The ILO also supports the framing of labour rights as human rights. Social justice can be attained by placing workers' rights and their needs at the centre of the economic and social policy.[67] According to the ILO: 'employees and their labour are not like other things that should be bought and sold; they have dignity and rights.'[68] It is therefore submitted that the employment relationship should be governed by human rights principles, not only the law of contract.

---

[61] Mantouvalou (2012), p. 171.

[62] Stefano and Antonio (2019), p.

[63] Collins (2022), p. 15.

[64] Collins (2022), p. 15.

[65] Collins (2022), p. 15.

[66] Mantouvalou (2012), p. 172.

[67] https://www.ilo.org/resource/article/international-labour-standards-human-rights. Date visited 13 September 2025.

[68] https://www.ilo.org/international-labour-standards/benefits-international-labour-standards#:~:text=In%20the%20Declaration%20of%20Philadelphia%20%281944%29%2C%20the%20international,for%20the%20highest%20profit%20or%20the%20lowest%20price. Date visited 13 September 2025.

This study supports this school of thought and concludes that labour rights cannot be separated from human rights. Improvement of the strict protection of human and labour rights will increase the number of decent jobs. In turn, such will contribute to the reduction of poverty.

2.5 Arguments Against the Classification of Labour Rights as Human Rights

The scholars against the classification of labour rights as human rights include Compa, Dawkins, Youngdahl, and Parriotti. The main argument of this group of scholars is philosophical in nature. Parriotti argues that human rights should have the following features:

> (i) Firstly, the list of human rights should be very short so that only a limited set of rights; Secondly, human rights are understood as a toolbox at the disposal of individuals to protect their (negative) liberty, their bodily security and their life from governmental abuse and thirdly, the protection of these human rights can legitimise the use of force at the international level.[69]

It is submitted that the above definition sets strict criteria and only a few labour rights would qualify to be classified as human rights.

The second major argument against labour rights being framed as human rights, regards human rights as basic moral entitlements that accrue equally to people solely by virtue of their humanity and regardless of the prevailing legal or social structures or their spatial location.[70] Viewed from this perspective, the list of basic rights must be quite short and the social guarantees required by the structure of a right are not supposed to act against all possible threats, but only against standard threats.[71]

Three human rights are thought to be basic: the right to (physical) security, the right to subsistence (minimal economic security), and the right to liberty. For instance, subsistence includes water, food, clothing, shelter, health care and unpolluted.[72] Under this approach, labour rights would be viewed to be less important than human rights, since the state is not compelled to grant such rights.

Scholars in favour of this approach, argue that labour rights primarily affect private actors whilst human rights primarily affect states.[73] Human rights regulate and apply to the relationship between states and individuals.[74] These scholars suggest

[69] Pariotti (2018), p. 137.

[70] Dawkins (2022), p. 24.

[71] Pariotti (2018), p. 137.

[72] As above.

[73] Mantouvalou (2012), p. 4.

[74] Hertel (2009), p. 288 states that International human rights law has historically obliged states, not companies, to respect, protect, and fulfil human rights. Despite what activists on the ground may assert, human rights law only applies directly to companies in instances where corporations are liable for certain war crimes and crimes against humanity through complicity with states.

that 'the regulation of the employment relationship requires the application of private law rules, in particular law of contract'.[75] They submit that the employment contract is the same with other contracts, such as sale contracts.

Therefore, there should be a minimal intervention of public law institutions or states in employment relations.[76] State intervention in their view could disturb the contractual freedom of both the employer and the worker. To them, the employment contract is a legal mechanism that helps to curb the employers' bargaining power and ensure the principles of fairness between the employees and the employers and correct the distributional implications of a labour market that may be unjust.[77]

A further reason why there has been resistance to human rights in the labour relationship is that state intervention in the labour market is seen as a threat to market flexibility. This is because MNEs will incur transaction costs that make them less competitive both on a local and global level.[78] This study rejects such reasoning as it promotes profit-making interests more than workers as human beings. A balance should be found which will promote both workers' rights and profit-making interests. The sections that follow, analyse whether labour rights are human rights.

2.6 Tests to Determine If Labour Rights Are Human Rights

According to Mantouvalou, three recognised approaches are used to determine whether labour rights are human rights, namely: the positivist approach, an instrumental approach, and a normative approach.[79] In the section that follows, these approaches are analysed in more detail:

2.6.1 The Positivist Approach

The first test is the positivist approach in terms of which a list of rights is categorised as human rights insofar as certain treaties or directives recognise them as such.[80] This study agrees with this test for the following reasons. The test is uncomplicated. If particular labour rights are included in human rights documents such as international treaties or any country's constitution, such rights should be classified as human rights. If the labour rights are not included in the human rights documents, they are not deemed as human rights.

---

75 Compa (2008), p. 11.

76 Youngdahl (2009), p. 32.

77 Youngdahl (2009), p. 32.

78 Mantouvalou (2012), p. 7.

79 Mantouvalou (2012), p. 172.

80 Mantouvalou (2012), p. 152.

Several international organisations, such as the ILO, the UN, the EU and the African Union (AU) have adopted and implemented treaties that promote human rights. In the sections that follow, key human rights documents will be surveyed to determine if labour rights should be classified as human rights or not.

2.6.1.1 The Universal Declaration of Human Rights of 1948

According to Pocar, the concept of human rights existed from time immemorial. Its significance was acknowledged by the global community in the Universal Declaration of Human Rights (UDHR) for the first time.[81] The first paragraph of the preamble to the UDHR states that 'human rights are both equally possessed by all members of the human family and inalienable to all members of the human family'.[82]

The UDHR aims to attain a world in which the dignity and value of each human being are valued and protected. It affirms several labour rights to be human rights. For instance, article 23 of the UDHR provides that 'everyone' has the right to work, to 'free choice of employment', 'equal pay for equal work', and 'join trade unions for the protection of their interests'. Such rights form part of a comprehensive list regarded as 'inalienable human rights'.[83]

It is of significance to note that the UDHR has been hugely influential in so far as its principles have made their way into several hard law international instruments such as the International Covenant on Civil and Political Rights 1966 (ICCPR)[84] and the International Covenant on Economic, Social, and Cultural Rights (ICESCR)[85] 1966. Sun argues that even though the UDHR does not have any legal enforceability, legal experts nonetheless accept that its principles have attained the force of customary international law over time.[86] It is submitted that there can be no doubt in terms of the positivist approach test that labour rights constitute human rights in terms of the UDHR.

---

[81] Pocar (2015), pp. 43–53.

[82] Preamble to the Universal Declaration.

[83] https://www.ohchr.org/en/what-are-human-rights/international-bill-human-rights. Date visited 13 September 2025.

[84] Article 8 (1) of the ICCPR prohibits all forms of slavery and forced labour. It provides that everyone has the right to freedom of association, including the right to form and join trade unions.

[85] Article 6 of ICESCR recognises the right of everyone to the enjoyment of just and favourable conditions of work which ensure remuneration which provides all workers with fair wages and equal remuneration for work of equal value.

[86] Sun (2009), p. 19.

2.6.1.2 The United Nations Guiding Principles on Business and Human Rights

The United Nations Guiding Principles (UNGPs) was the first major and comprehensive authoritative instrument adopted by an international organisation to regulate business conduct.[87] Prior to its adoption, the United Nations (UN)[88] has drafted a Code on Transnational Corporations (TNCs) in the 1970s which was shelved due to role players' disagreement on its texts.[89] An attempt to revive the Code was made in 2004, but again the UN member states failed to reach an agreement on the texts of the code.

The UNGPs were developed by Professor John Ruggie (the then special representative of the Secretary-General of the UN). The framework accepts internationally recognised human rights as those expressed in the UDHR and the principles concerning fundamental rights set out in the ILO's Declaration on Fundamental Principles and Rights at Work.[90]

The framework rests on three independent but mutually supporting pillars: The first pillar is the state's duty to protect against human and labour rights abuses by third parties, including MNEs. In this regard, the states are required to adopt and enforce appropriate laws and regulatory mechanisms requiring MNEs to respect and adhere to human and labour rights.[91] In the event of breach, the states should investigate, punish, and redress such abuse. As indicated in Chap. 1, some governments of poor states are in a weaker position due to a need for FDI associated with MNEs.[92]

It is, therefore, very difficult for such states to set stricter legislation and high labour standards for MNEs. It is submitted that this challenge can be resolved if all countries were to implement higher standards. Under such an approach, the MNEs would not have an opportunity to relocate businesses to countries with lower standards.

---

[87] Buhmann (2015), p. 416. The UNGPs was adopted by the United Nations member states in 2011.

[88] The UN was formed in 1945 after the end of the Second World War. The UN replaced the League of Nations, which was established in 1919 after World War I, under the Treaty of Versailles. The League of Nations' main goal was to promote international cooperation and to achieve peace and security. The establishment of the UN was necessitated by the failure of the League of Nations to prevent World War II. The UN has evolved over the years to keep up with a rapidly changing world. The UN and its work are guided by the purposes and principles contained in its founding Charter. Amongst others, its main goals are to promote fundamental human rights, human dignity, equal rights of all men and women, and respect for the obligations arising from sources of international law. https://www.bing.com/search?q=History+of+the+United+Nations+%7C+United+Nations&cvid=7078cf05879540418e03b01a59aa09be&gs_lcrp=EgZjaHJvbWUyBggAEEUYOTIGCAEQRRhAMgcIAhBFGPxV0gEIMTQ4NmowajSoAgCwAgA&FORM=ANAB01&PC=U531. Date visited 13 September 2025.

[89] See also Chap. 1 para 1.3.

[90] Baxi (2017), p. 167.

[91] UNGP para 3.

[92] See Chap. 1 para 1.2.

The second pillar of the framework is the corporate responsibility to respect human and labour rights, which requires MNEs to avoid infringing on the rights of others and to address adverse impacts with which a business is involved.[93] In order to address the adverse human rights impacts, MNEs are required to take adequate measures for their prevention, mitigation and, where appropriate, remediation. It is argued that whilst it is easier for MNEs to draft instruments containing a list of obligations for themselves and their suppliers, unfortunately, the same cannot be said in respect of remediation for breaches of the same obligations.

The MNEs may not become their own police and punish themselves in favour of workers who are victims of their conduct. There is also little evidence that MNEs have done so since the adoption of the UNGPs. It is argued that whenever the labour rights interests' conflict with profit interests, MNEs will choose the latter.[94]

The last pillar of the framework emphasises the need for access to effective judicial and non-judicial remedies for victims of MNEs.[95] It is argued that this is the most challenging part of the framework. Currently, none of the regulatory instruments create a list of remedies for employees of MNEs. Therefore, it is left up to MNEs to decide what to do whenever they breach human and labour rights. There are, however, signs that the NGOs responsible for dispute resolution of MNEs are beginning to introduce a hard law approach to cases referred to them.[96]

The standards contained in the UNGPs have since been adopted in other international legal instruments. In particular, the OECD Guidelines followed this route.[97] The recent International Organisation for Standardisation (ISO 26000) Guidance on corporate social responsibility standards also reflects the UNGPs in its human rights provisions.[98] The UNGPs seek to ensure that labour rights are protected and where they are violated by MNEs, the workers should have access to remedies. As such, it is concluded that in line with the positivist approach labour rights contained in UNGPs are indeed human rights.

---

[93] UNGP para II.

[94] See Chap. 1 para 1.2.

[95] UNGPs para III.

[96] See Chap. 4 para 4.4 for cases where the NCPs found MNEs guilty of breach of OECD Guidelines. See also Chap. 5 para 5.2 where a number of NGOs managed to secure remedies for employees who were victims of labour and human rights abuse by MNEs.

[97] See Chap. 4 para 4.1 for detailed discussion on OECD Guidelines.

[98] ISO (International Organisation for Standardisation) is an independent, NGO with a membership of 168 national standards bodies. ISO standards are internationally agreed upon by experts. ISO 26000 is deigned to empower organisations to make meaningful contribution to sustainable development. It urges organisations to surpass mere legal compliance, acknowledging that adherence to the law is a fundamental obligation for any organisation. Organisations should proactively consider societal, legal, organisational diversity, while also adapting to various economic conditions, all while upholding international norms of behaviour. The primary focus of the ISO26000 is on labour practices, encompassing employment relationships, working conditions, social protection, social dialogue, health and safety at workplaces, human development and training the workplace.

2.6.1.3 The ILO MNE Declaration

The ILO MNE Declaration was adopted by the ILO Governing Body (GB) in 1977 and has been amended four times, the latest being in 2022.[99] According to Goldstein: 'the ILO MNE Declaration is the only ILO instrument that provides direct guidance to MNEs on social policy and inclusive, responsible and sustainable workplace practices'.[100] Globally, the ILO MNE Declaration is the only instrument that regulates the conduct of MNEs that was discussed and adopted by governments, employers and employees. Apart from the UNGPs and the OECD Guidelines, the ILO MNE Declaration is regarded by the ILO as one of the three leading instruments recognised by the international community that seek to ensure that MNEs comply with human rights and labour rights.[101]

The ILO MNE Declaration is also recognised by the UN in the Ruggie framework as one of the instruments that regulates compliance with human and labour rights by MNEs. In addition to the above, the Ruggie framework mentions that MNEs must comply with the rights contained in the ILO Declaration on Fundamental Principles and Rights at Work. Such rights are, amongst others, the elimination of forced labour, the abolition of child labour, and equal opportunities.[102] These rights are also contained in the ILO MNE Declaration.

MNEs must use their purchasing influence to ensure that the third-party companies involved in their supply chain comply with recognised human and labour rights and that they provide remediation where violation occurred.[103] The rights in question are contained in the UDHR and the principles concerning fundamental rights set out in the ILO Declaration on Fundamental Principles and Rights at Work.[104]

It is submitted that the ILO MNE Declaration is a human rights instrument for the following reasons. It is recognised in certain prominent human rights instruments such as the UNGPs. Further, the rights that it seeks to protect are also contained in other human rights instruments. For example, the UNGPs and UDHR. To the extent that the freedom of association and elimination of child and forced labour are listed in the ILO MNE Declaration, there remains no doubt that they are to be deemed as human rights. In the part that follows, the South African Constitution is briefly discussed.

---

[99] https://www.ilo.org/empent/areas/mne-declaration/lang%2D%2Den/index.htm. Date visited 13 September 2025.

[100] Goldstein (2020), p. 1265.

[101] https://www.ilo.org/resource/other/what-ilo-mne-declaration. Date visited 13 September 2025.

[102] ILO MNE Declaration para 25 to 31.

[103] Clause 65 of the ILO MNE Declaration.

[104] Para 10 of the ILO MNE Declaration.

2.6.1.4 The Constitution of the Republic of South Africa, Act No 108 of 1996

The Constitution of the Republic of South Africa (the Constitution, 1996) was enacted after the historic release of Nelson Mandela and the end of apartheid in South Africa. Although the Constitution, 1996 does not fall under the category of international treaties and conventions, this study will not be complete from a South African perspective without covering this milestone document.

According to the acclaimed human rights authors, Heyns and Brand, the South African Constitution, 1996 provides arguably one of the most sophisticated and comprehensive systems for the protection of socio-economic rights of all the constitutions in the world today.[105] In South Africa, labour rights are listed in Chap. 2 of the Constitution under a 'Bill of Rights' which forms the cornerstone of democracy in South Africa.

It enshrines the rights of all people in the country and affirms the democratic values of human dignity, equality, and freedom.[106] The state must respect, protect, promote, and fulfil the rights in the Bill of Rights and all legislative instruments should be aligned to its fundamental principles.[107] Such rights may only be limited by a law of general application in terms of section 36 of the Constitution which is acceptable in an open and democratic country.

Section 23 of the Constitution provides various individual employee and collective labour rights to employees. For example, the section includes every person's right to fair labour practices, the right to form and join a trade union, the right to strike, and the right to collective bargaining. The Constitution, 1996 has been influential in the development of South African labour law. So, for example, the Labour Relations Act,[108] the Employment Equity Act,[109] and each seeks to give effect to the labour rights contained in the Constitution, 1996.

In *NUMSA v Baderbop*, the Constitutional Court held that South African courts are obliged to take ILO conventions and recommendations into account when interpreting South African legislation.[110] However, litigants are not entitled to bypass the legislation and rely directly on a constitutional right unless the litigant claims that it falls short or is unconstitutional. This is referred to as the 'principle of subsidiarity' which *South African National Defence Union v Minister of Defence and Others*[111] confirmed.

It is submitted that there can be no doubt that labour rights should be deemed to be human rights in the South African context.

---

[105] Heyns and Brand (1998), p. 153.

[106] Section 7(1) of the Constitution of the Republic of South Africa.

[107] Section 7(2) of the Constitution of the Republic of South Africa.

[108] 66 of the Act 1995.

[109] 55 of the Act 1998.

[110] At para 26.

[111] [2007] 9 BLLR 785 (CC). See para 44.

2.6.2 Instrumental Approach

The second test to determine whether labour rights are human rights is an instrumental approach.[112] Mantouvalou states that this method started to emerge in the 1970s, after it was realised that collective bargaining could not provide all the protection employees needed.[113] Scholars in favour of this test, examine which labour rights constitutes human rights in accordance with the specific documents, and they analyse how institutions and civil society organisations performed in safe guarding them.[114] This approach evaluates the outcomes of litigation, and if they are successful, the labour rights in question will be regarded as human rights.[115]

The European Court of Human Rights receives most claims submitted by employees who allege that their national government has violated their human rights protected under the ECHR. In *Siliadin v France*[116] the ECtHR upheld the right to work in decent conditions. The facts of the case were that the employer (spouse) took the employee's passport and forced her to work as an unpaid domestic worker. She was later lent to another employer who decided to keep her as an unpaid housemaid and child caretaker, working 15-hour days, seven days a week. Before the EctHR, both employers were found guilty and sentenced to 12 months imprisonment each, seven months of which were suspended.

It is submitted that this court's decision indicates that the courts are willing to find that labour rights are human rights. However, this study does not rely on the instrumental test as it is expensive and complicated to enforce human rights through court processes in developing countries.

2.6.3 The Normative Approach

The final approach to the question of whether labour rights are human rights is a normative one. It examines whether labour rights in question qualify as human rights per the definition of human rights, namely, 'the rights that are accorded to all human beings by virtue of their humanity'.[117] If the labour right is found to have key features of human rights, it will be classified as a human right.

According to Atkinson, the normative approach examines human rights as a matter of theory and considers their implications for labour law.[118] To determine whether

---

[112] As above.

[113] Mantouvalou (2012), p. 157.

[114] As above.

[115] Warikandwa (2014), p. 251.

[116] https://ec.europa.eu/anti-trafficking/siliadin-v-france-application-no-7331601_en. Date visited 13 September 2025.

[117] Mantouvalou (2012), p. 152.

[118] Atkinson (2018), p. 1.

labour rights are human rights, this approach accepts that human rights are universal moral rights that make up a distinct body of norms, and they exist independently of any legal or institutional recognition. Unlike the positivist approach which takes the lists of rights contained in international treaties or domestic constitutions as human rights, the normative approach differs. Instead, questions about which rights are human rights, and the nature and content of these rights, must be answered by a philosophical theory.[119]

Under this approach, labour rights will be framed as human rights, if it represents the urgency and compelling moral claims compared to traditional human rights like the right to life.[120] Certain labour rights such as access to trade union representation may not be as urgent as a right to life. This study does not rely extensively on this test either as the definition against which it should be measured is relatively wide and may incorrectly exclude many labour rights from the list of human rights.

2.7 Conclusion

This Chapter has argued that labour rights are human rights and that such a finding is foundational to the attainment of decent work in the context of the regulation of MNEs. Where there are doubts on such a finding, it has been shown that human rights cannot be fulfilled when labour rights are ignored. Therefore, the attainment of sound labour rights is a vehicle for the fulfilment of human rights such as the right to life. It is hard to imagine that the right to a dignified life can be attained without decent work.

This Chapter has also illustrated that even though some scholars may not agree with the argument that labour rights do constitute human rights, there can be no doubt viewed from a South African context that the Bill of Rights, contained in the Constitution, 1996 sets out several labour rights as human rights. As such, MNEs operating in South Africa will be bound by these rights in so far as human rights are enforceable.

It has been demonstrated that regulation of labour rights through other means which exclude human rights principles will only reduce labour to a commodity. This is particularly relevant in the case of MNEs where means should be sought to counter a race to the bottom in developing countries. Such may open an opportunity for workers' rights to be abused. The workers have dignity and their rights as human beings must be respected. Therefore, labour law has an important role in ensuring that human rights, such as the right to decent work, are properly protected in the workplace. Reformulating the right to decent work as a human right that must be respected under international law can begin a process of change, particularly in the international context.

[119] Warikandwa (2014), p. 253.

[120] Collins (2020), p. 494.

References

Anker R, Mehran F, Egger P, Chernyshev I, Ritter J (2003) Measuring decent work with statistical indicators. Int Labour Rev

Atkinson J (2018) Human rights as foundations for labour law. Oxford University Press

Baxi U (2017) Towards socially sustainable globalisation: reflections on responsible contracting and the UN guiding principles on business and human rights. Indian J Int Law

Bellace J (2011) Achieving social justice: the nexus between the ILO's fundamental rights and decent work. Employee Rights Employ Policy J

Buhmann K (2015) Business and human rights: understanding the UN Guiding Principles from the perspective of transnational business governance interactions. Routledge

Cohen T, Moodley L (2012) Achieving 'decent work' in South Africa? Potchefstroom Electron Law J/Potchefstroomse Elektroniese Regsblad

Collins H (2020) Labour Rights as Human Rights: The Derivation of Labour Rights from Civil and Political Rights under the European Convention on Human Rights. Capital University Law Review

Collins P (2022) Putting human rights to work: labour law, the ECHR, and the employment relation. Oxford University Press

Compa L (2008) Labour's new opening to international human rights standards. J Labour Soc

Dawkins C (2022) Disciplining the notion of 'labour rights as human rights'. Global Labour J

Frey D, MacNaughton G (2016) A human rights lens on full employment and decent work in the 2030 Sustainable Development Agenda. J Workplace Rights

Ghai D (2003) Decent work: concept and indicators. Int Labour Rev

Goldstein A (2020) Dirty business: accountability for harmful pesticide use in Brazil. Int Comp Policy Ethics Law Rev

Grogan J (2017) Workplace Law. Juta South Africa

Hepple B (2003) Rights at work international. Institute for Labour Studies Geneva

Hertel S (2009) Human rights and the global economy: bringing labour rights back. Mayland J Int Law

Heyns C, Brand D (1998) Introduction to socio-economic rights in the South African constitution. Law Democr Dev

Kolben K (2010) Labour rights as human rights. Va J Int Law

Mantouvalou V (2012) Are labour rights human rights. Eur Labour Law J

Okpaluba C (2012) Law and contemporary South African society. New Africa Books

Okuwa B (2020) Job Creation and Decent Work in Oyo State Nigeria. Scientific Research Publishing

Pariotti E (2018) Human Rights as Basic Rights: Path to Universality. Persona Y Derecho Journal

Piasna A, Bruchell B (2020) Decent work: conceptualisation and policy impact. Springer

Pocar F (2015) Some thoughts on the Universal Declaration of Human Rights and the 'generations' of human rights? Intercult Hum Rights Law Rev

Rombouts B, Zekic N (2020) Decent and sustainable work for the future?' (2020). Univ Calif Los Angeles J Int Law

Stefano V, Antonio A (2019) Fundamental labour rights, platform work and human rights protection of nonstandard workers. Labour Bus Hum Rights Law J

Sun P (2009) On significance of the birth of the Universal Declaration of Human Rights. Hum Rights J

Sychenko E (2017) Infringement proceedings in EU Law. Wolters Kluwer

Van Eck S (2013) Regulated flexibility and the Labour Relations Amendment Bill of 2012. De Jure

Van Eck S, Vettori S (2001) The Unemployment Insurance Bill: A relic of the past? South African Mercantile Law Journal

Van Eck S, Pamhidzai B, Chanda C, Kalula E (2020) Celebrating the ILO 100 years on reflections on labour law from a South African perspective. Juta

Warikandwa T (2014) Human rights, core labour standards and the search for a legal basis for a trade-labour linkage in the multilateral trade regime of the World Trade Organisation. Law Democr Dev

Youngdahl J (2009) Solidarity first labour rights are not the same as human rights. New Labour Forum

Chapter 3
The Monitoring of MNEs by the ILO

3.1 Introduction

The ILO was established in 1919, as part of the Treaty of Versailles that ended the First World War.[1] According to Deranty and MacMillan, at the time of its establishment, the ILO's founding members believed that universal and lasting peace could be attained only if it was based upon social justice.[2] As early as in 1919, the ILO recognised that its urgent and main priority was to promote the creation of humane working conditions free from hardship, privation, and injustice.[3] In its preamble, the ILO identified a number of priorities which were necessary for the attainment of social justice. The preamble includes the following core elements:

> the regulation of the hours of work, the regulation of the labour supply, the prevention of unemployment, the provision of an adequate living wage … recognition of the principle of freedom of association and social protection.[4]

Many scholars commended the ILO for its achievements in setting the minimum labour standards. For instance, Weiss states that the achievements of the ILO in 'standard setting are undoubtedly a success story … almost 200 conventions and even more recommendations, … are an impressive output'.[5] The ILO's advantage lies in its unique tripartite structure that reflects the significance of consulting with governments, employees, and employers in setting economic policy.[6]

---

[1] Van Niekerk and Smit (2019), p. 23.

[2] Deranty and MacMillan (2012), p. 386. See also the official website of the ILO; https://www.ilo.org/resource/other/ilo-constitution. Date visited 13 September 2025.

[3] Preamble of the ILO Constitution.

[4] Preamble of the ILO.

[5] Weiss (2013), p. 9.

[6] Dahan et al. (2013), p. 693.

F. Maluleke, *Compliance with Decent Work Standards by Multinational Enterprises*, European Yearbook of International Economic Law 48,
https://doi.org/10.1007/978-3-032-21261-0_3

However, the ILO has been criticised for poor monitoring and enforcement of the set minimum labour standards.[7] As stated in Chap. 1, the rapid globalisation which favours the operations of MNEs at the expense of human and labour rights, has led to a reduction in regulations that protect workers.[8] It is submitted that the ILO should find new ways to engage its traditional partners and private actors participating in a global labour market.

This chapter sets out the ILO's structures and main bodies concerning norm-setting. Second, it explains the ILO's monitoring and enforcement mechanisms, and it highlights the positive and negative aspects about it. Third, the chapter highlights the binding effect and enforcement mechanisms of the ILO MNE Declaration. Fourth, it analyses the ILO's evolving role in responding to challenges posed by globalisation, particularly through private partnerships with other international organisations.

3.2 The Main Bodies of the ILO and Norm-Setting

The ILO accomplishes its work through three main bodies, namely: the Governing Body (GB), the International Labour Office, and the ILC.[9] The structures are discussed in more detail in the sections that follow.

3.2.1 The Governing Body

The GB is the executive body of the ILO and is regarded as the secretariat of the organisation.[10] The initial task of the GB was that of drawing up the agenda of the International Labour Conference (ILC) and providing direction to the ILO.[11] However, this role has evolved and currently its powers go beyond its original mandate. The GB also elects and appoints its Director General without any formal need for the agreement of the ILC.[12] It also has the power to create a commission of inquiry.[13] In addition, it also prepares the ILO's budget based on the proposals of the Director General.

[7] Van Eck et al. (2020), p. 7.

[8] See Chap. 1 para 1.2.

[9] https://www.ilo.org/global/about-the-ilo/how-the-ilo-works/lang%2D%2Den/index.htm date visited 13 September 2025.

[10] Van Niekerk and Smit (2019), p. 25.

[11] Gironde and Carbonnier (2019), p. 43.

[12] As above.

[13] See para below for a detailed discussion on the commission of inquiry.

3.2.2 The International Labour Office

First and foremost, the International Labour Office is the permanent secretariat of the ILO.[14] It is responsible for the ILO's day to day activities, which it performs under the supervision of Governing Body.[15] Additionally, the ILO is tasked with conducting research under two categories. The first category encompass research produced internally by current officials of the ILO.[16] The second category includes research produced by independent academics whose publications are driven by scientific interest and theoretical inquiries, without personal ties to the organisation.[17]

3.2.3 The ILC

The ILC is the apex body of the ILO and it can be viewed as an international parliament of labour where social and labour questions of importance to the entire world are discussed freely.[18] The ILC is tasked with the important responsibility of crafting and adopting minimum labour standards in the form of conventions.[19] Conventions are 'legal instruments drawn up by the ILO's constituents (governments, employers, and workers) and setting out basic principles and rights at work'.[20] Recommendations serve as non-binding guidelines. Conventions become binding on an ILO member state only after the member state has ratified them.[21]

In 2013, Weiss warned that many conventions need updating, and that there is a decline in the signing of new conventions.[22] Further, it is regrettable that many

---

[14] Van Niekerk and Smit (2019), p. 25.

[15] As above.

[16] Van Deale (2008), p. 487.

[17] Van Deale (2008), p. 488.

[18] https://streetnet.org.za/international-labour-conference/ date visited 14 September 2025.

[19] International Labour Standards (ILS) refer to the conventions agreed upon by international actors (workers, employers, and government representatives) which emerged from a series of value judgements, principles for the protection of worker rights, enhances job security among workers, and improve on their terms and conditions of employment on a global scale (ILO, 2004). The purpose of such standards is to prevent inhumane labour practices among the ILO member states through the adoption and implementation of such measures. The ILO member countries may ratify conventions at any time once they are adopted by the ILC.

[20] https://www.ilo.org/global/standards/introduction-to-international-labour-standards/conventions-and-recommendations/lang%2D%2Den/index.htm date visited 14 September 2025.

[21] Chau et al. (2001), p. 113. See also Van Niekerk and Smit (2019), p. 25. Once a standard is adopted, the ILO member states should in terms of article 19(6) of the ILO Constitution, submit it to their national parliaments for consideration within a period of twelve months. If the parliament ratifies the convention, it should come to force in that country after twelve months from the date of the of ratification.

[22] Weiss (2013), p. 9.

countries still have to ratify all the fundamental and priority conventions.[23] As stated in Chap. 1, this tendency has the potential to affect the labour market negatively because countries with low labour standards tend to attract many MNEs.[24] This phenomenon gives such countries an unfair advantage by attracting more MNEs to their jurisdiction.[25]

At the ILC, the minimum labour standards are adopted by a two-thirds majority vote of ILO constituents. It is argued that because of this high threshold requirement, the standards contained in the ILO conventions are regarded as universally acceptable.[26] However, it has the effect of reducing the number of conventions to be adopted.

In the parts that follow, the monitoring and enforcement mechanisms of the ILO are discussed in more detail.

3.3 The Monitoring and Enforcement Mechanisms of the ILO

In addition to setting minimum labour standards, the ILO also has the task of ensuring that its member countries adhere to such standards. In this regard, the ILO has a unique reporting supervisory system, which tracks the progress in implementation of ratified conventions by its member states. The system allows the ILO to review reports, interview state officials, and visit its member states to inspect the level of their application of the conventions.[27] The reporting system consists of two main elements: a regular supervisory process and three special procedures which are discussed below.

3.3.1 The Regular System of Supervision

This supervisory system creates an obligation for the ILO member states to submit reports on measures they have taken to give effect to ratified conventions.[28] The report is an important indicator of the progress made in fulfilling their international labour standards obligations. These reports must be submitted every three years,

---

[23] Those countries are amongst others Afghanistan, Brunei Darussalam, China, Japan, Marshall Islands, Myanmar, Palau, Tonga, Tuvulu, Republic of Korea, Tonga, and USA.

[24] See Chap. 1 para 1.1–1. 2.

[25] As above.

[26] Deranty and MacMillan (2012), p. 386.

[27] Payne (2017), p. 609.

[28] Article 22 of the ILO Constitution states that 'each of the members agrees to make an annual report to the International Labour Office on the measures which it has taken to give effect to the provisions of Conventions to which it is a party'.

and they must provide detailed steps taken in law and practice on applying any of the eight fundamental and four governance conventions that they have ratified.[29] The reports should be provided every six years with respect of all other conventions. This excludes conventions that have been 'shelved' and therefore no longer subject to regular supervision.[30] The ILO may, however, at its discretion, request reports on the application of conventions at shorter intervals.

It is worrisome that the traditional supervisory procedures of the ILO ignore the impact of MNEs on human and labour rights violations. The existing procedures only require ILO member states to account for violations of human and labour rights in their countries. Furthermore, poor countries may not have the necessary resources to hold MNEs accountable. To bridge the gap and emphasise on the importance of ILO based compliance instruments, Alhambra, Ter Haar and Kun recommended for introduction of a transnational inspectorate at the ILO level which will be responsible for carrying out inspections of compliance by MNEs.[31] Such reasoning finds support from this study as evidence demonstrates that MNEs impact human and labour rights in a significant way.[32]

It is also concerning that the levels of compliance with the existing supervisory systems are very low. Some ILO member states fail to submit reports even after direct requests have been made. (See the detailed discussion on the Committee of Experts on the Application of Conventions and Recommendations below).

3.3.2 The Committee of Experts on the Application of Conventions and Recommendations

The Committee of Experts on the Application of Conventions and Recommendations (CEACR) was established in 1926 to examine the growing number of government reports on ratified Conventions.[33] Today it is composed of 20 eminent jurists who are considered experts. They come from different geographic regions, legal systems, and cultures appointed by the GB for three-year terms.[34] The role of the CEACR is to provide an impartial and technical evaluation of the application of international labour standards in ILO member States.[35]

---

[29] As above.

[30] As above.

[31] Alhambra et al. (2020) *ILR* 236.

[32] See Chap. 1 para 1.2.

[33] https://www.ilo.org/global/standards/applying-and-promoting-international-labour-standards/committee-of-experts-on-the-application-of-conventions-and-recommendations/lang%2D%2Den/index.htm date visited 14 September 2025.

[34] As above.

[35] As above.

The CEACR produces two kinds of conclusions: observations and direct requests. Observations are generally used 'in more serious or long-standing cases of failure to fulfil obligations'.[36] They also 'address the absence of measures to give effect to a Convention or to take appropriate action following the Committee's requests'.[37] The observations are published in the CEACR's annual report.

Direct requests, on the other hand, are technical in nature and they facilitate continuous dialogue between the CEACR and governments of the ILO member states.[38] They can, amongst others, be used to clarify certain points when the submitted information does not enable a full appreciation of the extent to which the obligations are fulfilled. Unlike the published observations, the direct requests are not published in the report but are communicated directly to the governments concerned.

The CEACR reports are tabled at the ILC for analyses by the Committee on the Application of Standards (CAS), a standing body of the ILC. The CAS 'is mandated to draw up conclusions about a selection of observations from the reports'.[39] Rombouts argues that such reports have a political flavour and that they highlight specific issues of particular concern about countries. However, he warns that ILO member states being investigated may not accept the reports as they may be seen as instruments to force a regime change.

In 2023, the CEACR made 656 observations and 1,263 direct requests.[40] The 2023 CEACR report indicates that several countries did not submit their reports on ratified fundamental conventions, and some member countries[41] failed to report in successive years. Such a failure denies the CEACR an opportunity to assess the level of compliance with important minimum labour standards by the said ILO member states. In some cases, some ILO member states like Equatorial Guinea failed to submit reports in fifteen successive years and 14 reports are due on fundamental and technical conventions.[42]

Predictably, commenting on the failure to submit reports by the mentioned ILO member states, the CEACR noted with great concern the non-submission and hoped that the governments of such countries would comply with direct requests.[43] Further,

---

[36] Report of the Committee of Experts on the Application of Conventions and Recommendations (2023) para 106.

[37] As above.

[38] As above.

[39] Rombouts (2019), p. 137.

[40] Report of the Committee of Experts on the Application of Conventions and Recommendations (2023) Para 107.

[41] The ILO member states in question are amongst: Afghanistan, Antigua and Barbuda, Chad, Comoros, Dominica, Gabon, Haiti, Lebanon, Saint Lucia, Slovenia, Somalia, Syrian Arab Republic, Timor-Leste, Tuvalu, Vanuatu, and Yemen.

[42] As above.

[43] Report of the Committee of Experts on the Application of Conventions and Recommendations (2023) para 90.

the ILO indicates its availability and willingness to provide technical assistance to the concerned ILO member states should they request it.[44]

In order to exert pressure on ILO member countries failing to submit reports, the ILO launched an urgent appeal procedure which applies to states that have failed to submit reports for more than three years.[45] The process draws their attention to the fact that if they fail to submit reports which are due, the committee may go ahead and examine the level of application of the conventions concerned based on public information at its position. However, there are still many ILO member states failing to submit reports. It is argued that the ILO is powerless in this situation as it cannot impose any sanction, even in cases of deliberate and consistent failure to submit reports.

As a result of the said deficiencies in the reports, it can thus be concluded that the CEACR reports do not provide a true reflection of the level of compliance by ILO member states. It is concerning that the details of direct requests are deliberately omitted in the ILO publication. It is submitted that such an omission only protects the ILO member states against public shaming which frustrates the very purpose of publication. The part that follows analyses the positive and negative aspects of the ILO's existing monitoring and enforcement procedures.

3.4 Positive Aspects of the ILO's Monitoring and Enforcement Procedures

Scholars who believe that the ILO supervisory mechanisms are effective are, amongst others, Tapiola and Swepston. These scholars argue that the ILO's supervisory mechanism is 'complex' and has many avenues to exert pressure on governments of ILO member states to ensure compliance with human and labour standards.[46] Contrary to the views of many observers, Bendix argues that the ILO acts as a watchdog and expresses censure on countries not adhering to ratified conventions.[47] The ILO's monitoring mechanisms allow for the publication of a list of ILO member states failing to comply with the ratified conventions. South Africa is one such example in that it resigned from ILO due to pressure from supervisory mechanisms.

---

[44] As above.

[45] https://guide-supervision.ilo.org/reporting/reports-on-ratified-conventions-are-due-every-three-or-six-years-depending-on-the-convention-and-the-alphabetical-order-of-the-countrys-name/. Date visited 14 September 2025.

[46] Tapiola and Swepston (2010), p. 515.

[47] Bendix (2015), p. 98.

Further, experience has shown that the naming-and-shaming technique has the effect of producing compliance.[48] The governments of ILO member states fear being publicly exposed and criticised by the international community and may even feel a sense of shame or embarrassment about their wrongdoings. In the Australian case, the government passed a new law which had a detrimental impact on collective bargaining and Australian workers. The initial response of the Australian government was that the issue was neither sufficiently important to 'warrant immediate consideration' at international level. However, despite the reluctance of the Australian government to be publicly criticised, the ILO continued the criticism until the Act was repealed.[49]

It is argued that naming and shaming may produce compliance through different pathways and under certain conditions. A country may incur reputational and social costs by mobilising various reform-minded groups and transnational actors.[50] However, it is not sufficient, and more research is required to increase the rate of compliance.

3.5 Negative Aspects of the ILO's Monitoring and Enforcement Procedures

Maupain, Payne, and Fraterman have criticised the ILO supervisory procedures for their lack of enforcement power, which they attribute to non-compliance with its recommendations by offending ILO member states. They argue that the ILO's supervisory system makes no provision for issuing penalties or sanctions in the event of non-compliance, but instead it focuses on dialogue, recommendations, persuasion, and technical assistance. Maupain submits that the ILO's failure to successfully enforce compliance with its set standards is attributable to the gamble

[48] In June 1998, the ILO publicly criticised Sudan for violating one of the organisation's fundamental conventions: the abolition of forced labour. The ILO asserted that there was strong evidence of the practice of slavery and slave trading in the country. After being exposed as a norm violator to the international community, and subsequently criticised by other members of the ILO, the Sudanese representative called the allegations unreasonable and dishonest. The government representative declared that the allegations constituted a 'slap in her face' and that she 'felt embarrassed' by the accusations (ILO, 1998). While the government of Sudan denied the existence of slavery practices, the ILO's criticism put pressure on the government to introduce new reforms intended to abolish forced labour. In a similar vein, the Australian government was publicly named and shamed by the ILO for the Workplace Act, which gave preference to individual agreements on the labour market, violating the ILO's fundamental convention on the right to organise and collective bargaining.

[49] Similarly, when Belarus was targeted by the ILO as one of the worst violators of international standards, the Belarusian government not only rejected the allegations but found it unacceptable to be compared to countries like Qatar and Ethiopia.

[50] Koliev (2018), p. 4.

taken by its founders of entirely relying on instruments of persuasion to achieve its purpose, as opposed to binding instruments.[51]

Fraterman notes that once sanctioned by the ILC, an offending state could always renounce its adherence to the convention in question, thereby evading punishment.[52] Further, the ILO does not view its monitoring bodies as judicial or quasi-judicial mechanisms. As a result, the ILO's GB cannot deliver binding decisions on infringements of human and labour rights or shame the perpetrators of such infringements.[53] It is submitted that the ILO has no other solution for its member state that refuses to implement its recommendations. Payne is of the view that the mobilisation of shame through the publication of a member state's failure or violation is not strong enough to effect real change.[54]

Further, the ILO does not offer remedies like compensation to the affected individuals. Instead, it focuses on the future conduct of the offending member state. It is argued that this situation does not assist the victims of human and labour rights violations. This area must be revisited to ensure that victims are not only protected against future violations but also get remedies for violations already suffered.

In the sections that follow, the binding effect of the ILO MNE Declaration is discussed.

3.6 The Binding Effect and Enforcement of the ILO MNE Declaration

As discussed in Chap. 2, the ILO MNE Declaration's goal is the provision of effective dispute resolution regarding MNEs in global supply chains.[55] As part of their duty to protect workers against business-related human and labour rights abuses, governments are compelled to provide judicial means and remedies.[56] Where the governments fail to implement such an obligation or did not ratify certain conventions, MNEs should use their influence to promote compliance with internationally recognised labour standards by all their business partners. They should also make it a requirement for their business partners to provide remediation of abuses of internationally recognised human rights.[57]

All employees employed by MNEs, acting individually or jointly with other employees who believe that they have grievance(s), should be allowed to refer their complaint without any threat of retaliation. Such a complaint should be investigated

[51] Maupain (2013), p. 1.

[52] Fraterman (2011), p. 879.

[53] Kagan (2011), p. 217.

[54] Payne (2017), p. 609.

[55] See Chap. 2 para 2.6.

[56] Clause 64 of the ILO MNE Declaration.

[57] As above.

through an appropriate procedure. This is specifically important whenever the MNE conducts businesses in countries which do not adhere and respect ILO conventions.

This is challenging because MNEs are not always directly responsible for violation of human and labour rights.[58] Such rights are often violated by the subcontractors and suppliers doing business with MNEs. In its current form, the ILO MNE Declaration indicates that MNEs should use their leverage to ensure that their business partners involved in their supply chains also comply with labour standards. As such, it is left to the individual MNE to determine the meaning of such leverage. There is a need for the parameters of the expectations from MNEs to be clarified and properly defined. For instance, it would need to be indicated under which conditions the MNE is expected to terminate the relationship with the business partners for violation of human and labour rights.

In terms of the ILO MNE Declaration, governments and MNEs are required to at least adopt conciliation and arbitration procedures to assist in the prevention and settlement of industrial disputes between employers and employees involved in their supply chain.[59] The procedure should be free of charge and preferably be expeditious.[60] It is argued that the expectation for the MNEs to participate in establishing dispute resolution procedures is not practical and reasonable. It would imply that the MNE plays a dual role or being the alleged violator of labour rights and at the same time be responsible for resolution of such disputes. As such, the process will lack legitimacy and credibility.

It is not surprising that most MNEs only opted to have conciliation of disputes and excluded arbitration from their codes of conduct.[61] Instead of adopting a similar provision, the ILO MNE Declaration adopted an interpretation procedure as a method to resolve disputes. The procedure is discussed below.

3.6.1 The Interpretation Procedure

The interpretation procedure is a voluntary tool, and it is used to interpret the provisions of the ILO MNE Declaration when the need arises to resolve the members' disagreement on their meaning.[62] Several principles apply to this procedure. The request for interpretation must arise from a factual situation between two or more parties to whom the ILO MNE Declaration applies.[63] The requester must be a government of an ILO member state, a national organisation of employers or workers'

[58] See Chap. 1 para 1.3.

[59] Clause 67 of the ILO MNE Declaration.

[60] As above.

[61] See Chap. 5 para 5.3 for detailed discussion.

[62] Heric and Cernic (2009), p. 31.

[63] Para 1 of the ILO MNE Declaration.

representative at the national and or sectoral level, or an international organisation of employers or workers on behalf of a representative national affiliate.[64] Second, the procedure in the particular case may not duplicate existing national process or that of the ILO.[65]

Therefore, the ILO will refuse to process a case if the requester already followed another process at the national level. Second, the request for interpretation may only be made where the concerned government has declined to submit the request to the ILO or three months have elapsed since the requesting organisation addressed the issue to the government.[66] It is submitted that the requirement that only a government is entitled to refer a case to the interpretation procedure is absurd. It presupposes that the violators can only be a government. This ignores MNEs which violate human and labour rights.

It is not surprising that after the decades of this procedure having been introduced, only a limited number of cases were referred for such interpretation. Thus far, only twenty-one cases have been referred for the interpretation procedure.[67] Further, the details of the parties, including the names of the MNEs involved, are withheld. It is submitted that such confidentiality of basic details undermines the efficacy of the procedure. The interpretation procedure is by its very nature limited since it cannot be invoked to challenge violations of internationally recognised labour standards by MNEs.[68]

The employees who feel that their labour rights were violated by MNEs have no option but to rely on remedies catered for by their national laws. Further, the procedure does not offer any real solution to individual employees. It can thus be concluded that the interpretation procedure does not create an additional platform for employees who are victims of human and labour rights violations by MNEs. Instead, the employees must still rely on ineffective national laws. In some instances, employees must use highly complex and costly civil procedures.[69]

The interpretation procedure falls short of the standard expected in Ruggie framework as it fails to ensure that the employee rights are protected and respected and where the violation occurred, so that the employees are provided with effective remedies.[70] Hepple described the ILO MNE Declaration as another example of soft international law which is disappointing.[71] Neither is it legally enforceable, and it

[64] As above.

[65] Annexure II clause 2 of the MNE Declaration declares that to avoid duplication, the following disputes cannot be referred for interpretation. The procedure should not be in conflict with other dispute resolution procedures catered for in the country concerned. Thus, it cannot be invoked: (a) in respect of national law and practice; (b) in respect of international labour Conventions and Recommendations; and (c) in respect of matters falling under the freedom of association procedure.

[66] Paragraph 2 of the ILO MNE Declaration.

[67] Heric and Cernic (2009), p. 35.

[68] Annexure II clause 2 of the ILO MNE Declaration.

[69] Schoeman (2019), p. 446.

[70] See Chap. 2 para 2.6.

[71] Hepple (2003), p. 26.

cannot be invoked before national courts or tribunals. It has been ineffective because of the absence of sanctions to secure compliance with its standards, even by countries which adopt them.[72]

The part that follows discusses the ILO's experience in supervision of international organisations outside of its traditional supervisory procedures.

3.7 Partnerships Between the ILO and Other International Organisations

3.7.1 The Supervision of the Accord on Fire and Building Safety in Bangladesh

The Accord on Fire and Building Safety in Bangladesh (the Accord) is an 'independent, legally binding agreement' concluded by two global trade unions (IndustriALL and UNI Global) with over 190 MNEs and 1600 factories involved in their supply chains.[73] The Accord was concluded after the Rana Plaza factory building collapsed on 24 April 2013, which resulted in death of 1,133 workers and others sustained critical injuries. Furthermore, prior to the Rana Plaza building collapse, several factory fires occurred in Bangladesh. The Accord was adopted to enable a safe working environment in which no employee is exposed to risk of fires or other preventable accidents.[74]

In contrast to many earlier voluntary regulatory instruments, the Accord is a 'binding and enforceable agreement'.[75] Further, its scope extends beyond MNEs, and includes obligations on suppliers to comply with safety requirements. It sees apparel MNEs and retailers at the top of the supply chain as jointly responsible, along with contractors, for certain conditions. The Accord imposes on MNEs financial obligations to help suppliers pay for safety upgrades and major repairs while guaranteeing the payment of workers' salaries for time lost at work.

Due to its binding nature, some MNEs such as Walmart declined to sign on to the accord and instead, decided to partner with the Gap, and they together established the Alliance for Bangladesh Worker Safety (the Alliance), which is a voluntary organisation.[76] The Alliance differs from the Accord in that the former (a) does not require high amount of money from its member MNEs apart from administrative

[72] Hepple (2003), p. 26.

[73] https://bangladeshaccord.org. Date visited 13 September 2025.

[74] As above.

[75] Ter Haar and Keune (2014), pp. 16–25. See also Salminen (2018), p. 411 who mentions that the Accord takes the form of an enforceable contract that directly connects MNEs with worker representatives of the host nations.

[76] https://www.theguardian.com/business/2016/may/31/rana-plaza-bangladesh-collapse-fashion-working-conditions. Date visited 14 September 2025.

fees and a non-obligatory loan program; (b) furthermore, the Alliance lacks enforcement provisions; and (c) another crucial factor is that, the Alliance was developed without worker or trade union participation.[77]

3.7.1.1 How the Accord works

All factories producing for Accord signatory MNEs are required to undergo independent and regular fire, electrical, and structural safety inspections.[78] MNEs should disclose such suppliers and subject them to safety inspections led by recognised and independent experts. Such reports should be: (a) transparent and made public through disclosure of inspection reports; (b) paying suppliers prices that make repairs and renovations possible; (c) the safe operation of factories and maintaining supplier relationships throughout the five-year length of the program; and (d) guaranteeing certain rights to workers.

3.7.1.2 Bodies Created by the Accord

The Accord is governed through a steering committee which comprise three representatives from trade unions and three signatory MNEs, as well as a neutral chairperson from the ILO.[79] The steering committee is supposed to reach decisions by consensus, otherwise through majority votes. The Accord has two offices - one in Dhaka and the other in Amsterdam - to oversee and coordinate its activities, with 95 staff members.[80]

3.7.1.3 Monitoring and Enforcement Mechanisms

The Accord creates an independent complaints mechanism which is operated by 'The Ready Made Garments Sustainability Council' (RSC) which is an independent safety monitoring body.[81] It comprises representatives from three constituents from the industry, MNEs, and global trade unions.[82] In terms of the mechanism, workers and their representatives have a right to refuse unsafe work and can raise complaints with the RSC.[83] Upon receipt of the complaint, the RSC is required to assess the complaint and timely issue a resolution that ensures the remediation of hazards and remedy for any harm done.

---

[77] Salminen (2018), p. 419.

[78] Salminen (2018), p. 419.

[79] Huber and Schormair (2019), p. 464.

[80] Khan et al. (2015), p. 15.

[81] Huber and Schormair (2019), p. 464.

[82] RSC Quarterly Aggregate Report (2023) 3.

[83] As above.

For a complaint to be investigated, the factory involved should be listed in the Accord and there should be identifiable MNEs that procure from such MNEs. On 23 January 2023, the complainant alleged to have been assaulted by a named Factory Manager. The complaint was closed as 'not processed … the factory is not a listed supplier of the Accord'.[84] In as much as the Accord is binding, its membership remains voluntary. As such, MNEs and factories that do not want to be exposed to litigation risks may easily escape liability by refusing to become members or by resigning.

The outcomes of complaints are published on the official website of the Accord. However, complainants, MNEs, and factories have the right to have their names withheld. For instance, in one case, the Accord's official website indicates that a complaint was filed on 08 February 2023 and the names of the complainant, factory, and MNEs involved are withheld. It is argued that the non-disclosure of names of parties may not deter factories from violations of the Accord. Such factories may not suffer reputational harm from the negative findings of the independent complaints' handler.

Further, this study agrees with Anner, Bair, and Blasi who criticised the Accord: '[The Accord] covers only one area of labour standards worker safety'. This is even though there are several complaints which cover the whole labour relations spectrum from complainants. Complaints falling outside the purview of safety violations are closed by indicating that such cases are non-occupational health and safety issues. For instance, on 23 January 2023, a complainant filed a non-payment of due earned wages. The complaint was closed as 'non-OSH complaint … not processed'.[85] It is suggested that future Accords should consider expanding their scope to include other equally important matters such as wage theft.

Upon receipt of a complaint, the RSC should assess the complaint on time and thereafter produce findings on MNEs and the management of the factory. The complaints are finalised expeditiously which is a good sign of a departure from voluntary initiatives where complaints take an unreasonably long time to be finalised.[86]

Another significant area of the Accord is that it creates an arbitration process to resolve complaints which cannot be resolved by means of mediation. Under the Accord's dispute resolution process, disputes concerning implementation are first submitted to the steering committee. Any decision of the steering committee may then, at the request of either party, be appealed to a process of binding arbitration. Dispute resolution under the Accord is based on the standard international commercial arbitration model.[87] The arbitrator's award may be enforced in a court of law of the home country of the signatory party against whom enforcement is sought.

---

[84] https://internationalaccord.org/workers/complaints-mechanism/ date visited 14 September 2025.

[85] https://internationalaccord.org/workers/complaints-mechanism/ date visited 14 September 2025.

[86] See Chap. 4 para 4.6.

[87] Khan et al. (2015), p. 15.

There are two known cases that were arbitrated under the auspices of the Accord. The first one was initiated by the trade union parties against global fashion MNEs which allegedly failed to comply with the standards contained in the Accord. It is unfortunate that the name of the MNE was not named but it participated in the dispute resolution process which resulted in the settlement agreement of $2 million to improve safety measure in over 150 garment factories in Bangladesh. Furthermore, an amount of $300 000 would be paid to the complainants (two trade unions IndustriALL Global Union and UNI Global). The said trade unions were required to set up a fund responsible for projects and initiatives to ensure safety in garment supply chain.

In another case, the trade unions representing Bangladeshi textile workers have reached a landmark settlement agreement wherein the MNE accused of delays in introducing measures to safeguard the lives of employees agreed to pay $2.3 million.[88] It is also reported that IndustriALL and UNI trade unions concluded another settlement agreement with a MNE which sourced from more than 200 factories in Bangladesh. It is disappointing that the terms of the settlement were highly confidential.

Another significant area of the Accord is the explicit requirement of the MNEs to suspend or terminate relationships with factories that fall behind too far in the remediation process or otherwise do not fully participate in the programme and can be suspended and eventually terminated after an escalation procedure. Accord signatory companies and Alliance members are required to terminate business with these suppliers' factories. As of 2018, the list of the Accord contains 93 suppliers - with each one or more production locations - which were terminated by MNEs.[89]

In conclusion, it is argued that the Accord's model for the remediation process appears to be functioning well in getting the necessary remediation implemented up to a good level.[90] The project resulted in the government of Bangladesh upgrading the Chief Inspector of Factories and Establishments Office to a department and creating over 679 new staff positions in the Directorate, including 392 new positions for inspectors. On 22 January 2014, training of the first batch of newly recruited labour inspectors started in Dhaka, focussing on capacity building.

3.7.2 Cooperation Between the ILO and the European Union

3.7.2.1 Background

The cooperation between the ILO and EU dates to 1953 when the EU was established.[91] Since then, the relationship between the two institutions continued to grow, and today they have a significant number of areas in common. For instance, both

[88] https://www.theguardian.com/business/2018/jan/22/bandgladesh-textile-factory-safety-unions-settlement date visited 14 September 2025.

[89] Wiersma (2018), p. 19.

[90] Wiersma (2018), p. 23.

[91] Korda and Pennings (2008), p. 135.

institutions have a tripartite representation in areas such as policymaking.[92] The EU is not a member of the ILO, and it cannot attain membership of the ILO since it is not a country. It has, however, been argued that the EU is not only a legal sovereignty, but it can be seen as a hybrid and international organisation and group of governments at the same time. It, however, continues to contribute to the work of the ILO and the most recent document is the C190 Violence and Harassment Convention.[93]

The partnership between the ILO and EU is allowed in terms of article 12 of the ILO Constitution. The other important area where the two institutions worked together is social security. In this regard, the EU developed a Code of Social Security (ECSS). The ECSS is discussed in detail below.

3.7.2.2 The European Code of Social Security

The European Code of Social Security (ECSS) is an instrument adopted in 1964 by the Council of Europe, which establishes minimum social security standards that member states should provide.[94] It is the same with the ILO Convention No. 102 but the ECSS provides for a higher level of protection.[95] Whilst the ILO Convention No. 102 only requires ILO member countries to comply with three of the nine standards, the ECSS requires the ratification of a minimum of six standards.[96] Further, the preamble of the ECSS states that it has the goal to 'establish a European Code of Social Security at a higher level than the minimum standards embodied in International Labour Convention No. 102 concerning Minimum Standards of Social Security'.[97]

Michoud argues that social security benefits contribute to maintaining a certain social cohesion in Europe by reducing poverty.[98] Such a view finds support in this study. There is also concrete evidence to support the argument in favour of cooperation to increase social security benefits. Countries seeking membership of the EU, are, amongst others, required to satisfy the requirements of the ECSS which increases the levels of social security. For example, in Estonia the unemployment insurance scheme was created which resulted in the improvement of the old-age and invalidity pensions. Furthermore, an annual relief was established to satisfy the standards of the ECSS.[99] The supervision of the ECSS has been given to the ILO and is discussed in the section that follows.

---

92 Koldinská (2019), p. 174.

93 Koldinská (2019), p. 175.

94 Michoud (2018), p. 65.

95 Dijkhoff (2012), p. 178.

96 Dijkhoff (2012), p. 178.

97 Preamble to the Code.

98 Michoud (2018), p .65.

99 Dijkhoff (2012), p. 186.

3.7.2.3 Supervision by the ILO's Committee of Experts

Despite several years of cooperation between the EU and the ILO in economic and social policy, the EU is an international organisation, and it does not have a formal participation status at the ILO.[100] As such, the efficacy of the legislation adopted by the EU can only be evaluated against the purposes as set by the EU itself.

All EU member countries are required to submit annual reports concerning their progress in the application of the ECSS.[101] Each report should include, 'full information concerning the laws and regulations by which effect is given to the provisions of this Code covered by the ratification; and evidence of compliance with the statistical conditions specified'.[102] The Secretary-General should submit the reports to the Director General of the International Labour Office.[103]

It is worrisome that the ILO cannot impose sanctions if it finds that specific countries do not comply with the ECSS.[104] However, the system is to some extent effective as governments do not like to be on the 'special list' of countries that are yet to bring their legislation in line with their international obligations. However, from a legal point of view, the regulatory system is not fully effective. The governments can cancel their ratification if they believe that they are highly limited in their policy choices.[105]

The positive aspect of the relationship between the ILO and the EU is that the EU can influence its member countries to adopt international standards. Furthermore, the EU can also play a part in enforcement of international standards through its procedures.[106] It is therefore submitted that the EU legislation and the ILO international norms can complement each other even establish positive synergies.

3.8 Conclusion

This chapter has shown both successes and failures of the ILO monitoring and enforcement procedures. However, successes were mainly based on the will of concerned ILO member countries. At times, the recommendations of the ILO structures were accepted by offending countries due to the latter's fear of reputational damage. Therefore, the ILO's pressure through recommendations should continue to be applied. However, it is argued that where the offending ILO member state

[100] Dijkhoff (2012), p. 175.

[101] Article 74 (1) of the ECSS.

[102] As above.

[103] Section 74(4) of the ECSS.

[104] Dijkhoff (2012), p. 188.

[105] Dijkhoff (2012), p. 188.

[106] Garben (2018), p. 81.

disregards all the ILO's attempts to bring about compliance, there should be a binding enforcement procedure.

Such is attainable by the establishment of a tribunal in terms of Article 37 of the ILO Constitution.[107] The ILO's GB may submit to the ILO conference for approval rules providing for the establishment of a tribunal to be responsible for the determination of any dispute or question relating to the interpretation of a convention.[108] However, calls for the establishment of a World Court for Human Rights to hear claims against MNEs are controversial and highly unlikely to yield results due to the current *realpolitik* of world powers.

This chapter has shown that the ILO can lead successful projects outside its traditional structures. Such was the case in respect to its supervision of the implementation of the European Code of Social Security and the Accord on Fire and Building Safety in Bangladesh. It is interesting that in the Accord, the ILO worked with labour NGOs such as the WRC and Clean Clothes Campaign.

It is argued that the ILO can achieve positive results through partnerships with like-minded international organisations. This is particularly important with respect to MNEs, which are not directly accommodated in the traditional ILO procedures. It is suggested that further research be conducted to establish whether the monitoring mechanisms and supervisory function of the ILO can be extended to private NGOs that handle complaints against MNEs.

References

Alhambra A, Ter Haar B, Kun A (2020) Harnessing public institutions for labour law enforcement embedding a transnational labour inspectorate within the ILO. Int Organ Law Rev

Bendix S (2015) Industrial relations in South Africa. Juta

Chau N, Kanbur R, Harrison A, Morici P (2001) The adoption of international labor standards conventions: who, when and why? Brookings Institution Press

Dahan Y, Lerner H, Milman-Sivan F (2013) Shared responsibility and the international labour organisation. Mich J Int Law

Deranty J, MacMillan G (2012) The ILO's decent work initiative: suggestions for an extension of the notion of decent work. J Soc Philos

Dijkhoff T (2012) The contested value of international social security standards in the European Union. Eur J Soc Secur

Fraterman J (2011) Article 37(2) of the ILO Constitution: can an ILO interpretive tribunal end the hegemony of international trade law. Georgetown J Int Law

Garben S (2018) The problematic interaction between EU and international law in the area of social rights. Camb Int Law J

Gironde C, Carbonnier G (2019) The ILO @ 100: in search of renewed relevance. J Hist Int Law

Hepple B (2003) Rights at work international. Institute for Labour Studies Geneva

Heric L, Cernic J (2009) Corporate Responsibility for Human Rights: Analyzing the ILO Tripartite Declaration of Principles Concerning Multinational Enterprises and Social Policy. Miskolc Journal of International Law

[107] Article 37(2) of the ILO Constitution.

[108] As above.

Huber K, Schormair M (2019) Progressive and conservative firms in multistakeholder initiatives: tracing the construction of political CSR identities within the accord on fire and building safety in Bangladesh. Springer
Kagan J (2011) Making free trade fair: how the WTO could incorporate labour rights and why it should. Georgetown J Int Law
Khan I, Mohd R, Wichterich C (2015) Safety and labour conditions: the accord and the national tripartite plan of action for the garment industry of Bangladesh. International Labour Organisation
Koldinská K (2019) The international labour organisation and the EU- old friends with new goals. Hung J Leg Stud
Koliev F (2018) Naming and shaming the politics and effectiveness of social pressure in the ILO. Stockholm University
Korda M, Pennings F (2008) The legal character of international social security standards. Eur J Soc Secur
Maupain F (2013) The future of the international labour organisation in the global economy. Oxford Hart Publishing
Michoud A (2018) The accountability of transnational corporations for the adverse impacts of their business activities: an international and comparative law study. Dublin University Law Society
Payne T (2017) Retooling the ILO: how a new enforcement wing can help the ILO reach its goal through regional free trade agreements. Indian J Global Leg Stud
Rombouts B (2019) The International Diffusion of Fundamental Labour Standards: Contemporary Content, Scope, Supervision and Proliferation of Core Workers' Rights under Public, Private, Binding, and Voluntary Regulatory Regimes. Columbia Human Rights Law Review
Salminen J (2018) Accord on fire and building safety in Bangladesh: a new paradigm for limiting buyers' liability in global supply chains. Am J Comp Law
Schoeman E (2019) Litigating about where to litigate: Vendenta Resources Plc v Lungwe [2019] UKSC 20' (2019). Comp Int Law J South Afr
Tapiola K, Swepston L (2010) The ILO's contribution to improving the welfare of workers globally, especially in Asia and Africa. J Asian Multicult Res Soc Sci Study
Ter Haar B, Keune M (2014) One step forward or more window-dressing? A legal analysis of recent CSR initiatives in the garment industry in Bangladesh international. J Comp Labour Law Ind Relat
Van Deale J (2008) The International Labour Organisation (ILO) in past and present research. Internationaal Instituut voor Sociale Geschiedenis
Van Eck S, Pamhidzai B, Chanda C, Kalula E (2020) Celebrating the ILO 100 years on reflections on labour law from a South African perspective. Juta
Van Niekerk A, Smit N (2019) Law@work. LexisNexis
Weiss M (2013) International labour standards: a complex public-private policy mix. Int J Comp Labour Law Ind Relat
Wiersma E (2018) Fire safety in the ready-made garment industry in Bangladesh, Five years after Rana Plaza. Bangladesh University of Engineering and Technology

Chapter 4
The Organisation for Economic Cooperation and Development

4.1 Introduction

In 1948, the Organisation for European Economic Cooperation (the OEEC) was established to oversee the implementation of the Marshall Plan, a programme funded by the US aimed at reconstructing Europe in the aftermath of the Second World War.[1] Encouraged by the success and the prospects of carrying its work forward on a global stage, Canada and the US joined other OEEC members and they signed the Convention of the Organisation for Economic Co-operation and Development (OECD).[2] This convention transformed the OEEC into the OECD and it was signed in Paris on 14 December 1960 and entered into force on 30 September 1961. Since then, the number of member countries has increased from 18 original

[1] Leimgruber and Schmelzer (2017), p. 23.

[2] As above.

F. Maluleke, *Compliance with Decent Work Standards by Multinational Enterprises*, European Yearbook of International Economic Law 48,
https://doi.org/10.1007/978-3-032-21261-0_4

members[3] to 37 member countries[4] worldwide. The OECD also has five key partners, namely: Brazil, China, India, Indonesia and South Africa.[5]

In its founding convention, the members of the OECD set themselves three key goals. Through its policies, the OECD seeks first, to promote economic growth and high standard of living in its member countries. Second, the OECD aims to contribute to expansion of none-OECD countries' economy. Third, the OECD strives to contribute to 'expanding world trade on a multilateral, non-discriminatory basis following international obligations'.[6]

Whereas the labour market has changed fundamentally since over 60 years ago when the OECD was established, this study supports the view that the goals identified at its inception are still relevant to date. It is submitted that the goals of the OECD are akin to the ones contained in the decent work agenda.[7] One of the key components of the decent work agenda is the creation of employment of acceptable quality and to improve the standard of living of everyone. This challenge is also relevant to the OECD. As confirmed by the ILO in 2019:

> Globally, the number of people who are not employed continues to increase. In addition to the above, over 3.3 billion people employed globally in 2018 had inadequate economic security, material well-being and equal opportunities.[8]

MNEs have been identified as a counter-weight to the identified challenges. It has been estimated that one out of seven jobs (excluding informal forms of work) in the world are created by MNEs.[9] Brincikova and Darmo state that 'MNEs contributed significantly to increased employment, transfer of knowledge, skills and

---

[3] Austria, Belgium, Denmark, France, Greece, Iceland, Ireland, Italy, Luxembourg, Netherlands, Norway, Portugal, Sweden, Switzerland, Turkey, United Kingdom, and Western Germany (originally represented by both the combined American and British occupation zones [The Bizone] and the French occupation zone). see https://www.oecd.org/general/organisationforeuropeaneconomicco-operation.htm#:~:text=The%20OEEC%20originally%20had%2018%20participants%3A%20Austria%2C%20Belgium%2C,zones%20%28The%20Bizone%29%20and%20the%20French%20occupation%20zone%29. Date visited 14 September 2025.

[4] Australia, Austria, Belgium, Canada, Chile, Colombia, Costa Rica, Czech Republic, Denmark, Estonia, Finland, France, Germany, Greece, Hungary, Iceland, Ireland, Israel, Italy, Japan, Korea, Latvia, Lithuania, Luxembourg, Mexico, Netherlands, New Zealand, Norway, Poland, Portugal, Slovak republic, Slovenia, Spain, Sweden, Switzerland, Turkey, United Kingdom, and United states. See https://www.oecd.org/about/document/ratification-oecd-convention.htm date visited 14 September 2025.

[5] Yildiz (2019), p. 2. See also https://www.oecd.org/about/document/ratification-oecd-convention.htm date visited 14 September 2025.

[6] Article 1 of the OECD Convention.

[7] As discussed in Chap. 1 paras 1.1–1.4, above, decent work includes job creation, social dialogue, social protection, and protection of rights at work. The achievement of decent work for all men and women everywhere was identified as the main goal of the ILO. See Chap. 2 para 2.2.

[8] https://www.ilo.org/global/research/global-reports/weso/2019/lang%2D%2Den/index.htm date visited 14 September 2025.

[9] Ruggie (2017), p. 317.

technology to economies of many developing countries'.[10] This study agrees that there is evidence showing that MNEs do create jobs which have the potential of raising the standard of living of workers, and therefore contribute to the achievement of one of the decent work goals.[11] Due to the above, MNEs gained much influence over the governments of their host nations. Such influence can be traced from the fact that their production is mobile and the governments want to remain competitive.[12]

However, the operations of MNEs are often associated with non-compliance with internationally recognised labour standards which negatively affect some of the other decent work initiatives.[13] This is challenging because MNEs are often not held accountable when they violate human and labour rights in respect of their employees. Davarnejad argues that 'MNEs can avoid controls and regulations imposed by the laws of their host nations due to their ability to move operations from one country to the other'.[14]

To bridge the legal vacuum and out of their own initiative, MNEs adopted several voluntary codes of conduct as part of private self-regulation mechanisms.[15] In response to international calls to the above challenges, the OECD has adopted the OECD Guidelines, which sets forth principles and standards for responsible business conduct across an array of issues such as human rights and labour rights.[16] Through the OECD Guidelines, the OECD encourages its member countries to implement internationally recognised labour standards to ensure that all MNEs play by the same rules.[17]

One of the major global challenges is the absence of credible complaint mechanisms through which employees can lodge their grievances against MNEs. Responding to this challenge, the OECD Guidelines established National Contact Points (NCPs), the institutions tasked with the responsibility for resolving complaints regarding breaches of OECD Guidelines cases by MNEs.[18]

The role of the OECD in setting labour standards is discussed below.

---

[10] Brincikova and Darmo (2014), p. 7. Also, see the 2016 study of the ILO which found that global supply chains and MNEs have enabled workers to access employment requiring a higher level of skills and offering better pay and conditions.

[11] See Chap. 3 para 3.2.

[12] Bilchitz (2021), p. 597.

[13] See Chap. 1 para 1.1.

[14] Davarnejad (2011), p. 354. See also Chap. 1 paras 1.1.

[15] See Chap. 5 paras 5.1.

[16] Maheandiran (2015), p. 205.

[17] OECD (2021) 4.

[18] Para 11 of the OECD Guidelines.

4.2 The Role of the OECD in Setting Decent Work Standards

The OECD originally adopted the OECD Guidelines in 1976 and has since reviewed the instrument six times, with the latest revision occurring in 2023.[19] The OECD Guidelines utilise a risk management approach of due diligence to ensure that MNEs comply with international human and labour rights. The OECD Guidelines defines 'due diligence' as:

> the process through which enterprises can identify, prevent, mitigate and account for how they address their actual and potential adverse impacts as an integral part of business decision-making and risk management systems.[20]

Cernic argues that 'even though the OECD Guidelines are not legally enforceable, it nevertheless represents the expectations of governments of the adhering countries for MNEs' behaviour'.[21] However, the role of the OECD Guidelines evolved to be a dispute resolution instrument. It is argued that this soft law instrument surprisingly led to the obligation upon adhering countries to establish an alternative dispute resolution mechanism that operationalises the Guidelines.[22]

The OECD should be commended for creating a platform for countries which are non-members of the OECD to adopt the OECD Guidelines without taking up membership of the OECD.[23] However, it appears that many countries are not yet persuaded to utilise this opportunity. It is therefore imperative that the OECD member countries should promote the OECD Guidelines to have a wider reach. Alternatively, it is proposed that there should be greater cooperation between the OECD and other international organisations such as the ILO, which is already supported by many countries.

The rights in the chapter on employment and industrial relations in the OECD Guidelines are like those in the ILO 1998 Declaration on Fundamental Principles and Rights at Work and the ILO's MNE Declaration.[24] This reinforcement of rights and standards is necessary since the ILO currently has no similar agreed-upon

---

[19] The OECD Guidelines are recommendations addressed by governments to MNEs. https://www.oecd.org/daf/inv/mne/48004323.pdf. Date visited 14 September 2025.

[20] Para 14 of the OECD Guidelines.

[21] Heric and Cernic (2009), p. 79.

[22] Perillo (2022), p. 40.

[23] https://www.oecd.org/about/members-and-partners/ date visited 17 September 2025. It is stated that, thus far, ten countries have adopted the OECD Guidelines without being part of the OECD, namely, Argentina, Brazil, Colombia, Costa Rica, Egypt, Latvia, Lithuania, Morocco, Peru, Romania, and Tunisia.

[24] Blackett and Trebilcock (2025), p. 97 mention that the rights include: 'freedom of association; elimination of all forms of forced or compulsory labour; equality of opportunities and treatment'. https://www.oecd.org/daf/inv/mne/48004323.pdf date visited 14 September 2025. See also Chap. 2 para 2.2.

instrument in the regulation of MNEs. The mentioned chapter also refers to the worst forms of child labour.[25]

This study supports the OECD Guidelines, in so far as it requires MNEs to comply with labour rights or standards irrespective of the country where they operate. Oshionebo confirms that the responsibility of MNEs to respect employee rights is independent of the host country's ability or willingness to protect the labour rights of its employees.[26] In addition to the stated expectation, MNEs should comply with relevant national laws where they operate.[27] In this regard, the OECD Guidelines provide that in the event that the laws of the host nations are less favourable to the home nation standards, MNEs should adhere to employment relations standards not less favourable than those observed by comparable employers in the host country.[28]

MNEs are further required to ensure that the health and safety standards are adhered to throughout their operations.[29] However, experience shows that MNEs have consistently prioritised making a profit ahead of health and safety standards of employees. For instance, between 1984 and 2005, more than 11 000 mine workers died in South African mines which are operated by various MNEs.[30] It is disappointing that the death toll remains high; 270 mine workers died in 2003, and it was reduced by only 24% in 2010. The government and the mining companies reached an agreement to reduce mining fatalities by 20% per annum.[31] It is submitted that the aim should be to eliminate the number of fatalities in the mines.

In this respect, the OECD Guidelines must be applauded insofar as they expect MNEs to adopt higher health and safety standards in all parts of their operations, even where this may not formally be required by existing regulations in host countries where they operate.[32] Further, the OECD Guidelines also create a right of

[25] Article 3 of Convention 182 - Worst Forms of Child Labour Convention describes the worst forms of child labour as '(a) all forms of slavery or practices similar to slavery, such as the sale and trafficking of children, debt bondage and serfdom and forced or compulsory labour, including forced or compulsory recruitment of children for use in armed conflict; (b) the use, procuring, or offering of a child for prostitution, for the production of pornography or pornographic performances; (c) the use, procuring, or offering of a child for illicit activities, in particular for the production and trafficking of drugs as defined in the relevant international treaties; (d) work which, by its nature or the circumstances in which it is carried out, is likely to harm the health, safety, or morals of children'.

[26] Oshionebo (2013), p. 2.

[27] Heric and Cernic (2009), p. 79. See also para 8 of the OECD Guidelines.

[28] Para 4 of the OECD Guidelines.

[29] Para 57 of the OECD Guidelines provides that 'MNEs are expected to follow prevailing regulatory standards and industry norms to minimise the risk of accidents and injury to health arising out of course of employment'.

[30] https://www.dmr.gov.za/mine-health-and-safety/mine-accidents-and-disasters date visited 14 September 2025.

[31] https://www.dmr.gov.za/mine-health-and-safety/mine-accidents-and-disasters date visited 14 September 2025.

[32] Para 57 of the OECD Guidelines.

employees to remove themselves from a work situation which presents an imminent risk to their health and safety.

Additionally, MNEs are expected to create employment in their host nations. MNEs must, in their operations, to the greatest extent reasonable and practicable, employ local persons and provide training to improve skill levels, in cooperation with representatives of employees and governmental authorities. As previously stated, experience unfortunately illustrates that MNEs do not comply with such standards. Although unreported, the case of *Department of Employment and Labour v Huawei* (a Chinese MNE) sheds some light.[33]

In this instance, Huawei was granted a permit in line with the Immigration Regulations requiring it to employ 60% South Africans and 40% foreign nationals. However, Huawei was found to have employed over 90% foreign nationals. The department sought to fine the firm an amount of R1.5 million ($99 151) or 2% of the local firm's annual 2020 turnover for the alleged rule breaches.[34] The matter was, however, resolved by the parties in favour of the Department and Huawei indicated its commitment to complying with national laws.[35]

The monitoring mechanisms of the OECD are discussed in detail below.

4.3 Monitoring and Enforcement Mechanisms of the OECD

It is submitted that, in addition to improving labour standards, the OECD should also have appropriate responses to situations of violation of internationally recognised human and labour rights by MNEs. This includes guidance to MNEs on risk mitigation efforts, including suspension and termination of the relationship with suppliers.[36] According to Castermans and Van Woensel, the monitoring processes of the OECD also include the obligation on MNEs to terminate relationships with third parties that do not comply with the OECD Guidelines.[37]

It must be indicated that, thus far, there is no known evidence that such power was invoked by any MNE. First, this may, amongst others, be because of the absence of the enforceable law which creates an obligation for MNEs to terminate relationships with third parties involved in their supply chains in the event of consistent and repeated serious labour rights violations. Second, the OECD Guidelines contain no provision governing such an area.

In addition to the absence of law, the OECD Guidelines recognise that there are practical limitations on the degree of leverage MNEs have or may be able to build

[33] https://www.business-humanrights.org/en/latest-news/south-africa-huawei-sued-by-labour-department-as-90-of-employees-are-foreign-nationals/ date visited 14 September 2025.

[34] As above.

[35] https://www.reuters.com/technology/south-africa-takes-huaweis-local-unit-court-over-employment-rule-breaches-2022-02-11/. Date visited 14 September 2025.

[36] Para 25 of the OECD Guidelines.

[37] Castermans and van Woensel (2017), p. 93.

to effect change in the behaviour of entities with which they have business relationships.[38] These are, amongst others, related to product and/or service characteristics, the number of suppliers and other business relationships, the structure and complexity of the supply chain, or the nature of a business relationship or adverse impact in question.

It is therefore submitted that there is a need for OECD Guidelines to provide a step-by-step approach which provides guidance to MNEs on how they should manage the third parties that do not adhere to OECD Guidelines. This may include warnings, suspension, and termination of business relationships by the MNE. Failure to do so by the MNE where there is glaring evidence of labour and human rights violations by its suppliers should attract some penalties for the MNEs concerned. To overcome such a challenge, the OECD Guidelines established two institutions to monitor compliance with the OECD Guidelines by MNEs, namely, National Contact Points (NCPs) and the Investment Committee (CIME).

In the parts that follow, the OECD's two monitoring and enforcement mechanisms will first be discussed before the specific procedures are covered.

4.3.1 The NCPs

The governments of adhering countries to the OECD Guidelines are obliged to set up an NCP[39] to further the implementation of the OECD Guidelines.[40] According to Perillo, 'the OECD Guidelines despite the non-binding nature, they resulted in the creation of a legal obligation on the part of adhering states'.[41] The NCP's mandate is first, to promote adherence to OECD Guidelines and to make the NPC known by amongst governments and other stakeholders. Second, to provide a grievance mechanism to resolve cases (referred to as specific instances) relating to the violation of the OECD Guidelines by MNEs.[42]

Specific instance means 'a case that is submitted to the NCP concerning a company's alleged breaches of the OECD Guidelines'.[43] For over 20 years, the OECD Guidelines and NCPs have been resorted to continuously by victims and advocates for labour rights in holding MNEs to account for various violations and misbehaviour in their supply chains.[44] The NCP was designed as a conciliation and mediation tool that offers the relevant parties an opportunity to address human rights and

[38] Para 24 of the OECD Guidelines.

[39] According to the OECD Watch, the NCP is a government-supported office whose core duty is to advance the effectiveness of the OECD Guidelines. https://www.oecdwatch.org/oecd-ncps/national-contact-points-ncps/ date visited 14 September 2025.

[40] Para I (1) of the OECD Guidelines. See also Rombouts (2019), p. 78.

[41] Perillo (2022), p. 40.

[42] Ruggie and Tamaryn (2015), p. 99.

[43] Ruggie and Tamaryn (2015), p. 99.

[44] Perillo (2022), p. 39.

labour rights breaches and other concerns identified in the OECD Guidelines in a voluntary, consensual, and non-adversarial manner.[45]

4.3.2 *Composition of NCPs*

The structure of NCPs may be organised in various forms as governments have discretion on this aspect. However, the structure should comply with certain requirements. Sbovada mentions that:

> the NCP structure must satisfy the core criteria based on four basic principles: visibility, accessibility, transparency, and accountability. In addition, the NCPs should resolve complaints in a manner that is impartial, predictable, consistent, and equitable.[46]

According to the OECD Watch, (the NGO that monitors the implementation of the OECD Guidelines), the governments of the adhering countries are allowed to organise and locate their NCPs in different ways, including involving representatives from one or more ministries.[47] The adhering governments may also choose whether to constitute NCPs with or without formal involvement of labour, business and other social partners.[48] The OECD Guidelines advise that these advisory and oversight bodies should be 'multistakeholder in nature'.[49] Below is a simplified analysis of various recognised structures and their advantages and disadvantages (see Table 4.1).

This study argues that the selection of the structure should be based on the unique attributes of the specific OECD-adhering country. For instance, a country with a

Table 4.1 Structure of NCPs

Structure	Composition	Advantage	Disadvantage
a) Monopartite NCP Structure	One individual from a single ministry	Expeditious resolution of the complaints	Perceptions of bias and limited expertise
b) Inter-agency	Several representatives from several ministries	Increase expertise due to diverse opinions	Delay in finalisation of cases
c) Multipartite	Several government officials and stakeholder representatives	Less prone to bias	Delay in finalisation of cases
d) Expert-based	Experts external of government	Impartial	Perceived bias if experts are appointed by the government

[45] Perillo (2022), p. 44.

[46] Svoboda (2018), p. 4.

[47] Daniel et al. (2015) *OECD Watch, www.oecdwatch.org* 33. Date visited 14 September 2025.

[48] Daniel et al. (2015) *OECD Watch, www.oecdwatch.org* 33. Date visited 14 September 2025.

[49] At Para 12.

higher number of disputes may utilise a monopartite structure due to its expeditious resolution capacity. However, to avoid its inherent bias, the country may ensure that its decision makers are appointed through independent processes, which is an attribute of the expert-based structure.

4.3.3 The Investment Committee

The investment committee is a body established by the OECD, and it oversees the implementation of the OECD Guidelines.[50] Further, it is responsible for considering requests for assistance from NCPs, including by providing clarifications, guidance, and information on the interpretation of the OECD Guidelines in respect of cases.[51] Unfortunately, due to the non-binding nature of the OECD Guidelines, the investment committee is precluded from acting as a judicial or appellant mechanism. Nor should the findings and statements made by the NCP (other than interpretations of the OECD Guidelines) be questioned by a referral to the investment committee. The provision that the investment committee shall not reach conclusions on the conduct of individual MNE has been maintained in the decision itself.[52]

4.4 The NCP-Specific Procedure in Terms of the OECD Guidelines

The OECD adopted three main procedures for handling of cases, namely, the initial assessment, the mediation of cases, and finally the conclusion of procedures. After traversing procedures, the processes will be evaluated by considering a selection of relevant case law and statistics.

4.4.1 The Initial Assessment

The purpose of the initial assessment phase is to determine whether a complaint warrants further examination and whether it raises a bona fide issue that is relevant to the OECD Guidelines. The commentary to the procedural guidance lists six specific criteria that NCPs should consider in the initial assessment which are as follows: (a) the identity of the party concerned and its interest in the matter; (b) whether the issue raised is material and substantiated; (c) whether there seems to be a link

[50] Para 4 of the OECD Guidelines.

[51] Para 56 of the OECD Guidelines.

[52] Para 57 of the OECD Guidelines.

between the enterprise's activities and the issue raised; (d) the relevance of applicable law and procedures; (e) including court rulings; how similar issues have been, or are being, treated in other domestic or international proceedings and whether the consideration of the issues would contribute to the purposes; and (f) effectiveness of the OECD Guidelines.[53]

At this stage, the NCP decides whether to offer mediation to assist parties to resolve the case. This phase should be completed within 90 days from the date when the case was lodged.[54] However, additional time may be granted for purposes of collection of evidence necessary for an informed decision. Where the NCP decides that the issue raised does not merit further consideration, it should issue a statement which describes the issue and the reasons for the NCP's decision.[55]

The OECD Watch raised an alarm that despite these clear factors, there are several examples in which initial assessments consider additional factors that are unrelated to the criteria listed in the procedural guidance.[56] Such a practice has the effect of undermining the accessibility and credibility of the NCPs. It is submitted that the trend affects the predictability, consistency, and transparency of the process and make it more difficult for complainants to determine in advance whether they have a viable case.[57] This can be resolved by amending the OECD Guidelines to include lessons learned through the case law that took place in various NCPs.

4.4.2 Conciliation/Mediation of the Case

The second stage is the actual assistance to the parties in their efforts to resolve the issues raised. Where the issue raised merits further examination, the NCP should conduct a conciliation or mediation process to facilitate access to consensual and non-adversarial means to resolve the issues.[58] The NCP should strive to facilitate the resolution of the issues expeditiously. However, since progress through mediation and conciliation, entirely depends upon the parties involved, the NCP should, after consultation with the parties, establish a reasonable timeframe for the discussion between the parties to resolve the issues raised.[59]

---

[53] Para 25 of the OECD Guidelines

[54] Para 51 of the OECD Guidelines.

[55] Para 27 of the OECD Guidelines.

[56] Daniel et al. *OECD Watch, www.oecdwatch.org* 27. Date visited 14 September 2025.

[57] Daniel et al. *OECD Watch, www.oecdwatch.org* 27. Date visited 14 September 2025.

[58] Para 25 of the OECD Guidelines provides that 'in making an initial assessment of whether the issue raised merits further examination, the NCP will need to determine whether the issue is bona fide and relevant to the implementation of the OECD Guidelines'.

[59] In *FOCO & Friends of the Earth Argentina v. Shell Capsa,* the Argentine NCP closed a complaint that had been open for over 12 years. https://www.oecdwatch.org/complaint/foco-friends-of-the-earth-argentina-vs-shell-capsa/ date visited14 September 2025.

If they fail to reach an agreement within the prescribed timeframe, the NCP should engage the parties on the importance of continuing the process. The NCP should draft and issue the statement if it is of the view that mediation is unlikely to resolve the dispute.[60] It is unfortunate that the nature of conciliation and (or) mediation processes are voluntary and can only be utilised if the parties are genuinely committed to the process. As a result, the victims of labour and human rights violations can only find assistance if the MNE concerned is willing to resolve the disputes.

4.4.3 Conclusion of the Procedures

The NCP should strive to conclude the procedure within 12 months from receipt of the case.[61] It is recognised that this timeframe may need to be extended if circumstances warrant it, such as when the issues arise in a non-adhering country. At the conclusion of the mediation procedures and after consultation with the parties involved, the NCP is expected to make the outcome publicly available, considering the need to protect sensitive business and other stakeholder information.[62] Santner argues that the finding of breach may be effective if such a decision is publicly available, since it can significantly affect stakeholders.[63]

This information is understood to include the facts and arguments brought forward by the parties. Nonetheless, it remains important to strike a balance between transparency and confidentiality to build confidence in the OECD Guidelines procedures and promote their effective implementation.[64] Thus, while the proceedings associated with implementation of the OECD Guidelines are normally confidential, the results will normally be transparent.[65] The NCP should issue its statement or report within three months after the conclusion of the procedure.[66]

Where parties have reached an agreement on the issues raised, the statement should describe the issue raised, the procedures the NCP initiated in assisting the parties, and the time the agreement was reached.[67] However, the information on the

---

[60] Para 25 of the OECD Guidelines.

[61] Para 41 of the OECD Guidelines.

[62] Para C3 of the OECD Guidelines.

[63] Santner (2011), p. 384.

[64] Former Employees of Bralima v. Bralima after reaching agreement, the parties agreed to only inform the public that the matter was resolved. There are reports suggesting that monetary compensation was awarded to the former employees. https://www.oecdguidelines.nl/documents/publication/2017/08/18/final-statement-notification-bralima-vs-heineken date visited 14 September 2025.

[65] Para 38 of the OECD Guidelines.

[66] Para 35 of the OECD Guidelines provides that such a statement should contain the identity of parties concerned, the issues involved, the date on which the issues were raised with the NCP, any recommendations by the NCP, and any observations the NCP deems appropriate to include on the reasons why the proceedings did not produce an agreement.

[67] Para C3 (b) of the OECD Guidelines.

content of the agreement will only be included insofar as the parties involved agree thereto.[68] If the NCP believes that, based on the results of its initial assessment, it would be unfair to publicly identify a party in a statement on its decision, it may draft the statement to protect the identity of the party.[69]

The NCP procedure is also important in that it allows the parties to seek its assistance in following up on the implementation of the concluded agreements, and the NCP may do so on terms agreed between themselves and the NCP.[70] This is an important mechanism since the agreements reached under the auspices of the NCPs are not enforceable through the courts. It is my view that the follow-up should not only be done if the parties agree but should form part of NCPs' dispute resolution procedures. It is interesting to note that the resolutions of disputes by NCPs ignore the fact that the disputes arose from real facts. They are mostly trying to prevent future disputes from recurring, which is still an important and commendable task.[71] This area can be resolved by making NCPs' outcomes binding on parties.

4.5 A Selection of Cases Handled by NCPs

This study selected several landmark cases that were dealt with by various NCPs. The outcomes of such cases will reveal the negative and positive aspects of the OECD Guidelines. After such analysis, this study will be able to recommend the improvement of the OECD Guidelines. This will be done by following a set of questions and uses applicable case law to demonstrate how NCPs dealt with the situations.

4.5.1 Are OECD Guidelines Applicable to Supply Chains of MNEs?

4.5.1.1 Global Witness v Afrimex[72]

In this case, the UN panel of experts filed a complaint against OECD-based companies for violating the OECD Guidelines in the Democratic Republic of Congo (DRC). Amongst others, the complaint indicated the life-threatening conditions in

[68] As above.

[69] As above.

[70] Para 46 of the OECD Guidelines.

[71] https://www.business-humanrights.org/en/latest-news/specific-instance-regarding-the-fédération-internationale-de-football-association-fifa-submitted-by-the-building-and-wood-workers-international-bwi/ date visited 13 September 2025.

[72] https://www.oecdwatch.org/complaint/global-witness-vs-afrimex/ date visited 17 December 2025.

cassiterite mines and that employees were forced to work. Further, there were children who were employed to work at the workplace.

The UK-based NCP held that Afrimex breached the OECD Guidelines. It held that the MNE should take proactive steps to influence the responsible conduct of the entities involved in its supply chains.[73] It was further held that mere assurances by suppliers that they will act in compliance with the OECD Guidelines are not sufficient to satisfy the due diligence requirements of the OECD Guidelines.

Oshionebo states that following the decision above, 'the MNEs will only be able to satisfy their due diligence responsibilities under the OECD Guidelines, by ensuring that they monitor the behaviour of their suppliers'.[74] It is concluded that MNEs' obligations in terms of the OECD Guidelines are not limited to their own workplaces but extend to their supply chains in various countries.

4.5.2 What Happens When the MNE Refuses Mediation?

4.5.2.1 Survival International v Vedanta Resources plc[75]

In this case, amongst others, it was alleged that the MNE utilised forced labour. The UK NCP contacted the MNE about the complaint, and the company responded by refuting all allegations. The NCP's offer for mediation was rejected by the company. Further, the MNE did not provide evidence to support its case.

The UK NCP conducted the investigation and concluded that the company did not have a concrete human rights policy or any mechanism for assessing the impact of its operations on human rights despite its published commitments. The NCP recommended that Vedanta should consider implementing Ruggie's[76] suggested key steps for a basic human rights' due diligence process. It further recommended that the company should adopt a human rights policy which is not simply aspirational but practically implementable.

[73] https://www.oecdwatch.org/complaint/global-witness-vs-afrimex/ date visited 14 September 2025. In October 2002, a UN panel of Experts accused 85 OECD-based companies of violating the Guidelines for their direct or indirect roles in the illegal exploitation of natural resources in the Democratic Republic of Congo (DRC). The complaint also highlights the life-threatening conditions in cassiterite mines and the use of forced labour and child labour. the NCP issued its final statement, concluding that Afrimex did not comply with Chapter II (General Policies) and Chapter IV (Employment and Industrial Relations) of the Guidelines. Throughout the period that the NCP was investigating the case in 2007 and 2008, Afrimex continued buying minerals from eastern DRC. Furthermore, one of the company's main suppliers was cited by the UN Group of Experts as trading in minerals produced by the FDLR, one of the main armed groups in eastern DRC.

[74] Oshionebo (2013), p. 571.

[75] https://www.oecdwatch.org/complaint/survival-international-vs-vedanta-resources-plc/ date visited 17 December 2025.

[76] See Chap. 2 para 2.4.

The NCP issued a decision with strong findings of non-compliance. Although the decision did not directly lead to any change in the company's behaviour on the ground, it played a role in convincing several shareholders to put pressure on the company to improve its human rights policy, which it ultimately did.

4.5.2.2 Communal Land-Owners vs Excellon Resources[77]

In this case, a group of communal land-owners from the Ejido 'La Sierrita de Galeana' (La Sierrita) and several Canadian and Mexican civil society organisations allege that Excellon Resources has breached OECD Guidelines provisions on disclosure, human and labour rights standards. It was alleged that specifically, the MNE infringed their rights to collective bargaining and freedom of association. They further complained that the company engaged in worker intimidation.

The Mexican NCP rejected the complaint and cited the company's unwillingness to participate in any possible NCP-facilitated mediation as a reason for rejecting the case.[78]

4.5.2.3 Are NCPs Empowered to Pronounce Whether the MNE Breached the OECD Guidelines?

Raid v Das Air[79]

In this case, the UN panel of experts accused 85 OECD based MNEs of violating the OECD Guidelines. Amongst others, the MNEs were accused of failure to respect human rights and forced labour. DAS Air denied the allegations in the complaint and strongly objected to the allegations that it contributed to the human and labour rights infringements. In July 2008, a strongly worded final statement was issued.

The NCP concluded that DAS Air breached the human and labour rights provision. DAS Air was also found to have failed to undertake due diligence regarding its supply chain; the company's contention that it had no knowledge of the source of production of the minerals it was responsible for their transportation was rejected given its intimate understanding of the situation and the conflict.[80] This case is a prime example of the NCP going beyond the OECD Guidelines. It was for the first

---

[77] https://www.oecdwatch.org/complaint/communal-landowners-vs-excellon-resources/ date visited 17 December 2025.

[78] Daniel et al. *OECD Watch www.oecdwatch.org* 28. Date visited 14 September 2025.

[79] https://www.oecdwatch.org/complaint/raid-vs-das-air/ date visited 17 December 2025.

[80] See also Fenceline Community for Human Safety and Environmental Protection v Shell's Pandacan oil depot. After receiving the complaints, the Dutch NCP offered mediation which was rejected by the MNE. Despite the rejection of mediation offers, the NCP investigated the allegations and issued a final statement. The published statement was not directly implemented by the MNE. However, the parties used it to resolve the dispute on their own.

time in the history of NCPs, that a company was found to be, amongst others, in violation of its human and labour rights responsibilities under the OECD Guidelines.

4.5.2.4 What Happens If There Is No NCP in the Host Nation?

ECCHR and Others v TÜV Rheinland[81]

In this case, the European Center for Constitutional and Human Rights (ECCHR), together with FEMNET, Medico International, Garment Workers Unity Forum, the Comrade Rubel Memorial Center, and survivors of the Rana Plaza Factory collapse, filed a complaint against TÜV Rheinland AG and its subsidiary TÜV Rheinland India Pvt. Ltd. for carrying out an inadequate social audit of a factory in the Rana Plaza building in June 2012 and breaching the OECD Guidelines in the process. The complainants further alleged that the company failed to accurately report on the various labour rights violations occurring at the Phantom Apparels Ltd. factory and described the construction quality of the building in the report as good.

Some of the human and labour rights infringements allegations in the factory at the time included child labour, discrimination against women, the absence of trade unions, and forced overtime. The complainants asked the German NCP to assess the company's breach of the OECD Guidelines and facilitate mediation. The complainants sought financial compensation from TÜV Rheinland to cover psychological treatment of the employees who were survivors of the Rana Plaza Factory disaster, as well as the company's commitment to work with the Bangladesh Government.

In this case, the German NCP decided that it had the requisite jurisdiction to facilitate the resolution of the dispute based on being home to the parent company since there was no NCP in Bangladesh and India where the MNE operated.

4.5.3 Can NCPs Impose Sanctions on MNEs?

4.5.3.1 Canada Tibet Committee v China Gold International Resources Corp. Ltd[82]

In this case, the Canadian NCP went against the OECD Guidelines by imposing sanctions against the MNE despite the latter's unwillingness to cooperate. In 2013, the Chinese state media reported that 83 mine workers died following the landslide at the Gyama Copper Polymetallic Mine in Central Tibet. The management of the

[81] https://www.bundeswirtschaftsministerium.de/Redaktion/EN/Beschwerdefaelle-NKS/Abschliessende-Erklaerung/ecchr-against-tuev-rheinland.pdf?__blob=publicationFile&v=1 date visited 17 December 2025.

[82] https://www.oecdwatch.org/complaint/canada-tibet-committee-vs-china-gold-int-resources/ accessed on 14 September 2025.

mine, a subsidiary of China Gold International Resources, described the incident as a natural disaster. In 2014, the complainants filed a complaint with the Canadian NCP alleging amongst others that the company violated human and labour rights.

The Canadian NCP offered mediation to the company and the company did not respond to the NCP. The NCP proceeded with the investigation and thereafter issued a final statement wherein it imposed sanctions on the company for violations of human and labour rights.

4.5.3.2 Forum and Friends of the Earth Norway v Cermaq ASA[83]

In this case, Cermaq was accused of multiple breaches of the OECD Guidelines arising from the fish farming and fish feed operations of the company's subsidiary Mainstream. In July 2011, the parties reached a settlement agreement that entailed commitments by Cermaq to ensure the respect of human and labour rights in its supply chain. The NCP issued a final statement wherein it amongst others invited the parties to a follow-up meeting to be held twelve months thereafter to provide update on progress made on the implementation thereof.

It is disappointing that the NCP did not conduct any follow-up meetings as described in the final statement. However, the parties were of the view that the company adhered to the settlement agreement. The complainant made follow-ups after six months and they appointed two independent consultants to examine to what extent the agreement had led to a change of conditions of employment. It is concerning that the findings were that the employment conditions did not change which shows that the impact of the NCPs outcome was not effective.

4.6 Evaluation of Cases

The OECD should be commended for being accessible. Interested stakeholders (trade unions, NGOs, and individual employees) can bring allegations of contravention of the OECD Guidelines by MNEs to the adhering country's NCP. This is irrespective of where the specific instance giving rise to the damage occurred.[84] The NCPs should also be applauded for having provided simplified referral procedures and able to accept referrals from individual employees. The employees with no legal training can be able to refer such cases.

However, NCPs have a high percentage of rejected cases. According to the OECD Watch, the high percentage of case rejection affects the accessibility of the NCPs. The OECD Watch recommended that the standard of proof at the initial

[83] https://www.oecdwatch.org/complaint/forum-and-friends-of-the-earth-norway-vs-cermaq-asa/ date visited 14 September 2025.

[84] Santner (2011), p. 383.

assessment phase should not place an overly high burden of proof on the complainants.[85] Further, the evidentiary requirements for initial assessments need not be like those required in legal proceedings due to the voluntary nature of participation in NCP mediation.[86]

The rejection of cases due to the unwillingness of the MNE to form part of the conciliation and (or) mediation process is regrettable. In addition to the above, it is concerning that several NCPs have rejected cases due to the refusal of the MNE to participate in mediation. This seems to be a glaring omission in OECD Guidelines. In a case of *Lead Education and Abatement Design (LEAD) Group v Innospec*, the US NCP determined that the issues raised merited further consideration and stated that it would have been prepared to offer its mediation but ultimately decided to reject the complaint because Innospec had refused to engage in mediation.[87]

There is a risk that NCPs may reject cases at the initial assessment phase when successful mediation is unlikely, and only accept relatively easy cases that can be solved through mediation and dialogue.[88] According to the OECD Watch, NCPs often miss the opportunity to further the OECD Guidelines and instead reject important cases.[89] As a result, disputes which do not fit the mediation criteria are not catered for in the OECD Guidelines.

Sanchez suggests that where an NCP's offering for mediation is rejected or if it fails, it should be empowered to conduct a thorough examination of facts and to make a finding as to whether the concerned MNE breached the OECD Guidelines.[90] According to Sanchez, such power encourages the parties to comply with the OECD Guidelines. Given this reality, it appears to be a glaring omission that the NCP has not been explicitly given the powers to conduct a thorough examination of facts to determine whether the OECD Guidelines were breached by the concerned MNE.[91]

Further, the OECD Guidelines provide that when the parties fail to reach an agreement or when the MNE refuses to take part in mediation process, the case should be closed as unresolved.[92] It is suggested that the NCPs should draft their final statements in a way that include recommendations on the implementation of the OECD Guidelines where relevant. It is also suggested that where the parties fail to reach agreement or if the MNE is unwilling to participate in mediation, the concerned NCP should issue a final statement, which include such reasons.[93]

---

[85] The OECD's Guide for NCPs on the initial assessment of specific instances states that the initial assessment should not be unnecessarily onerous and that some NCPs have framed this standard as one of plausibility.

[86] OECD Watch (2021) 4.

[87] Daniel et al. *OECD Watch, www.oecdwatch.org* 28. Date visited 14 September 2025.

[88] https://www.international.gc.ca/trade-agreements-accords-commerciaux/ncp-pcn/2019-03-19-ncp-pcn.aspx?lang=eng accessed on 14 September 2025.

[89] OECD Watch (2015) 22.

[90] Sanchez (2015), p. 89.

[91] https://wwwsearch.oecd.org/daf/inv/mne/48841231.pdf accessed on 14 September 2025.

[92] Para 4 of the OED Guidelines.

[93] Sanchez (2015), p. 89.

It is regrettable that the 2023 amended OECD Guidelines did not improve the said position despite various NCPs having moved in this regard. This is a reflection that the OECD Guidelines are outdated and should be amended to empower NCPs to make such decisions as may be reasonably necessary in cases which are not amenable for resolution by mediation. It is suggested that the OECD Guidelines should be amended to make participation in mediation procedures compulsory.

Further, it must be noted that the rejection of many cases was not only because of the unwillingness of MNEs to participate in mediation but the views of NCPs that such cases did not merit further investigation. It is argued that the real issue lies in the clarification of the jurisdiction of the NCPs. It is argued that it is not in the interest of justice that NCPs receive all kinds of cases without a strict criterion. Such may unnecessarily affect the budget of NCPs with complaints without merits. Therefore, more efforts should be made to educate the employees and employers on the jurisdiction of the NCPs.

Unlike the courts and other statutory tribunals, where the violation of labour rights is confirmed, NCPs do not recommend a remedy such as a compensation or reinstatement but only focus on preventing future re-occurrence. Such is falling short of the Ruggie framework and the UNGP which require that a remedy be provided to employees. It is suggested that the OECD Guidelines should be amended to empower the NCPs to recommend that MNEs should provide remedies.

It can thus be concluded that some NCPs view their dispute resolution function to be limited to mediation not adjudication. For instance, NCPs such the Canadian NCP believes that its purpose in dispute resolution is not to determine whether the MNE breached the OECD Guidelines.[94] However, some NCPs, such as the Germany and UK view their role differently. Their final statements pronounce the guilt or otherwise of the MNE.[95] It is only after such a finding is made that the NCP will recommend corrective measures. It is argued that the NCP should be empowered to assess the facts and evidence submitted to make a recommendation. This could be possible if the NCP made a pronouncement on whether there was a breach of OECD Guidelines.

Notably, the OECD Guidelines encourage the use of appropriate international dispute settlement mechanisms, including arbitration, to facilitate the resolution of legal problems arising between enterprises and host country governments.[96] However, such a process is hardly used at any stage of NCPs' complaints handling procedures. This study argues that such a process would be important to cater for many complaints that remain unresolved during mediation procedures. This study submits that the OECD Guidelines fail to consider that not all disputes are amenable to mediation.

In the part that follows, the statistics of cases are discussed in detail.

[94] Oshionebo (2013), p. 581.

[95] As above.

[96] Para 10 of the OECD Guidelines.

4.7 Statistics of Cases Handled by NCPs

The NCP is one of the world's largest grievance-handling mechanisms by case referral in global supply chains. The NCPs handled over 620 known cases or specific instances since 2000.[97] The following terminology is necessary for the reader to understand the number of cases referred.

a) Cases closed means cases submitted during the year and include rejected and all cases finalised in that year.
b) Cases concluded during the year are those that the NCP found to merit further examination after the initial assessment and that have subsequently been closed.
c) Cases rejected during the year are those that the NCP found not to merit further examination or cases that have been withdrawn prior to the completion of the initial assessment and that have therefore been closed.
d) Cases settled means cases on which parties reached an agreement.

In 2020, a total of 58 cases were received, which was the highest number of cases received by NCPs in a twelve months period. In the same year, a total of 38 cases (65%) were closed with the status of unresolved. Further, 14 cases were rejected at the preliminary stage, which translates to 24% of the cases. There were, however, nine cases (15%) which were settled.[98] A total of 15 cases (25%) were closed without a resolution.

In 2021, 48 new cases were received which was the third highest in the history of NCPs and 43 cases were closed. During the same year, seven cases (including those coming from the previous year) were resolved.[99] 22 cases were concluded, and 11 cases were rejected. Only two cases were settled.

In 2022, 41 cases were received and 41 cases were closed. The number of cases received in 2022 is lower than previous submission numbers per year within the NCP Network, which saw 48 in 2021 and 58 in 2020. While 41 submissions represent a decrease compared to the last couple of years, it is still slightly higher than the historical average since 2011 (38). Amongst the 41 cases that were closed in 2022, 33 were already in progress from 1 January 2022 and eight were submitted during the year. It is therefore correct to say that only seven of the 41 received in 2022 were closed during the year. Fourteen cases were rejected, which translates to 34%. Four cases were settled, which translates to 10%. However, the settlement rate is higher when measured against concluded cases and excluding rejected cases. In this instance, the settlement rate is 30%.

The analysis of the three previous reports reflects an increase in a number of cases referred to NCPs. Regrettably, there is a high number of cases that are rejected at the preliminary stage and cases which remain unresolved after mediation and

[97] OECD Annual NCP report (2021) 6.

[98] https://www.international.gc.ca/trade-commerce/ncp-pcn/report-2020-rapport.aspx?lang=eng date visited on 13 September 2025.

[99] OECD Annual NCP report (2021) 10.

remain as such. Such non-resolutions are attributable to the absence of other mechanisms above the conciliation and mediation processes. It is therefore suggested that more stringent mechanisms be established which would make it compulsory for MNEs to participate in the dispute resolution processes prescribed by the OECD Guideline.

4.8 The Negative Aspects of the OECD Guidelines

The fundamental weakness of the OECD Guidelines is that their observance by MNEs is voluntary and not legally enforceable. It is submitted that there is no law which makes it mandatory for MNEs to participate in dispute resolution processes. Ruggie and Tamaryn argue that 'the OECD Guidelines make no provision for sanctions, even for serious and repeated breaches of the OECD Guidelines'.[100] Further, the OECD Guidelines make no provision for remedies for victims where their rights are found to have been violated by MNEs.

Although NCPs may reach agreements through voluntary mediation or conciliation between parties, it is disappointing that there are no consequences for failing to comply with such agreements. As a result, MNEs do not incur any consequences when they fail to implement the agreements reached.[101] Such could have easily been achieved by declaring that the settlement agreements concluded under the auspices of OECD Guidelines are enforceable in national courts or other statutory tribunals. The OECD member countries would domesticate such in their legislations.

In addition to the above, the OECD Guidelines follow very strict confidentiality requirements in respect of their proceedings. The parties to the dispute are given discretion as to which information is to be published.[102] The effectiveness of the OECD Guidelines is impeded by absence of legal sanctions for violations of human and labour rights and confidentiality requirements which would name and shame the MNE. It appears that the solution lies in the amendment of the OECD Guidelines to empower the NCPs to publish certain basic and relevant details such as the name of the MNE and complainant as well as factories involved in the supply chain and a summary of the main issue at hand.

Another significant weakness of NCP procedures is that settlement agreements are not adequately followed. In its current form, the follow-up of commitments made in settlement agreements can only be made if the parties included such

[100] Ruggie and Tamaryn (2015), p. 99.

[101] See https://www.oecdwatch.org/complaint/forum-and-friends-of-the-earth-norway-vs-cermaq-asa/ date visited 14 September 2025.

[102] Para 73 of the OECD Guidelines provides that 'at the conclusion of the procedures, the NPC will make a statement publicly available after consultations with the parties involved and taking into account the need to preserve the confidentiality of sensitive business and other information. Information, such as the identity of individuals involved in the procedures, should be kept confidential'.

provision in the final statement. As a result, MNEs can simply agree to improve the conditions of employment in their supply chains but fail to do so without incurring any legal consequences.[103] It is submitted that concluding the settlement agreement does not bring the case to the end since same is not enforceable.

It is submitted that the factor that restrains the efficacy of the OECD Guidelines is the absence of appellate or review mechanism through which complainants who are not happy with the process and outcome of the NCPs can have their cases reviewed for reconsideration. In this respect, the investment committee strives to perform the oversight role over NCPs. However, it does not have the power to overrule outcomes of NCPs. The OECD Guidelines make no provision for NCP processes to be questioned. It is submitted that this is a fundamental weakness because there are no worthwhile checks and balances on the NCPs' activities.[104]

It is submitted that guaranteeing the independence of NCPs is crucial for their processes and outcomes to be legitimate and reliable. This study concludes that several NCPs do not satisfy the prerequisites to be perceived to be independent. It is suggested that the OECD Guidelines should have a clause which regulates the structures of NCPs.

4.9 Positive Aspects of the OECD Guidelines

The OECD must be commended in that the established NCP procedures are relatively easy to operate, they are flexible, and they do not require judicial expertise and experience. Further, the financial risk is limited and as such they are more acceptable to both MNEs and complainants.[105] The employees may refer cases without fear of paying legal costs in the event of losing cases. The effective implementation of the OECD Guidelines may reduce costs incurred through statutory dispute resolution procedures. The employees do not need legal representation to be able to refer cases to NCPs.

Further, the follow-up activities of the OECD are not costly or burdensome for NCPs as opposed to statutory enforcement mechanisms. For example, in a case regarding *Survival International v Vedanta Resources plc*, the NCP asked both parties to send written reports on the implementation of the NCP's recommendations after three months.[106] It is not surprising that NCPs are by far the most successful international institutions. Unlike other international institutions, NPCs received and

---

[103] OECD Guidelines 49.

[104] Oshionebo (2013), p. 578.

[105] Schuler (2008), p. 1756.

[106] https://www.oecdwatch.org/complaint/survival-international-vs-vedanta-resources-plc/ date visited 14 September 2025.

dealt with many complaints throughout the world.[107] There is also evidence of the successes of the NCPs in ensuring that decent work was attained.[108]

This study agrees with the argument expressed by Oshionebo that a finding by the NCP that a MNE has breached the OECD Guidelines is to some extent an effective sanction as it serves as a shaming device.[109] The desire to avoid negative publicity may spur the MNE to change its corporate behaviour and comply with the OECD Guidelines.

4.10 Conclusion

This chapter has demonstrated that the OECD Guidelines are an important instrument for setting higher human and labour rights standards. It has the capacity to ensure that international standards unrecognised in certain countries may find recognition through the OECD Guidelines, which benefit employees across the globe. As such, continuous promotion of the OECD Guidelines is important and necessary. Further, through NCPs, the OECD can deal with cases which otherwise would not find their way to the normal courts and statutory tribunals due to jurisdictional challenges.[110] As an example, bringing a case against the MNE in its home country is a complicated matter involving complicated legal principles of civil law.[111] However, such technicalities are avoided by the NCPs' simplified procedures.

However, despite some notable successes in complaints handled by NCPs, there are very few examples of cases leading to beneficial results for employees. It is argued that the right to a remedy for victims of labour rights violations is a tenet of every functioning judicial system. The effectiveness of all other rights rests on

[107] The NPCs began accepting complaints from people harmed by MNEs' non-compliance with the OECD Guidelines. Since then, the NPCs handled over 620 cases from NGOs, trade unions, and individual complainants. https://mneguidelines.oecd.org/Flyer-OECD-National-Contact-Points.pdf date visited 16 September 2025.

[108] The Czech-Moravian Confederation of Trade Unions filed a complaint to the Czech NCP alleging that a Czech subsidiary of the German company Bosch had violated the OECD Guidelines, specifically the human and labour rights by refusing the employees their right to collective bargaining. It alleged that employees were prevented from forming trade unions. This case was discussed at four meetings in the Czech NCP. The Czech NCP informed the German NCP as well as the German Embassy and offered a forum for negotiations. The MNE being the parent company decided to change the subsidiary's management team in order to enable constructive mediation. The parties finally concluded an agreement wherein the employees were allowed to establish a trade union. mneguidelines.oecd.org/database/instances/cz0001.htm date visited 14 September 2025.

[109] Oshionebo (2013), p. 586.

[110] https://www.oecdguidelines.nl/documents/publication/2017/08/18/final-statement-notification-bralima-vs-heineken date visited 14 September 2025.

[111] See Chap. 1 para 1.3.

access to effective legal remedies.[112] Unfortunately, most outcomes of NCPs encompass only future corporate policy changes. As a result, MNEs do not incur direct financial liability if they are found to have violated the OECD Guidelines but are merely expected to take steps to prevent the same from recurring.

It is submitted that NCPs have the potential to become the state-based non-judicial grievance mechanism envisaged by the UNGP. There are, however, several adjustments that must be made to meet the UNGP requirements. First, NCPs approach matters considerably different which impacts negatively on their consistency, predictability, and reliability. Such could ultimately undermine the impact of the OECD Guidelines.[113] In other words, compliance and implementation of the OECD Guidelines have different meanings for NCPs. This is a clear indication that the OECD Guidelines are outdated and are due for revision as a matter of urgency.

As a first step, the OECD Guidelines should be able at the very least to compel or encourage MNEs to participate and stay in the mediation procedure. When the MNE refuses to engage fully in the NCP process or fails to implement the NCP's recommendations, material consequences such as exclusion from privileges of public procurement contracts, export credit guarantees, private sector development aid, international trade, and investment services should result.[114]

Consequences should be attached to ensure that the OECD Guidelines are taken seriously. In the long term, the cooperation with the ILO in order to adopt wider and advanced monitoring and compliance mechanisms should be considered. Furthermore, since the OECD Guidelines are applicable not only in the adherent countries but also in non-adherent countries, in which an adherent country-based MNE operate, the OECD Guidelines should be introduced and promoted worldwide.[115]

References

Bilchitz D (2021) Fundamental rights and legal obligations on business. Cambridge University Press

Blackett A, Trebilcock A (2025) Conceptualising transnational labour law research handbook on transnational labour law. Edward Elgar Publishing

Brincikova Z, Darmo L (2014) The impact of foreign direct investment inflow on employment in V4 countries. Eur Sci J

Castermans A, van Woensel L (2017) CSR for young business lawyers. Eleven International Publishing

Davarnejad L (2011) In the shadow of soft law: the handling of corporate social responsibility disputes under the OECD guidelines for multinational enterprises. J Dispute Resolut

[112] Heric and Cernic (2009), p. 84.

[113] Davarnejad (2011), p. 352.

[114] Yildiz (2019), p. 22.

[115] Yildiz (2019) *SSRN* 21.

Heric L, Cernic J (2009) Corporate Responsibility for Human Rights: Analyzing the ILO Tripartite Declaration of Principles Concerning Multinational Enterprises and Social Policy. Miskolc Journal of International Law

Leimgruber M, Schmelzer M (2017) The OECD and the international political economy since 1948. Springer

Maheandiran B (2015) Calling for clarity: how uncertainty undermines the legitimacy of the dispute resolution system under the OECD guidelines for multinational enterprises. Harv Negot Law Rev

Oshionebo E (2013) The OECD guidelines for multinational enterprises as mechanisms for sustainable development of natural resources: real solutions or window dressing? Lewis Clark Law Rev

Perillo P (2022). The role of the OECD guidelines for multinational enterprises and the National Contact Points in shaping the future of corporate accountability. Int Community Law Rev

Rombouts B (2019) The International Diffusion of Fundamental Labour Standards: Contemporary Content, Scope, Supervision and Proliferation of Core Workers' Rights under Public, Private, Binding, and Voluntary Regulatory Regimes. Columbia Human Rights Law Review

Ruggie J (2017) Multinationals as global institution: power, authority and relative autonomy. Regul Gov

Ruggie J, Tamaryn N (2015) Human rights and the OECD guidelines for multinational enterprises: normative innovations and implementations challenges. Brown J World Aff

Sanchez J (2015) The roles and powers of the OECD National Contact Points regarding complaints on an alleged breach of the OECD guidelines for multinational enterprises. Nordic J Int Law

Santner A (2011) Soft law mechanism for corporate responsibility: how the updated OECD guidelines for multinational enterprises promote business for the future. George Wash Int Law Rev

Schuler G (2008) Effective governance through decentralized soft implementation: the OECD guidelines for multinational enterprises. German Law J

Svoboda O (2018) The OECD guidelines for multinational enterprises and the increasing relevance of the system of National Contact Points. Social Science Research Network

Yildiz A (2019) The OECD guidelines on multinational enterprises: strengths and weaknesses. Social Science Research Network

Chapter 5
The Role of Non-governmental Organisations in the Regulation of MNEs

5.1 Introduction

This chapter focuses on the role of non-governmental organisations (NGOs) in establishing, overseeing and enforcing international human and labour rights standards by MNEs. It is important to note that while NGOs play an increasingly significant role in international law-making and enforcement, the term 'NGO' lacks an authoritative definition within international law.[1] Scholars commonly define an NGO by highlighting what it is not, rather than providing a precise definition. According to Edwards, an NGO can be understood as 'a private, independent, non-profit, goal-oriented group not founded or controlled by a government'.[2] This distinguishing feature sets NGOs apart from international organisations, political parties, and profit-seeking companies.[3] NGOs encompass a range of categories including research institutes, political parties, educational and training institutions, human rights organisations, and trade unions.[4]

This study focuses on the role of human rights NGOs that specifically concentrate on MNEs. According to Bortolotto and Neyrinck, a human rights NGO aligns with the definition of a general NGO but places its primary emphasis on promoting and safeguarding human rights as outlined in international law, with obligations extending from the local level to the global stage.[5] Recently, human rights NGOs have become increasingly active in safeguarding labour standards. This surge in

[1] Kamminga (2005), p. 389.

[2] Edwards (2021), p. 329.

[3] Kamminga (2005), p. 390.

[4] Edwards (2021), p. 320.

[5] Bortolotto and Neyrinck (2020), p. 162.

F. Maluleke, *Compliance with Decent Work Standards by Multinational Enterprises*, European Yearbook of International Economic Law 48,
https://doi.org/10.1007/978-3-032-21261-0_5

activity is attributed to the failure of states to adopt a binding instrument capable of effectively addressing challenges posed by globalisation.[6]

As previously discussed in Chap. 1, in the early 1990s, various activist and media campaigns brought to light violations of workers' human and labour rights in global garment supply chains.[7] This resulted in mounting pressure for more effective government-centred mechanisms to hold MNEs accountable for the human and labour rights violations committed throughout their supply chains.[8] For example, in 1996, Life magazine published a story with the headline 'Six Cents an hour', with a photo of a Pakistani boy sewing Nike soccer balls.[9] The initial response from Nike was that it was not responsible for human and labour rights violations in its supply chain. At a later stage, Nike changed its view and its then CEO Phil Knight, undertook to reform the company operations to eradicate human and labour rights violations in its entire supply chain.

In response to such pressures, MNEs collaborated with NGOs and committed to adhering to corporate codes of conduct aimed at improving working conditions across their supply chains.[10] Revak defines a code of conduct as:

> the self-imposed ethical statement which sets out basic policy standards to guide employees and officers, but they also serve to assure consumers that the products they purchase come from a principled organisation.[11]

According to Bair and Palpacuer, codes of conduct serve as a commitment and assurance by MNEs that they will ensure decent working conditions in their supply chains and monitor compliance with human and labour standards by their factories and suppliers.[12] This approach led to the rise of a system of private regulation, where NGOs, rather than the government entities, are tasked with establishing and monitoring of labour standards by MNEs.[13] However, some scholars, such as Calatayud expressed scepticism about the sincerity of MNEs' commitments.[14]

Hepple argues that the commitments made by MNEs amount to a pledge to adhere to only basic standards.[15] He warns that re-writing ILO conventions in codes of conduct could dilute the binding nature of these laws, which are enshrined in international and national legal frameworks. It is unfortunate that only a few codes of conduct make explicit reference to wages that go above and beyond the legal

---

[6] Bortolotto and Neyrinck (2020), p. 162.

[7] Anner (2017), p. 56. See also Chap. 1 para 1.3.

[8] Revak (2012), p. 1667.

[9] https://www.theguardian.com/sustainable-business/2015/feb/09/corporate-ngo-campaign-environment-climate-change. Date visited 14 September 2025.

[10] Revak (2012), p. 1667.

[11] Revak (2012), p. 1667.

[12] Bair and Palpacuer (2015), p. 189.

[13] Ter Haar (2013), p. 93.

[14] See Chap. 1 para 1.3.

[15] Hepple (1999), p. 358.

minimum wage levels.[16] Nonetheless, this study argues that their inclusion serves as the reinforcement of rights and allows MNEs to focus directly on these rights.

The part that follows discusses the legal status of NGOs in international labour law.

5.2 Legal Status of the NGOs

There is consensus in today's international legal arena that NGOs are increasingly influential. These organisations are actively engaging on the global stage, advocating for their causes, and capturing the attention of international decision-makers and media.[17] Notably, various specialised UN agencies, including the ILO, the World Health Organisation, the Food and Agriculture Organisation collaborate with NGOs in several ways.[18] This study will specifically examine the roles of the UN and ILO in this context.

5.2.1 Accreditation of NGOs by the UN

According to Kamminga, the involvement of NGOs in international law-making and enforcement is usually restricted to the domestic level.[19] He argues that they do not have power to conclude treaties.[20] However, there are exceptions, such as the role of NGOs in UN and ILO, where certain NGOs are allowed to participate in creating binding laws. It is submitted that NGOs received legal recognition in the UN Charter, particularly in Article 71, which states that:

> The Economic and Social Council (ECOSOC) may make suitable arrangements for consultation with non-governmental organisations which are concerned with matters within its competence. Such arrangements may be made with international organisations and, where appropriate, with national organisations after consultation with the member of the United Nations concerned.[21]

While this article does not mandate consultation with NGOs, in 1996, ECOSOC adopted Resolution 1996/31, which updated the relationship to allow NGOs to be accredited by the UN if their aims align with the principles of the UN Charter.[22] It is submitted that NGOs can be accredited by the UN and granted consultative status,

[16] Anner (2017), p. 57.

[17] Le Roux (2006), p. 203.

[18] Moloo (2011), p. 10.

[19] Kamminga (2005), p. 390.

[20] Kamminga (2005), p. 390.

[21] Article 71 of the UN Charter.

[22] A NGOs guide to consultative status (2018) ILO 2.

which consists of general status, specialist status and roster status. As of now, nearly 5000 NGOs hold consultative status.[23]

The general status is given to NGOs which represent large segments of societies in several countries such as the International Organisation for Standardisation (IOS). Their area of work should cover most of the issues on the agenda of ECOSOC and its subsidiary bodies.[24] Furthermore, Special status, is reserved for NGOs that have a special competence and are concerned only with a few of the fields of activity covered by ECOSOC. These NGOs tend to be smaller and more recently established.[25] Lastly, the Roster status, is conferred on NGOs that have a technical focus and make occasional and useful contributions to the work of ECOSOC or its subsidiary bodies.[26]

It is submitted that the UN follows a rigorous process before the NGO can be granted the consultative status.[27] Once an application is approved, the accredited NGO can attend UN conferences and other official and unofficial UN hosted meetings, disseminate information, provide valuable expert advice, help monitor implementation of international agreements, raise awareness, advocate for policy, engage in education, and lend services and technical expertise.[28] When certain types of human and labour rights breaches are alleged, such NGOs might bring or facilitate bringing one or more of three different types of complaints to different U.N. bodies themselves as aggrieved parties, or on behalf of individual or group victims.[29]

To maintain their accreditation, NGOs must submit a quadrennial report outlining their contributions to the UN's work.[30] Failure to comply may lead to suspension or termination of membership.[31] This study argues NGOs are recognised within the UN system. While their role is primarily advisory, they can provide valuable contributions in various capacities. It is submitted that a clear, defined and more formal role for NGOs within the UN is crucial for their continued involvement in global decision-making processes.

---

[23] Edwards (2021), p. 335.

[24] A NGOs guide to consultative status (2018) ILO 38.

[25] As above.

[26] As above.

[27] See Edwards (2021), p. 339 who states that before an NGO begins its U.N. ECOSOC consultative status application, the NGO might be advised that: (a) the application process can take many months or years; (b) the application process can be quite taxing; (c) some NGO applications are rejected; and (d) if an application for consultative status is rejected, the NGO should consider applying again, and if rejected again, apply again, and apply until the application is accepted.

[28] Edwards (2021), p. 336.

[29] Edwards (2021), p. 338.

[30] Edwards (2021), p. 339.

[31] ECOSOC Resolution 2008/4.

5.2.2 Accreditation of NGOs by the ILO

It is submitted that the composition of ILO makes it a more relevant international organisation to analyse the problem of the inclusion of non-state participants.[32] Currently, the ILO has the highest level of NGO participation in the international arena, predominantly from trade unions and employers organisations.[33] Scholars such as Supiot advocates for expansion of the ILO' scope and facilitate open discussions involving external specialists, including MNEs, to remain relevant in the face of globalisation.[34] This study agrees with the said view since the traditional ILO structure is no longer fit to deal with challenges posed by globalisation, especially against MNEs.

While there are obstacles to broadening the ILO's scope to include NGOs beyond its traditional tripartite structure, it is important to note that ILO has never completely excluded NGOs.[35] It is argued that from its inception, the ILO created alternatives to allow for participants who did not necessarily fall in the tripartite structure to play some roles within the ILO. For instance, the status of technical adviser was created which allows the ILO's social partners to include NGOs with specific expertise to participate.[36] This study agrees with Gironde & Carbonnier and submits that just like the UN, the ILO has an accreditation procedure which allows NGOs' participation which process is allowed under article 12 of the ILO's constitution.[37] Section 12 provides that:

> The ILO may make suitable arrangements for such consultation as it may think desirable with recognised NGOs, including international organisations of employers, workers, agriculturalists and cooperators.[38]

It is submitted that the ILO's accreditation process allows for admission of NGOs under three categories.[39] The first category is general or regional consultative status which is reserved for international NGOs with important interest in a wide range of the ILO's work. As a result of such accreditation, NGOs may participate in all ILO meetings including regional meetings. To be admitted in this list, NGOs requesting accreditation must satisfy three requirements, namely, first, prove that it has international composition and that it is represented or have affiliates in several number of

[32] Gironde and Carbonnier (2019), p. 15.
[33] Barbaro (2022), p. 77.
[34] Supiot (2020), p. 128.
[35] Gironde and Carbonnier (2019), p. 53.
[36] Gironde and Carbonnier (2019), p. 53.
[37] Dey (2020), p. 3.
[38] Article 12 (3) of the ILO Constitution.
[39] Reports of the Officers of the Governing Body (2019) ILO.

countries.[40] Secondly, the NGO should demonstrate that its aims, goals and objectives are in accordance with the spirit and principles of the ILO Constitution.[41]

Thirdly, to be considered for invitation, the NGO should have formally expressed a clear interest specifically related to its own activities, as defined in its statutes and explicitly referenced in one of the agenda items of the ILO's conference session. Examples of NGOs admitted under this category are Asia and the Pacific and General Union of Chambers of Commerce, Industry and Agriculture for Arab Countries.[42]

The second category for ILO's accreditation is the special list. This category permits the admission of international NGOs other than trade unions and employers' organisations that uphold the principles and objectives of the ILO constitution and the UDHR.[43] It is submitted that the inclusion of NGOs on this special list hinges on NGOs demonstrating their interest in the programme of the ILO's meetings and main activities. Examples of NGOs admitted in this category include Amnesty International, International Centre for Human Rights and Democratic Development and International Federation of Human Rights.[44]

It is argued that NGOs that do not satisfy the requirements prescribed on the first and second categories, may be admitted on the third category (Roster status).[45] It is submitted that despite the ILO constitution legally permitting the participation of NGOs since its formation, they have been rendered ineffective because the power to make decisions are limited to the tripartite structure.[46] Furthermore, Wickramasekara criticised the ILO for exclusionary accreditation criteria and that the accreditation only allows NGOs to be observers and make no decisions.[47]

This study submits that NGOs should be given more formal powers, especially in regulating MNEs. It is recommended that a fourth category specifically responsible for MNEs should be established. It is suggested that only NGOs with expertise and a track record in handling complaints against MNEs should be accredited under his category. This study identifies several NGOs with the necessary expertise and experience in the regulation of MNEs.

In the sections that follow, the different approaches by the identified NGOs will be discussed in detail. These NGOs include the Fair Labour Association (FLA), Fair Wear Foundation (FWF), Social Accountability International (SAI), Worker Rights

---

[40] Van den Bossche (2005), p. 10.

[41] https://www.ilo.org/projects-and-partnerships/civil-society-ilo-partnership. Date visited 14 September 2025.

[42] https://www.ilo.org/partnerships/civil-society/ngos-regional-consultative-status date visited 14 September 2025.

[43] https://www.ilo.org/partnerships/civil-society/relations-ngos/ilo-special-list-ngos date visited 14 September 2025.

[44] https://www.ilo.org/partnerships/civil-society/relations-ngos/ilo-special-list-ngos date visited 14 September 2025.

[45] Van den Bossche (2005), p. 10.

[46] Gironde and Carbonnier (2019), p. 53.

[47] Wickramasekara (2015), p. 11.

Consortium (WRC), and Clean Clothes Campaign (CCC). The FLA, FWF, and WRC have similar approaches and therefore only the FLA will be discussed in full detail. There will be no discussion of the WRC as its approach is entirely like that of the FLA. Regarding the FWF, only two aspects which differ from the FLA and WRC will be discussed.

5.3 The FLA

5.3.1 Background

The Fair Labour Association (FLA) is a US-based NGO in which several high-profile MNEs in the apparel and sportswear industry work together with universities to promote compliance with internationally recognised labour standards within their supply chains.[48] Similar to other NGOs which are responsible for corporate social responsibility, the FLA was established as a direct response to the anti-sweatshop campaigns that emerged in the US during the early 1990s.[49] Regarding the FLA, the campaigns were led by a group of students, labour, and human rights organisations, who demanded that MNEs supplying US consumer markets take responsibility for labour conditions throughout their supply chains across the globe. Thus far, the FLA has 30 members.[50]

5.3.2 Governance Structure

The FLA has no direct government participation in its overall management. Instead, it is governed by a board of directors which are responsible for setting the association's strategic direction and overseeing its activities.[51] The FLA structure is unique and allows for the independence of the management team. The board comprises six industry representatives, six labour/NGO representatives, six university representatives, and a Chair.

Davies recommends that at least one-third of the board should be non-executive directors, most of whom should be independent.[52] It is argued that due to its diverse nature, it is expected that the FLA board should be impartial in its strategic direction

[48] https://www.fairlabor.org/about-us/ date visited 14 September 2025.

[49] Macdonald (2011), p. 1.

[50] https://www.fairlabor.org/members/fla-accredited/?member_type=fla-accredited&page=2 date visited 14 September 2025.

[51] https://www.fairlabor.org/about-us/ date visited 14 September 2025.

[52] Davies (2000), p. 21.

of the business.[53] The role of affiliated MNEs is to control terms of their contracts with suppliers and NGOs which are necessary for the organisation's credibility.[54] University participation is necessary to ensure the organisation's financial viability. In other words, the universities certify MNEs in return for fees, which increase the membership revenues on which the FLA's budget largely depends.[55]

5.3.3 *Monitoring and Enforcement Mechanisms*

Ter Haar argues that the organisations such as the FLA seeks to entice the affiliated MNEs to comply with labour standards to continue to receive a certification and strengthen their brands.[56] Indeed, the FLA accreditation is important to assist investors and consumers to make informed choices by showing that the member MNE is actively fulfilling the highest standards in human and labour rights.[57]

The FLA adopted the Fair Labour Code which sets out human and labour rights standards that promote decent work and fair working conditions. The code's standards are based on the ILO's labour standards and internationally accepted good labour practices.[58] According to the preamble of the FLA labour code, for MNEs to receive and retain FLA certification, they should undertake to uphold relevant and applicable laws of the country in which employees are based. Furthermore, they should comply with the standards prescribed by the code in their applicable workplaces. They are further required to monitor and enforce compliance with the code by their suppliers.[59]

Monitoring of the FLA code within individual factories is carried out by individual affiliated MNEs, and in part via external monitoring visits managed by FLA staff.[60] MNEs bearing the FLA accreditation are evaluated on an ongoing basis and must demonstrate continuous improvement efforts to address working conditions and protect workers' rights.[61] The affiliated MNE that fails to comply with the set standards may have its membership terminated by the FLA.[62] Perhaps the most

[53] https://www.fairlabor.org/about-us/ date visited 14 September 2025.

[54] As above.

[55] https://www.fairlabor.org date visited 14 September 2025.

[56] Ter Haar (2013), p. 93.

[57] https://www.fairlabor.org/accountability/fair-labor-accreditation/ date visited 14 September 2025.

[58] MNEs commitment to evaluation includes how companies can better monitor and address issues like discrimination, forced labour, unfair discrimination, health and safety, child labour, collective bargaining and hours of work. https://www.fairlabor.org/accountability/standards/manufacturing/mfg-code/ date visited 14 September 2025.

[59] Preamble of the Fair Labour Code.

[60] https://respect.international/wpcontent/uploads/2017/10/fla_workplace_compliance_benchmarks_rev_10.2020.pdf date visited 14 September 2025.

[61] https://www.fairlabor.org/members/fla-accredited/?member_type=fla-accredited.

[62] Macdonald (2011), p. 2.

important part of the FLA monitoring and enforcement mechanisms is the remediation processes in response to documented violations of the code.

Such remediation essentially consists of efforts to promote capacity-building among suppliers by combining some degree of technical assistance with support for processes of additional influence and learning.[63] It provides stakeholders with the third-party procedure to raise grievances against member MNEs.

5.3.4 *Complaint Procedure (Third-Party Procedure)*

The FLA has a third-party complaint mechanism which is open to all interested third parties.[64] According to the official website of the FLA, 'for a complaint to be admissible, it must contain reliable, specific, and verifiable evidence or information that the alleged non-compliance has occurred'.[65] As soon as the FLA receives a complaint, it will verify if the factory concerned produces for the MNE which is affiliated to FLA. If so, it will further determine if the complaint has verifiable allegations of non-compliance with the FLA Code.[66]

The FLA also determines whether other dispute resolution procedures were utilised to resolve the issues raised and what outcome they achieved. For instance, *Teksif Union v Hugo Boss Izmir*,[67] the matter concerned the dismissal of two employees due to alleged union activities. Due to the pursuit of local legal remedies, the FLA has terminated its complaint procedure. This was after the FLA learned that the two workers who were the subjects of the complaint had filed legal cases in local courts against Hugo Boss Izmir regarding their dismissals.

It is argued that such restriction is fair, and it avoids situations where employees may lodge the same complaint with multiple dispute resolution agencies. Such may result in different outcomes which are not in the interest of justice. It is, however, argued that the employees will choose the tribunals which is predictable and has powers to provide remedies as opposed to the FLA which is limited to making recommendations. The FLA accepts the complaint for review if it meets the above criteria and then contacts the MNE(s) sourcing from the factory in question.

It is submitted that the test for 'verifiable evidence' is highly technical and complex. Such may result in cases being wrongly rejected.[68] As of June 2023, the FLA

[63] Same as above.

[64] Third-party complaints are those that were lodged by external parties such as civil organisations or trade unions, or government officials.

[65] https://www.fairlabor.org/accountability/fair-labor-investigations/tpc/ date visited 14 September 2025.

[66] https://www.fairlabor.org/?s=THIRD+PARTY+COMPLAINT date visited 14 September 2025.

[67] https://www.fairlabor.org/wp-content/uploads/2021/09/hugo_boss_izmir_final_report_july_2016.pdf date visited 14 September 2025.

[68] https://www.fairlabor.org/accountability/fair-labor-investigations/tpc-tracking-chart/ 14 September 2025.

received a total of 70 third-party complaints. Thus far 21 cases were rejected which translates to 30% which is very high. The complaints ranged, amongst others, compensation, unfair dismissals, and harassment.[69]

Like other similar dispute resolution forums such as the OECD, the FLA complaint procedure provides for no review nor appeal mechanism against the decision of rejection of the case. As such, complainants whose claims may be unfairly rejected may be left without recourse. There is therefore a need for some clear criteria to be designed, and such a procedure should be predictable and certain. Where a decision of rejection of the complaint is made, at least the complainant should be provided with reasons and given a chance to challenge or make a representation to be reconsidered for the decision.

When a complaint is accepted by the FLA, a complaint-handling procedure will commence, and it includes the MNE and its external and independent monitors.[70] The MNE concerned has 45 days to conduct an assessment and develop a remediation plan.[71] It is argued that such an approach is not appropriate because it allows the MNE, which is alleged to have failed to prevent the human and labour rights abuse, to control the process for complaint handling, which is already referred to external bodies. It should be made clear that once the complaint is received by the external body, the factory or subcontractor should no longer have control over the outcome of the matter.

However, this study commends the FLA complaint procedures because it has the power to intervene in the investigation by engaging the services of third parties to investigate allegations and recommend remedial action.[72] Such power allows for independence in dispute resolution. It must be indicated that although the procedure is comprehensive, the dispute resolution often takes unreasonably long, and the investigation may become academic in situations where employees lose interest in the matter, or they may have resigned or been dismissed from work.

As previously submitted, expeditious dispute resolution is vital in labour relations cases.[73] For instance, in the case of *Deriteks trade union v factory Aydinli Deri Konfekslyon*, FLA-affiliated MNE Hugo Boss was actively sourcing from the factory at the time of the complaint. The complaint dealt with freedom of association, which was filed with the FLA in 2016 and remained unresolved until 2023.[74] There are, however, some successes registered under the FLA third-party complaint procedures.

[69] https://www.fairlabor.org/accountability/fair-labor-investigations/tpc-tracking-chart/ 14 September 2025.

[70] https://www.fairlabor.org/accountability/fair-labor-investigations/tpc-tracking-chart/ 14 September 2025.

[71] As above.

[72] https://www.fairlabor.org/accountability/fair-labor-investigations/tpc/ date visited 15 September 2025.

[73] See Chap. 1 para 1.3.

[74] https://www.fairlabor.org/wp-content/uploads/2021/09/final_report_aydinli_deri_december_2016.pdf date visited 14 September 2025.

For instance, in the case of *Union Federation Federación De Asociaciones Y Sindicatos Independientes de El Salvador (FEASIES) v Supertex*,[75] the union filed a complaint about freedom of association with the FLA. The trade union alleged that the Supertex factory in June 2022 had unfairly dismissed two leaders from the union. FLA commissioned the independent investigator and the investigator's final report concluded that the terminations of the four union leaders from work were not legal under national labour regulations. Supertex factory management agreed to reinstate them with back pay.[76]

It is argued that the procedure is only effective to the extent that the MNE is willing and has the capacity to insist on performance by the factory. It is most glaring that the absence of power to make a binding decision is a serious omission. It is also glaring that there are no remedies for employees who lodge complaints. Where there are remedies, the FLA only makes recommendations, and the MNE decides on how to implement them. In *C.S.A. Guatemala S.A. workers v C.S.A. Guatemala S.A*, the FLA found that the employees were owed money and recommended that, although factory buyers (MNEs) are not legally obligated to assume the payment of amounts owed by factories to the workers, it recommends that MNEs assume a subsidiary responsibility for those owed payments, and consider donating money to pay amounts owed to workers, including payment of social contributions not paid to the IGSS.[77]

Payment of owed termination pay-outs should include all six workers terminated in October 2018 for expressing the intention to form a union. The above remained recommendations, and there is no proof that the MNE implemented them.

5.3.5 *Investigations*

Apart from third-party complaints mechanisms, the FLA may conduct investigations when it is alerted or detects signs of non-compliance with labour standards.[78] According to the FLA website, two investigations were lodged in 2022. This number suggests that the procedures are not widely used. It is submitted that there is therefore a need to promote this procedure to all employees of the FLA member MNEs. Such may result in employees informing the FLA of the allegations of non-compliance by factories.

Paiement and Melchers argue that even when codes of conduct are referring to international labour standards, in practice it is very difficult for fundamental labour rights to be implemented in the context of private employment relationships in a

[75] https://www.fairlabor.org/reports/supertex-el-salvador/ date visited 14 September 2025.

[76] Supertex summary report 3. https://www.fairlabor.org/reports/supertex-el-salvador/ date visited 14 September 2025.

[77] https://www.fairlabor.org/wp-content/uploads/2021/09/csa_guatemala_tpc_report_final_english_for_publication.pdf date visited 14 September 2025.

[78] https://www.fairlabor.org/ date visited 14 September 2025.

manner consistent with the ILO's understanding of these rights.[79] The basis for the FLA's intervention is the relationship between the factory and the MNE. The FLA is powerless where the MNE and factory terminate their relationship, and it must discontinue the complaint procedure where such termination occurs.[80]

The approach by Fair Wear Foundation is dealt with in detail in the following section.

5.4 Fair Wear Foundation

5.4.1 Background

The Fair Wear Foundation (FWF) has a similar background to that of the FLA and WRC. They all have similar monitoring mechanisms and grievance procedures, adopt codes of conduct, and require MNEs to promote compliance with human and labour rights in their supply chains. The FWF distinguishes itself regarding two aspects, namely, an expedited procedure for certain types of cases and the procedures applicable to confidentiality requirements. The two aspects are discussed in detail below.

5.4.2 Expedited Procedure

The Code of Labour Practices (CoLP) classifies violations that pose immediate risks to employees' health or life as urgent matters.[81] Such complaints must be addressed in an expedited manner, with stricter monitoring. These include fire and building safety, child labour, payment below legal minimum wage, and any other situations that present an immediate risk to the health and safety of employees.[82]

The idea of prioritisation of urgent cases is commendable and there is some evidence that the process can deliver social justice.[83] In *Outdoor & Sports Co, Ltd*, the FWF received an advanced notice of a report on labour conditions and social issues in the export-oriented garment industry in Myanmar. Shortly thereafter the report was also shared by the Centre for Research on MNEs with all the FWF member MNEs that were sourcing in Myanmar. The FWF conducted the investigation which

[79] Paiement and Melchers (2020), p. 314.

[80] In *Ad Hoc Committee v Bienno factory Guatemala.*

[81] https://www.fairwear.org/about-us/labour-standards/ date visited 14 September 2025.

[82] As above.

[83] https://fairwear.force.com/public/s/complaints#!complaint-244-outdoor-&-sports-company-ltd.-mammut-sports-groupN 14 September 2025.

confirmed that there were workers under the age of 14 years who were working at the factory.

The investigation was unannounced to ensure its integrity.[84] After reviewing all the evidence and interviews, the investigation concluded that one child worker aged 15 years and 5 days at the time of the investigation, had been identified. The worker has been working in the factory's sewing department since the age of 13 at the time of recruitment. She has been working 8 hours per day, and she has the same job description as adult workers.

The FWF recommended that the worker aged below 16 stop working immediately, and her full salary be paid monthly to the family of the child worker until she reaches the acceptable age. Further, the company should arrange education or vocational training until she reaches an acceptable age and regain employment thereafter (at the same position and seniority) when she turns 16 and wishes to be reinstated. Lastly, a medical certificate of fitness would need to be arranged for all workers under 18. With the support of MNEs, the factory has committed to the above remediation steps. As previously discussed, labour relations matters should be handled expeditiously. This study supports this approach, and it is submitted that other similar institutions should consider the same approach.

5.4.3 Confidentiality Requirements

The FWF also distinguishes itself from other NGOs, in respect of being a transparent institution. The FWF publishes all complaints on its website.[85] Such transparency assists in development of the law in Corporate Social Responsibility. It is submitted that the approach further assists in the improvement of compliance with labour standards since MNEs would not want to be associated with labour rights violations.

After the conclusion of complaints, the FWF publishes all complaints and the information includes basic information of the complaint, the relevant labour standard, and the country. The FWF always include the name of the member MNE sourcing from the factory. To avoid negative consequences for the employees, the name of the factory for which a complaint is filed is not disclosed during the procedure. When a complaint has been successfully remediated, the involved parties, including the complainants, may agree on disclosing the name of the factory. If the involved parties agree, this information will be added to the public information on the FWF website.

---

[84] https://www.fairwear.org/about-us/labour-standards/ date visited 14 September 2025.

[85] https://www.fairwear.org/about-us/labour-standards/ date visited 14 September 2025.

5.5 Social Accountability International

5.5.1 Background

The Social Accountability International (SAI) is a private organisation established in 1997 which seeks to promote workers' rights across the globe.[86] To attain its goal, the SAI amongst others adopted the SA8000 standard which is based on the international labour standards of ILO conventions,[87] the UDHR[88] and the United Nations Convention on the Rights of the Child.[89] SAI is responsible for accreditation of auditing firms and providing training to auditors, employees on the SA8000 standard, and publishes the list of factories that satisfy the standard.[90]

The SA8000 system differs from the FLA in some regards, most notably on the issues of wages, worker representation, and certification. The SA8000 may be interpreted to include the requirement that factories pay workers a 'living wage', or what SAI refers to as a 'basic needs' wage, as opposed to the FLA's weaker requirements to pay the prevailing wage.[91]

5.5.2 Governance Structure

The SAI is a multi-stakeholder's forum which brings together MNEs and their suppliers, governments, trade unions, NGOs, and academic institutions to contribute towards improving working conditions.[92] In addition to the above, it has established an independent accreditation division, the Social Accountability Accreditation Services (SAAS), which determines whether the auditing qualify to award factories with SA8000 certification.[93] Only certificates issued by the accredited or

---

[86] Kaan (2010), p. 70.

[87] ILO Declaration on Fundamental Principles and Rights at Work.

[88] Article 23 of the UDHR provides that 'Everyone has the right to work, to free choice of employment, to just and favourable conditions of work and to protection against unemployment'.

[89] Article 32 of Convention on the Rights of the Child provides that 'States Parties recognize the right of the child to be protected from economic exploitation and from performing any work that is likely to be hazardous or to interfere with the child's education, or to be harmful to the child's health or physical, mental, spiritual, moral or social development'. https://www.ohchr.org/en/instruments-mechanisms/instruments/convention-rights-child date visited 14 September 2025.

[90] O'Rourke (2002), p. 14.

[91] O'Rourke (2002), p. 14.

[92] https://sa-intl.org/about/issue-areas/ date visited 14 September 2025.

[93] Courville (2003), p. 278.

certification bodies (CBs) are recognised by the SAI.[94] Over 5089 organisations have been certified through the SAAS accredited bodies world-wide.[95]

5.5.3 Monitoring and Enforcement Mechanisms

According to Bartley, the SA8000 programme is regarded as the most challenging and credible global factory certification standard. In addition to the expectation that factories comply with conventions and national laws of host nations, factories are also required to pay decent compensation and to adopt strict limitations on working hours and overtime.[96]

The SA8000 differs from other NGOs in that it certifies factories not MNEs. The rational for such is that MNEs will procure products from manufacturers that satisfy the SA8000 certification requirements.[97] To assist MNEs in making procurement decisions, the SAI discloses lists of certified factories and their countries where they are based. However, the SAI does not publish the list of factories that lost their accreditation. It is submitted that such confidentiality is unreasonable, as MNEs may continue to procure from uncertified facilities.

Some scholars cast doubts on the quality of the SA8000 standard. They submit that it is not practical and reasonable to confirm that the factory is adhering to the SA8000 standard based on a day audit, which is conducted once in twelve months.[98] Some NGOs also cast suspicion on the credibility of the SA8000 auditing processes. They argue that there is a perceived bias toward factories and that they have weak controls and monitoring procedures.[99]

---

[94] The following firms are currently accredited: TUV SUD Group (TUV Italia), TUV Rheinland, TUV Nord Group, SI Cert, SGS India private limited, Rina, Ozone Sustainability Management systems, LSQA, LRQA, Leverage limited, IQ Net Ltd, Intertek, International Associate limited, Institute of quality and control ltd, HK, GIC, C Certi Italy S.R.I, Euro Cert, ESTS (Extensive Standard Technical Services Co., Ltd.), DNV GL Business Assurance, CISE (Centro per l'Innovazione e lo Sviluppo Economico), Centre Testing International Group Co., Ltd. (CTI), Bureau Veritas Certification, BSI, Benchmarks Company Limited, BCC Inc, APCER, APAVE, Accordia Global Compliance Group, and ABS Quality Evaluations. https://sa-intl.org/resources/sa8000-accredited-certification-bodies/ date visited 14 September 2025.

[95] https://sa-intl.org/sa8000-search/#stats date visited 14 September 2025.

[96] Bartley (2018), p. 180.

[97] O'Rourke (2002), p. 15.

[98] O'Rourke (2002), p. 15.

[99] O'Rourke (2002), p. 15.

5.5.4 Requirements for Certification

To be certified under the SA8000 standard, the manufacturing facility must first conduct a preliminary internal assessment of compliance with SA8000 and make any changes to conditions or policies as required.[100] Thereafter, an auditing firm accredited by the SAI should conduct an initial assessment and provide corrective action if required. After making changes per the corrective action requests, the facility may contact the auditing company to arrange a full certification audit. If it passes the audit, the facility will be certified.[101]

The SA8000 certification is valid for three years, subject to on-site surveillance monitoring.[102] Surveillance monitoring includes a combination of announced and unannounced visits, typically twice per year, and independent evaluations to track improvements over time. The expectation is that in the factory that has been certified, the protection of employees would be better and that working conditions and wages would be superior.

The cost of obtaining an SA8000 certification is comprised of certification fees as well as corrective/compliance costs.[103] The certifying bodies are paid directly by the facilities but are not allowed to offer consulting services to certified production facilities. Sethi and Rovenpor argue that the continuous reliance on funds from MNEs is the greatest threat to the credibility of the SAI. The CBs may be interested in developing long-term relationships with MNEs and this could affect their objectivity.[104]

Further, SAAS is entitled to terminate a relationship with a CB that fails to uphold its ethical standards. Recently, SAAS has suspended the India accreditation scope of four SA8000 CBs. This is the result of findings from SAAS surveillance visits undertaken following allegations of conflicts of interest between auditors, consultants, and certified organisations. The affected CBs are Bureau Veritas Certification, RINA, SGS, and TUV Rheinland. Such suspension implies that the four suspended CBs must temporarily cease all SA8000 activities in India. Such a decision is acceptable.

This study does not support the SAAS decisions insofar as the suspensions are only applicable in India operations, and all four firms may continue SA8000 activities outside of India under their respective scopes of accreditation. Further, the details of why suspensions were effected remain unknown as they are kept private. It is submitted that such action may not be sufficient to deter other auditing firms from embarking on such behaviour.

It appears that the penalty was made to have the minimum negative impact on the auditing firms in question. The suspensions will be lifted upon the CBs taking

---

[100] https://sa-intl.org/resources/sa8000-getting-started/ date visited 14 September 2025.

[101] As above.

[102] Bartley (2018), p. 183.

[103] Lin (2007), p. 328. See also Sethi and Rovenpor (2016), p. 23.

[104] Sethi and Rovenpor (2016), p. 21.

appropriate corrective actions addressing findings of non-conformity.[105] It, however, appears that the SAI reluctantly invokes the power to de-certify CBs. Courville states the SIA grants more opportunities to CBs even after committing serious misconduct.[106]

Another weakness of the SAI and SAAS is that they do not make the actual audit reports of production facilities available for public scrutiny. Sethe and Rovenpor criticised this restriction because it makes it impossible to determine the level of compliance achieved by a given facility and which facilities did not comply and did not get a certification.[107] Further, the checklist audit approach may not be suitable to assess conformity with the prevention of unfair discrimination.

5.5.5 *Grievance Procedure*

The affected employees or third parties who have reasons to believe that an SA8000 certified facility has breached the requirements of the standard have three forums to resolve their grievance.[108] The first forum is to refer the grievance to the certified organisation itself. Certified organisations are required to maintain an effective grievance process so that employees and other stakeholders can raise concerns and those concerns should be thoroughly investigated.[109] The procedure does not state how the certified organisation should attempt to resolve the complaints once received. This creates uncertainties and unpredictability of the outcomes.

However, should the complaint remain unresolved, the affected party may refer the issue to the CB that certified the facility. The aggrieved party may as a last resort refer the matter to the final forum, namely, the assurance division, SAAS. The SAI does not publish details of complaints lodged against its certified facilities on its website. As such, it is not possible to assess the effectiveness of the complaint procedure. Lack of transparency creates doubts on the credibility of the procedures.

However, in the rare known complaint against Delmonte Royal factory, a SA8000-certified facility, the factory was accused of carrying out several human and labour rights abuses, including paying employees lower than minimum wages

[105] https://sa-intl.org/wp-content/uploads/2020/02/SA8000-Performance-Indicator-Annex-1.pdf 14 September 2025.

[106] Courville (2003) *L&P* 285.

[107] Sethi and Rovenpor (2016), p. 25. Also see Bartley (2018), p. 72, who stated that 'SAI discloses only a list of SA8000-certified facilities, with no information on the auditing process. there is a channel for complaints and appeals, but watchdogs would have to mobilise their won documentation'.

[108] https://sa-intl.org/services/assurance/sa8000-complaints-and-feedback/ date visited 14 September 2025.

[109] https://sa-intl.org/services/assurance/sa8000-complaints-and-feedback/19 date visited 14 September 2025.

and prohibiting them from organising.[110] The employees filed a written complaint to the CB, Coop Italia. The CB investigated the process and confirmed that the allegations were confirmed. In resolving the issues, the CB decided to work with the factory to improve its human and labour rights performance. After several interventions, the facility achieved certification to SA8000.[111]

The SAI's approach is to withhold information in respect of breaches of the standards by the MNES. This is done to avoid negative publicity for the MNE which may result in them deciding not to participate again. Instead, companies can learn from the feedback provided in the initial inspection exercises and improve their performance. Only when certification is granted is this fact made public. SAI provides a list of all SA8000-certified facilities on its website.[112] Similarly, companies that look for an SA8000 certificate when selecting suppliers expect that the certificate is credible and represents the same level of social performance no matter where it was issued.[113]

The SIA therefore keep the non-compliance confidential until the certification is published. This may confirm views that the SAI accreditation is used for MNEs to improve their chances of obtaining lucrative contracts and not improve working relations.

5.6 The Clean Clothes Campaign

5.6.1 Background

The Clean Clothes Campaign (CCC) was founded in the Netherlands in 1989 and at the time it was called 'Schone Kleren Campagne (SKC)'.[114] Its campaigners were mainly female activists who wanted the world to know that women were responsible for making clothes under inhumane working conditions.[115] Encouraged by the progress made by SKC, the activists and consumers in other European countries organised their own campaigns, and later joined the association.[116] The CCC continued to grow and it now forms a worldwide network of more than 250 organisations,

[110] Kamunda (2019), p. 8.

[111] Courville (2003), p. 286.

[112] Courville (2003), p. 290.

[113] https://sa-intl.org/the-value-of-accreditation/ date visited 14 September 2025.

[114] Sahan (2022), pp. 42–43.

[115] Ascoly (2005) Clean Clothes Campaign. https://ecommons.cornell.edu/bitstream/handle/1813/99675/CCC_Made_by_Women.pdf?sequence=1&isAllowed=y. Date visited 14 September 2025.

[116] https://cleanclothes.org/about date visited 15 September 2025.

including trade unions, which are committed to ensuring decent working conditions in the clothing industry.[117]

The CCC network's vision is that 'all people working in the global garment and sportswear industries enjoy and exercise their human and labour rights at work ... and can defend and improve the implementation of those rights'.[118] Traditionally, the exploitation of employees within the clothing industry occurred in Asia, where cases of poverty wages, unsafe, and inhumane working conditions are well documented.[119] However, these problems are experienced throughout the clothing industry globally.[120]

5.6.2 Governance Structure

The CCC is governed by three self-steering teams, namely, the board, international secretariat, and the back office. The details are briefly discussed below.[121] The board is mainly responsible for supervision of the goal setting and functioning of the International Secretariat and the back office. The board consists of five members who do not earn honorariums, salaries, or other forms of compensation from the foundation.

An international secretariat is responsible to coordinate the international activities and campaigns. It facilitates the international campaign structures and channels. It also coordinates and/or facilitates urgent international appeals.[122] The back office provides services to both the International Secretariat.[123] It is responsible for administrative tasks, human resource management, external information services, websites, finances, and facilities.

[117] Its network connects actors across the garment and sportswear industry, linking home-based worker organisations, grass-roots unions, women's organisations, and trade unions to labour rights and feminist organisations, CSOs, and activists in both garment-producing and consumer market countries. https://www.schonekleren.nl/over-ons/ date visited 15 September 2025.

[118] https://cleanclothes.org/about/our-global-strategic-framework. Date visited 14 September 2025.

[119] Clean Clothes Campaign (2014) Stitched Up: Poverty wages for garment workers in Eastern Europe and Turkey. https://ecommons.cornell.edu/bitstream/handle/1813/102209/CCC_2014_Report_Stitched_Up.pdf?sequence=1 page 5. Date visited 14 September 2025.

[120] As above.

[121] Annual report (2007) ILR 4–5.

[122] Annual report (2007) ILR 4–5.

[123] As above.

5.6.3 Monitoring and Enforcement Mechanisms

To ensure the protection of human and labour rights by MNEs, the CCC embarks on the mobilisation of consumers, lobbies MNEs and governments at regional and national levels to campaign outside of its network.[124] The CCC may, amongst others, initiate days of action, panel discussions, information desks, learning opportunities, speeches, fashion shows, or movie screenings coming with the hope of a bigger media exposure.[125] The campaigns may be started at CCC's initiative or at the request of employees.

For instance, in 2012, the CCC, on its own discretion, ran an online campaign titled 'killer jeans'.[126] The campaign sought to secure a ban on sandblasting in the jeans production industry. It used the term 'Killer Jeans' dramatically to refer to a dangerous technique in the production process of jeans, specifically the use of sandblasting to fabricate fashionably worn-out-look jeans, which exposed employees to lung diseases. Consumers were requested to send protest letters to select MNEs, national governments, and the EU to reach an agreement to ban sandblasting products.

The CCC also adopted the urgent appeals system in cases of concrete violations of the employees' rights.[127] Kryst described urgent appeals as 'a call for solidarity and address consumers with the appeal to complain to companies about labour rights violations'.[128] It does so by calling MNEs and governments to account for abuses and exploitation in their territory, but also: by connecting trade unions, factory owners, clothing brands, and governments to reach binding agreements.

In the part that follows, a detailed discussion is presented on urgent appeals.

5.6.4 Urgent Appeals

Any garment employee or activist may refer a case of human and labour rights violation to a local organisation which is part of the global network of the CCC.[129] Upon receipt of the case, the CCC will explore possible ways to support the employees or activists, together with local organisations in the country where the alleged violation took place.[130] If the matter is urgent, the CCC will classify such a case as

[124] https://cleanclothes.org/about date visited 14 September 2025.

[125] Kryst (2012), p. 114.

[126] Kryst (2012), pp. 101–102.

[127] https://www.schonekleren.nl/over-ons/ date visited 14 September 2025.

[128] Kryst (2012), p. 114.

[129] Merk and Stolwijk (2014), p. 2.

[130] As above.

an urgent appeal. Thereafter, the CCC may prepare online letters and transmit them to the MNE agents in the places of production or to their customers.[131]

The CCC must be commended for having created a simple referral procedure for employees who allege that their human and labour rights have been infringed. The CCC may also accept such cases even in situations where there is no formal referral.[132] For instance, in *Angelica Manole v Tanex clothing factory*, the Romania-based factory makes clothing for MNEs such as Ted Baker.[133] In 2020, the factory withheld half of the employees' wages without giving any reason. One of the aggrieved employees, Manole, posted a photo of her paycheck online. Her post received 996 responses and was shared 2682 times. Through the support of international trade unions, organisations from the network of CCC and supporters worldwide, Manole and her colleagues were eventually paid their outstanding wages, and the Minister of Labour Inspectorate issued an apology.

In 2021 the CCC supported garment and sportswear employees and labour rights organisations in 29 cases in 14 different countries in their struggles against union busting, wage theft, gender-based violence, sexual harassment, and violations of reproductive rights, among other abuses.[134]

It is submitted that a criterion for assessing whether a case qualifies to be classified as urgent appeal is not written in any document. This area needs to be cleared as a matter of urgency to ensure certainty and predictability of cases. Over the years, the CCC classified certain types of cases as urgent appeals. Such cases are the following: theft of wages, severance payments, mass layoffs in cases of plant closures, unsafe or unhealthy situations, intimidation of employees, sexual harassment, and obstruction in the establishment of local trade unions.[135] As a starting point, it is suggested that these cases should be classified as urgent appeals. It is submitted further that such a list should be kept as broad as reasonable and practical. This is to ensure that most disputes which are excluded under normal dispute resolution can be covered under the urgent appeal system.

Another important issue relates to the transparency of cases. According to the CCC, not all urgent appeals should be made public.[136] Sometimes it is more effective to address the MNE or the government behind the scenes. If that does not produce sufficient results, it can still make the matter public if those who have asked for support want it.[137]

---

[131] As above.

[132] Check payyourworkers.org what you can do to help solve it. https://www.schonekleren.nl/urgent-appeal/het-verhaal-van-angelica/ date visited 14 September 2025.

[133] https://cleanclothes-ea.org/node/82. Date visited 17 December 2025.

[134] https://cleanclothes.org/file-repository/ccc-still-underpaid-report-2021-web-def.pdf/view date visited 14 September 2025.

[135] https://cleanclothes-ea.org/en-3 date visited 14 September 2025.

[136] https://www.schonekleren.nl/urgent-appeal/gestreden-voor-vakbond-sri-lanka/ date visited 14 September 2025.

[137] https://www.schonekleren.nl/urgent-appeal/gestreden-voor-vakbond-sri-lanka/ date visited 14 September 2025.

The main challenge facing the CCC is its heavy reliance on pressure tactics, particularly naming and shaming, as the sole strategy to encourage MNEs to uphold human and labour rights in their supply chains.[138] Unfortunately, these MNEs are not legally obliged to enforce compliance with human and labour rights in factories producing their products.[139] The weakness of naming and shaming strategy was apparent in the case involving Federasi Serikat Pekerja Metal Indonesia (FSPMI), and Fast Retailing and s.Oliver. In this case, the CCC filed a complaint with the FLA on behalf of the workers at the Jaba Garmindo factory in Indonesia concerning unpaid severance pay.[140]

Upon investigation, the FLA concluded that employees did not receive the severance pay they were legally entitled to.[141] The factory had closed overnight without informing the workers, which was a result of bankruptcy, following the withdrawal of major customers, including MNEs like Uniqlo. Despite efforts by the CCC, the workers did not receive their payment as recommended by the FLA, and the CCC is powerless to enforce compliance with the FLA's recommendations.[142]

Another challenge facing the CCC is that the urgent appeal system is not time-bound, and as a result, there is often a substantial delay in employees obtaining remedies for violations of their labour rights.[143] In the case of the migrant employees who worked for Kanlayanee factory in Thailand, the employees were owed their wages. The factory-made aprons for MNEs such as Starbucks, Terrible Ikke (*Despicable Me)* T-shirts for media company NBC Universal, and articles for Disney and the English supermarket chain Tesco.[144]

For two years, they were paid less than a euro an hour and forced into unpaid overtime.[145] Through the CCC campaigns, videos of employees were made—these videos stated: 'We worked seven days a week, and often fifteen hours a day'.[146] In September 2019, the workers told their story about the appalling working conditions in the media.[147] In response, Starbucks withdrew its orders and unexpectedly closed its doors.

---

[138] Sahan 44.

[139] As above.

[140] https://cleanclothes.org/news/2023/soliver-gives-100k-euros-to-jaba-garmindo-workers-owed-55-million-but-where-is-uniqlo date visited 17 December 2025.

[141] https://www.business-humanrights.org/en/latest-news/indonesia-former-jaba-garmindo-workers-write-open-letter-calling-for-uniqlo-soliver-to-pay-severance-pay/ date visited 13 September 2025.

[142] https://cleanclothes.org/news/2023/soliver-gives-100k-euros-to-jaba-garmindo-workers-owed-55-million-but-where-is-uniqlo date visited 13 September 2025.

[143] https://www.schonekleren.nl/urgent-appeal/het-verhaal-van-de-kanlayanee-arbeiders/ date visited 14 September 2025.

[144] https://cleanclothes.org/news/2023/soliver-gives-100k-euros-to-jaba-garmindo-workers-owed-55-million-but-where-is-uniqlo date visited 13 September 2025.

[145] As above.

[146] As above.

[147] As above.

With international support from the CCC network and trade unions, employees turned to MNEs Starbucks, Tesco, Disney, and NBC Universal. Organisations around the world joined the online campaign, inspired by NBC Universal's Terrible Me (*Despicable Me*) movies. Sympathisers addressed the MNEs online about their responsibility to pay. After two years, Tesco and Starbucks paid part of the amount owed.[148]

Further, where the MNE refuses to pay employees, there is currently no legal avenue the CCC can utilise. As such, the employees can only get the remedy to the extent that the MNE wishes and can. This is the case even in situations where the courts made binding orders. The MNE incurs no legal liability for an unjustified refusal of the CCC's requests. For years, the garment employees at the Violet Apparel factory in Phnom Penh made clothing for Nike and other MNE brands.[149] But in July 2020, the factory closed overnight, due to the sharp decline in demand for clothing due to the coronavirus and lockdowns. More than 1200 employees, most of them women, suddenly found themselves without work and income.[150] The employees demanded that their arrears of wages and the severance pay to which they were entitled be paid. They each claimed approximately 450 euros.

In its defence, Nike stated that it was not taking any action because it did not do business with Violet Apparel since 2006, but the employees convincingly demonstrated with photos and documents that Nike's claim was false.[151] The CCC was convinced that Nike was buying from at least fifteen other Ramatex factories. Unfortunately, even though Nike has a long-standing code of conduct, the employees were left without recourse.[152] In the parts that follow, the negative and positive aspects of a private regulatory system are discussed in detail.

5.7 Positive Aspects of the Regulation of MNEs Through NGOs

The role of NGOs in enforcing human and labour rights becomes crucial when governments have failed to impose sufficient standards for powerful MNEs.[153] For instance, the concerted pressure from NGOs prompted MNEs like Nike to commit

[148] https://www.business-humanrights.org/en/latest-news/thailand-migrant-workers-paid-below-minimum-wage-by-garment-factories-supplying-global-grands-launch-legal-action/ date visited 17 December 2025.

[149] Violet Apparel is one of the many subsidiaries of the Malaysian company Ramatex.

[150] http://www.schonekleren.nl/urgent-appeal/de-violet-apparel-zaak/ date visited 14 September 2025.

[151] As above.

[152] http://www.schonekleren.nl/urgent-appeal/de-violet-apparel-zaak/ date visited 14 September 2025.

[153] Daubanes and Rochet (2016), p. 32.

to upholding human and labour rights across their entire global supply chain.[154] According to Daubanes & Rochet, NGOs are effective institutions to enforce standards because MNEs are highly susceptible to reputational risks.[155]

Scholars in favour of regulation of MNEs through NGOs' system, amongst others, believe that it can reduce the capacity of states to resist emerging international law.[156] For instance; China is yet to ratify important ILO conventions such as working time and paid leave. As such, MNEs or their subsidiaries and suppliers operating in China are not obliged to comply with such conventions. However, NGOs may add ILO standards for MNEs even if they are not part of national laws.

By collaborating with NGOs, MNEs commit to be under scrutiny of the international law including the conventions not yet ratified by their host or home country. This system, amongst others, uses auditing as a form of monitoring tool to ensure compliance with the human and labour rights by MNEs. According to Baron, 'historically, audits have been used as a tool for internal business management, helping MNEs to minimise public relations risks and to reassure investors of the company's commercial viability'.[157] However, auditing has shifted from internal business management towards the governance of labour standards in global supply chains.[158]

Further, NGOs may establish higher standards than those of host countries. In addition to the above, complainants can refer a broad range of cases to NGOs without having to deal with complex and strict jurisdictional questions.[159] The expeditious resolution of complaints is also one of the advantages of private monitoring. Anner argues that 'instead of dealing with each case referred, this system is proactive in nature as opposed to reactionary dispute resolution. It can detect a trend of violations and address issues before they become disputes.[160] Perhaps the most important advantage of NGOs' system is that they complement state functions by providing alternative dispute resolution and help governments to save costs associated with such processes.

In terms of this system, MNEs are assessed and awarded certifications upon satisfying the prescribed requirements.[161] According to Marx and Wouters, 'certifications serve as proof that harmful practices involving amongst others; child labour, forced/compulsory labour and forced overtime hours are not used in the production processes'.[162]

In the part that follows, negative aspects of the NGOs' regulatory system are discussed in detail.

---

154 See Chap. 5 Para 5.1.

155 Daubanes and Rochet (2016), p. 32.

156 See Chap. 1 para 1.2.

157 Baron et al. (2017), p. 959.

158 Baron et al. (2017), p. 959.

159 Anner (2017), p. 57.

160 Anner (2017), p. 57.

161 See Chap. 6 para 6.1.

162 Marx and Wouters (2016), p. 438.

5.8 Negative Aspects of Regulating MNEs Through NGOs

The limitations of the system of regulating MNEs through NGOs are well documented. The main one is that its implementation is voluntary and is left to the goodwill of MNEs.[163] For instance, in 2005, some Chinese employees, Indonesia, and Swaziland instituted a civil action against Wal-Mart in the US courts for infringement of workers' rights[164] The code of conduct prescribes that its suppliers must adhere to conducive employment relations, a direct condition of supplying merchandise to Wal-Mart.

In this case, workers claimed that Wal-Mart failed to utilise its purchasing power over its suppliers, and they argued that such failure led to workers being subjected to unfair conditions of employment which were contrary to its code of conduct. Amongst others, workers alleged that there was a breach of minimum wages and forced labour and that the freedom of association was undermined. The question to be answered was whether Walmart's code could be viewed as a binding contract. The matter was, however, resolved.[165]

Hepple argues that the 'transplantation of international law into private codes of conduct could result in selective readings of international legal standards, limiting employees' rights, and workplace protections in the process'.[166] He argues that codes of conduct are more likely to offer their own definitions of fundamental labour law terms, which have well-established definitions in ILO conventions.[167] Paiement and Melchers share the sentiment and state why references to international law can lend legitimacy to codes of conduct. There is, however, a risk that they make only partial or selective references to international legal instruments, thereby creating an aura of labour rights protections while failing to systematically protect rights and create safe and fair working conditions.[168]

In *Kasky v Nike*, the US' supreme court was called upon to decide whether the MNE can incur legal liabilities for overstating or falsely claiming in codes of conduct that its products are produced in decent working conditions whilst such is not the case.[169] In this case, the plaintiff alleged that Nike, in response to public criticism, and to induce consumers to continue to buy its products, made false statements of facts about its labour practices and about working conditions in factories that make its products. Acting on behalf of the public, the plaintiff brought this

[163] Kenny (2007), p. 453.

[164] Kenny (2007), p. 453.

[165] Kenny (2007), p. 453.

[166] Hepple (1999), p. 358.

[167] Hepple (1999), p. 358.

[168] Paiement and Melchers (2020), p. 304.

[169] See the case of *Kasky v. Nike, Inc 539 U.S. 654 (2003)* https://www.lexisnexis.com/community/casebrief/p/casebrief-kasky-v-nike-inc date visited 14 September 2025.

action seeking monetary and injunctive relief under California laws designed to curb false advertising and unfair competition.[170]

The court found that workers were paid less than the prescribed minimum wages and that workers were forced to work more overtime hours than the prescribed hours of work. The court further held that some employees were subjected to sexual harassment and abuse, exposed to toxic chemicals which was in contravention of the national health and safety laws and regulations.[171] The majority judgement held that Nike's campaign constituted commercial speech and therefore merited protection.[172] However, the matter was settled by the parties and there was no further development on the matter. From the decision of the court, it can be deduced that Nike, Inc. might be accountable in a civil action for misleading statements it made to the press and to the public about its operations in Southeast Asia.[173]

Macdonald criticises auditing as a compliance tool and states as follows. 'Unlike state-based labour inspection programs, private auditing is not a neutral monitoring and enforcement mechanism, but it is for profit making'.[174] Further, there is an inherent and clear conflict of interest in that auditing firms are paid by MNEs and, as such, auditors are incentivised not to report conduct that undermines fair labour practices to please MNEs that commission the audits.[175]

Ter Haar and Keune argue that MNEs operate globally, and their supply chains extend through all continents.[176] As such, auditing firms may not have the capacity to have auditors everywhere in the world. Also, suppliers or subcontractors can develop audit fatigue when they manufacture and provide goods and products for many MNEs, each of which have their own set of norms and monitoring schemes. Global supply chain networks span not only multiple countries around the world but can also include very large numbers of suppliers and subcontractors: up to 1000 or, in some cases, even up to 10,000.[177]

In addition to the above, certain disputes, such as freedom of association rights, are not suitable for enforcement through auditing. According to Anner, the common method used by these voluntary programmes to resolve disputes about freedom of association rights is the development of policies and training.[178] It is argued that such processes fail to uncover many problems, and as such, they are ineffective. Anner argues that the state is seen as a legitimate arbitrator of these types of disputes.[179]

---

[170] 27 Cal 4th 946.

[171] At Para 70.

[172] At para A.

[173] Mayer (2015), p. 15.

[174] Macdonald (2011), p. 1.

[175] As above.

[176] Ter haar and Keune (2014), p. 8.

[177] Ter haar and Keune (2014), p. 8.

[178] As above.

[179] Anner (2017), p. 56.

Locke argues that without a capable government's involvement, the private enforcement of labour rights through codes of conduct is very weak.[180] In the study conducted by Locke, it was found that working conditions at various Nike suppliers produced mixed results. Some factories were almost fully compliant with Nike's code while others suffered from issues relating to wages, working hours, and health and safety.[181] The variation was because of the country effect (i.e., the ability of the labour inspectorate to enforce labour laws and standards in the country where the factory is located). Monitoring alone appears to produce limited or mixed results. He therefore recommended that proponents of international labour law should focus more on building capacity in developing countries.[182]

Bartley argues that auditing may also not be able to detect non-compliance with minimum wage. Both auditors and employees may find it difficult to determine since employees understand their wages largely as monthly sums, which may comprise of overtime, production bonuses, etc.[183] He states that 'the general response from auditors to these challenges by factory managers has been to produce false wage and hour records and to coach workers on the correct answers to give to auditors'.[184]

Hoang and Jones warned that another risk of third-party audits is that employees see themselves and managers as being on the same side.[185] The payment systems have a big influence on this tacit collusion. At times, the employees may receive bonuses when the company achieves good audit results. As a result, they are aware about audit results, awards and sanctions. They as a result, feel obliged to ensure that there is no negative or non-compliance findings. They may feel obliged to report positive things about the company for the collective good.[186]

Scholars against auditing as a form of regulation believe that the auditing process is not designed to improve labour rights but rather reduce the MNEs' legal and social liability to generate new business opportunities.[187] Terwindt and Armstrong warn that the auditing process is also challenged by a lack of due diligence by auditors themselves.[188] It is expected that the compliance certificate should only be granted to factories or sub-contractors that meet all the minimum requirements. However, evidence suggests that such is not the case.[189]

The incident in Ali Enterprises factory in Pakistan is one good example of auditing failures. The factory was awarded with the SA8000 certificate few weeks prior

---

[180] Locke et al. (2007), p. 20.

[181] Locke et al. (2007), p. 20.

[182] Locke et al. (2007), p. 20.

[183] Bartley (2018), p. 174.

[184] Bartley (2018), p. 174.

[185] Hoang and Jones (2012), p. 78.

[186] Hoang and Jones (2012), p. 78.

[187] Marx and Wouters (2016), p. 440.

[188] Terwindt and Armstrong (2019), p. 251.

[189] Terwindt and Armstrong (2019), p. 251.

to a fire breaking out and killed 260 employees and 32 sustained serious injured.[190] Terwindt and Armstrong argue that the auditing firm should have easily detected that the safety measures were inadequate. Instead of recommending the adequate improvements, the auditing firm issued the SA8000 certificate to the factory. It is submitted that such a certification misled MNEs to believe that the factory followed human and labour standards.

It is submitted that the important component of the auditing process is the recommendations of remedial actions of the auditors. After the remedial plan is issued, the factory is tasked with the responsible to implement the plan within the specified timeframe. Unfortunately, many factories fail to implement such measures. For instance, the audit was conducted by BSCI in respect of Tazreen fashions factory in Bangladesh.[191] The report with recommendations on health and safety measures was subsequently issued.[192] However, the recommended measures were not implemented, and 110 workers were killed by fire which broke out in 2012.[193]

5.9 Conclusion

This Chapter introduced a new system comprising of NGOs which reward MNEs for enforcing compliance with decent working standards throughout their supply chains. The reward system takes the form of certifications that are useful for obtaining contracts and projects by factories or suppliers and MNEs themselves. The system has complaints mechanisms through which trade union or workers who are victims of human and labour rights violations can report their cases. In addition to the above, the system has factory auditing procedures which seek to identify and remedy non-compliance with human and labour rights standards.

However, some MNEs chose to ignore outcomes of complaints mechanisms which are mandatory in nature. Further, the auditing system has several weaknesses and limitations ranging from a lack of capacity and inherent conflict by auditing firms, since they are paid by MNEs. Further, the penalties incurred by MNEs that fail to implement auditing recommendations are naming and shaming. Such a tool is effective, however, there is a high level of confidentiality in auditing outcomes. It

[190] Terwindt and Armstrong (2019), p. 251.

[191] Business Social Compliance Initiative is an NGO which was set up to ensure implementation of the international labour standards such as the ILO conventions and UNGP and OECD Guidelines. https://www.commonshare.com/standards/the-business-social-compliance-initiative-bsci date visited 14 September 2025.

[192] Business Social Compliance Initiative is an NGO which was set up to ensure implementation of the international labour standards such as the ILO conventions and UNGP and OECD Guidelines. https://www.commonshare.com/standards/the-business-social-compliance-initiative-bsci date visited 14 September 2025.

[193] Terwindt and Armstrong (2019), p. 252.

is argued that the lack of transparency in complaints and auditing mechanisms, can frustrate the efficacy of the system.

This chapter has however argued that the regulation of MNEs through NGOs is effective by bypassing the technical and jurisdictional challenges likely to be experienced in a statutory dispute resolution system. For example, the employer cannot be held accountable for violations of human and labour rights committed by third parties such as factories. However, NGOs can hold them accountable for a wide range of workplace issues. Further, where several MNEs procure from the same factory, they may be able to work together to protect the rights of the employees which cannot happen under traditional labour law.[194]

To advance labour rights in the global economy requires strong and effective regulation, follow-up, and enforcement mechanisms. This study suggests that the system entirely based on voluntarism is not effective especially in developing countries, as their laws are too fragile to monitor the behaviour of powerful MNEs.[195] It is suggested that a transparent and rigorous system of evaluating, monitoring, and verifying MNEs' performance against international standards, with a clear system of penalties when standards are breached, is urgently needed.

Such can be achieved by cooperation between the ILO and NGOs that are currently responsible for monitoring labour standards by MNEs. This should take place by incorporating the role of NGOs into ILO functions. However, for such an approach to be successful, the ILO should add the fourth category in addition to its current three accreditations statuses. The fourth category of accredited NGOs will focus on establishment, monitoring, and enforcement of internationally recognised labour standards by MNEs. In terms of the recommended procedure, the ILO will set requirements for accreditation to the list. This should also include requirements to remain accredited and the power of the ILO to suspend or cancel the accreditation. The details of the procedure are discussed in detail in Chap. 8 of this book.

---

[194] In PT Hansoll Hyun (a factory that was in Indonesia), the factory closed without paying workers millions of dollars in legally mandated severance and other compensation. Prior to its closure, Hansoll Hyun produced university-licensed apparel for Hanes brands. Other customers of the factory, for non-collegiate goods, included Abercrombie & Fitch, Hansoll Textile, and Kohl's, among others. The factory ceased operations and dismissed its entire workforce and the owners had set nothing aside to cover the millions of dollars in severance pay accrued by workers. The WRC found that Hansoll Hyun violated Indonesian law, and university and buyer codes of conduct, by failing to pay any of this severance and failing to pay back wages and mandatory payments to Indonesia's Social Insurance Administration. Through many months of engagement with Abercrombie & Fitch and Hansoll Textile, which sourced at Hansoll Hyun on Abercrombie & Fitch's behalf, the WRC was able to secure an additional $2.52 million contribution from Hansoll Textile to compensate the workers. Kesehatan (healthcare) https://www.workersrights.org/wp-content/uploads/2022/01/WRC-re-Hansoll-Hyun-Indonesia-01202022.pdf date visited 14 September 2025.

[195] Dawood (2021) *IJLS* 215.

References

Anner M (2017) Monitoring workers' rights: the limits of voluntary social compliance initiatives in labour repressive regimes. Global Policy Volume

Ascoly N (2005) Looking for a quick fix: how social auditing is keeping workers in sweatshops. Clean Clothes Campaign

Bair J, Palpacuer F (2015) CSR beyond the corporation: contested governance in global value chains. J Transnatl Aff

Barbaro E (2022) The role of NGOs in international law (Master thesis). Ca' Foscari University of Venice

Baron G, Lister J, Dauvergne P (2017) Governing global supply chain sustainability through the ethical audit regime, globalizations. Routledge

Bartley T (2018) Rules without rights: land, labour and private authority in the global. Oxford University Press

Bortolotto C, Neyrinck J (2020) Article 9. Accreditation of Advisory Organisations. Oxford University Press

Courville S (2003) Social accountability audits: challenging or defending democratic governance. Law Policy

Daubanes J, Rochet C (2016) The rise of NGO activism. CESIFO Working Paper NO. 5891, Munich

Davies P (2000) The board of directors: composition, structure, duties and powers. OECD

Dawood C (2021) Corporate social responsibility and MNCs: an appraisal from investment treaty law perspective. J Indones Leg Stud

Dey J (2020) Emerging challenges of International Labour Organisation (ILO). Social Science Research Network

Edwards G (2021) The United Nations and Human Rights Non-Governmental Organisations (NGOs) - Seventy-Five Years of Consultations, Collaboration, and Contributions. Pace International Law Review

Gironde C, Carbonnier G (2019) The ILO @ 100: in search of renewed relevance. J Hist Int Law

Hepple B (1999) A race to the top? International investment guidelines and corporate codes of conduct. Comp Labor Law Policy J

Hoang D, Jones B (2012) Why do corporate codes of conduct fail? Women workers and clothing supply chains in Vietnam. Global Soc Policy

Kaan C (2010) Social accountability international. Springer

Kamminga M (2005) The evolving status of NGOs under international law: a threat to the inter state system? In: Alston P (ed) Non-state actors and human rights. Oxford University Press

Kamunda J (2019) The effect of the multi-national Corporations on Human Rights in developing countries: a case of CIRIO Delmonte Limited in Kenya (1999–2017) (Master Dissertation). University of Nairobi 2019

Kenny E (2007) Code or contract: whether Wal-Mart's code of conduct creates a contractual obligation between Wal-Mart and the employees of its foreign suppliers. Northwest J Int Law Bus

Kryst M (2012) Coalitions of labour unions and NGOs: the room for maneuver of the German Clean Clothes Campaign. J Soc Move

Le Roux N (2006) NGOs at the world court: lessons from the past. Int Community Law Rev

Lin L (2007) Corporate social accountability standards in the global supply chain: resistance, reconsideration, and resolution in China. Cardozo J Int Comp Law

Locke Q, Fei Q and Brause A (2007) Does Monitoring Improve Labour Standards? Lessons from Nike? Industrial and Labour Relations Review

Macdonald K (2011) Fair labor association structure and activities. Polity Press, Cambridge

Marx A, Wouters J (2016) Redesigning enforcement in private labour regulation: will it work? Int Labour Rev

Mayer D (2015) Kasky V. Nike and the Quarrelsome Question of Corporate Free Speech. Cambridge University Press

Merk J, Stolwijk S (2014) A strategic-interaction analysis of an urgent appeal system and its outcomes for garment workers. Mobilization Int J
Moloo R (2011) The quest for legitimacy in the United Nations: role for NGOs. J Int Law Foreign Aff
O'Rourke D (2002) Outsourcing regulation: analysing non-governmental systems of labour standards and monitoring. Policy Stud J
Paiement P, Melchers S (2020) Finding international law in private governance: how codes of conduct in the apparel industry refer to international instruments. Indian J Global Leg Stud
Revak H (2012) Corporate codes of conduct: binding contract or ideal publicity? Hastings Law J
Sahan S (2022) Tactical changes in the Clean Clothes Campaign as a transnational advocacy network (PHD Thesis). Middle East Technical University
Sethi S, Rovenpor J (2016) The role of NGOs in ameliorating sweatshop-like conditions in the global supply chain: the case of Fair Labour Association (FLA), and Social Accountability International (SAI). Bus Soc Rev
Supiot A (2020) The tasks ahead of the ILO at its centenary. Int Labour Rev
Ter Haar B (2013) Love, Flirt or Repel: hybrid global governance of the ILO core labour standards. Eur J Soc Law
Ter Haar B, Keune M (2014) One step forward or more window-dressing? A legal analysis of recent CSR initiatives in the garment industry in Bangladesh International. J Comp Labour Law Ind Relat
Terwindt C, Armstrong A (2019) Oversight and accountability in the social auditing industry: the role of social compliance initiatives. Int Labour Rev
Van den Bossche P (2005) Rules on NGO accreditation: do existing legal arrangements facilitate the legitimization of the role of NGOs in international organisations? Universiteit Maastricht
Wickramasekara P (2015) International Labour Organization (ILO) and broader civil society: an uneasy relationship? ILO

Chapter 6
The International Framework Agreements

6.1 Introduction

The previous chapter shed light on the proactive measures taken by MNEs to tackle the challenges of globalisation. It detailed how MNEs adopted unilateral codes of conduct to ensure that their operations align with internationally recognised labour standards.[1] This forward-thinking strategy is encouraging, as it reflects the MNEs' willingness to prioritise ethical and responsible business practices. However, this unilateral approach is viewed with suspicion by trade unions who see it as a threat to their very existence.[2] It is submitted that due to their unilateral nature, the full implementation of these codes may lead to the exclusion of trade union representatives from playing any significant role in formulating workplace rules and standards.[3]

Buckett agrees and he suggests that the rise of codes of conduct happened in tandem with a global decrease in trade union membership.[4] However, Du Preez and Smit see an opportunity for workers and trade unions to exploit the codes of conduct to promote the respect for human and labour rights.[5] They suggest that MNEs and NGOs should cooperate to adopt international framework agreements. This highlights the need for a collaborative approach where MNEs and trade unions work together to ensure that the human and labour rights are protected while also meeting the global standards of business conduct.

---

[1] Du Preez and Smit (2017), p. 64. See also Chap. 5 para 5.2.

[2] As above.

[3] Burkett (2011), p. 82. See also Hernstradt (2007), p. 190 who mentions that the adoption of codes of conduct were described by trade unions as 'empty gestures aimed at satisfying conscious-laden consumers'.

[4] Burkett (2011), p. 82.

[5] Du Preez and Smit (2017), p. 68.

F. Maluleke, *Compliance with Decent Work Standards by Multinational Enterprises*, European Yearbook of International Economic Law 48,
https://doi.org/10.1007/978-3-032-21261-0_6

Van Leur submits that despite the rapid proliferation of private regulatory mechanisms aimed at achieving better working conditions, MNEs still maintain poor working conditions for their workers in their supply chains.[6] This is especially true for employees working for factories and suppliers linked to these MNEs, who lack the leverage to negotiate with such powerful entities. Holdcroft submits that the lack of meaningful collective bargaining at industry level is the main obstacle preventing the attainment of decent work for workers employed in global supply chains.[7] He submits that the solution lies in establishing industry-wide agreements.[8] Such a view finds support in this study and it is submitted that creating agreements at international level is crucial to eliminating labour cost disparities and promoting fair competition among countries.

By establishing a level playing field, all employees can benefit from improved working conditions, regardless of whether the company or factory they work for has a code of conduct or not.[9] Such agreements are understood to mean International Framework Agreement (IFAs).[10] The IFA is defined as:

> an agreement between an international trade union and the management of the firm at the transnational level and which aims at the international activities of this firm.[11]

Stevis and Fitcher argue that IFAs are 'the only instance of sustained formalised relations between labour and capital beyond national boundaries'.[12] Van Leur agrees with the sentiment and states that by adopting these agreements, parties recognise each other as legitimate labour relations partners at the global level and intend to work together in implementing these principles at the country (national) level.[13] To effectively negotiate with MNEs, global trade unions place a high priority on the establishment of IFAs.[14] Hennebert et al. agree with the sentiment and state that IFAs were considered as a 'trade union response' to limitations of codes of conduct.[15]

The first IFA was signed back in 1988 by Danone[16] and the hotels' chain, marking the beginning of a new era.[17] Since then, the number of IFAs has grown rapidly reaching 50 by the end of 2005 and since 2020 there are more than 140 registered agreements.[18]

---

6 Van Leur (2018), p. 4.

7 Holdcroft (2018), p. 96.

8 Holdcroft (2018), p. 96.

9 Holdcroft (2018), p. 101.

10 Stevis and Fichter (2012), p. 667.

11 Marzo (2011), p. 469.

12 Marzo (2011), p. 469.

13 Van Leur (2018), p. 8.

14 Rub (2006), p. 6.

15 Hennebert et al. (2023), p. 243.

16 French food MNE.

17 Zimmer (2020), p. 178.

18 Zimmer (2020), p. 178.

IFAs have been widely researched and are known to play a key role in promoting effective social dialogue between trade unions and MNEs. It is submitted that the focus of IFAs on creating social dialogue only, is a narrow approach. Under such system, the efficacy of IFAs is evaluated based solely on whether they include a pledge to engage in social dialogue.[19] Krause holds a similar view, and he submits that the aim of the IFA 'is not only to achieve social dialogue at the international level but also to safeguard core labour standards throughout the worldwide activities of MNEs, including their affiliates and in some cases also along the supply chain'.[20]

Although the literature on IFAs is increasing, there are significant gaps of their impact in the host countries and the supply chain of the signatory companies.[21] This book provides evidence to support the view that IFAs surpass basic labour rights and encompass critical matters such as living wages and working hours. The IFA between the International Federation of Building and Wood Workers (BWI) and Acciona is a remarkable example of how MNEs can prioritise the welfare of their employees.[22] The said IFA mandates not only basic labour rights but also guarantees fair compensation, worker well-being, and the safety of all employees, including migrant workers.[23]

It is submitted that evaluating the efficacy of IFAs solely by their potential to establish a forum for social dialogue falls short of appreciating their significant contribution to achieving decent working conditions. This chapter has three objectives. Firstly, it aims to thoroughly evaluate the significant contributions of IFAs in establishing and enhancing decent work standards. Secondly, section three of this chapter presents a critical assessment of the monitoring and enforcement mechanisms of these agreements. Thirdly, the chapter discusses the positive and negative aspects of these agreements.

In the following section, the role of IFAs in creating labour standards is discussed in detail.

---

[19] Thomas (2011), p. 280 mentions that the primary aim of IFAs is to 'promote unionisation across transnational supply chains by securing MNEs' commitment to respect freedom of association rights'.

[20] Krause (2012), p. 750. Also see, Rub (2006), p. 6. who states that IFAs aim to remedy working and employment conditions that violate fundamental rights and implement minimum working conditions at all sites of companies that have signed IFAs and furthermore, to implement them at their suppliers and contractors.

[21] Niforou (2012), p. 2.

[22] Acciona is one of Spain's principal business groups and a leader in infrastructure development and management. The BWI is the Global Union Federation, grouping free and democratic unions with members in the Building, Building Materials, Wood, Forestry, and Allied sectors. The BWI groups together around 350 trade unions representing around 12 million members in 135 countries. https://ec.europa.eu/employment_social/empl_portal/transnational_agreements/iFA_Acciona_EN.pdf date visited 13 September 2025.

[23] Para 1 - 10 of the Acciona IFA.

6.2 The Role of IFAs in Setting Decent Work Standards

Unlike codes of conduct that are unilaterally adopted by MNEs, IFAs are developed through direct negotiations between MNEs, and global trade unions involved in the entire supply chain. It is submitted that this collaborative approach fosters a sense of partnership and helps to build trust between all parties involved. Due to the status of such standards as bilateral agreements, the trade unions can influence their content and insist on incorporating employees' rights and interests in the IFA.

Hernstradt emphasises that for IFAs to be truly effective, they must meet four essential requirements.[24] First and foremost, their scope must encompass the entire MNE. Second, they must strive to comply with ILO core standards, and they should at a minimum explicitly include labour standards contained in conventions. Third, these standards must be enforceable in a transparent, meaningful, and effective manner.[25] Fourth, the implementation of these agreements must be carried out through communication and education to drive awareness and promote compliance.

Previously, only a few IFAs went beyond stating general principles or declaring adherence to basic norms and standards.[26] It is inspiring to see that the Global Union Federation (GUFs) and MNEs are taking positive steps towards ensuring decent work standards for employees. Their recent IFAs are commendable as they incorporate provisions that require third parties such as suppliers and sub-contractors of MNEs to comply with these standards. A prime example is the renewed IFA signed by Carrefour and UNI Global Union in 2018, which introduces new provisions that firmly addresses the issue of violence against women at work.[27]

It is worth noting that the labour standards established in the IFAs are already included in various other international instruments that were in place prior to their adoption and implementation.[28] As previously stated, these standards are not superfluous, as these rights are already enshrined in other international instruments. This should be seen as a positive development as it reinforces the importance of these rights, making them more likely to be implemented through special procedures. Further, it is important to note that IFAs include well-defined monitoring procedures

---

[24] Hernstradt (2007), p. 192.

[25] Hernstradt (2007), p. 192.

[26] De Koster and Van den Eynde (2009), p. 129. See also the IFA signed by Crédit Agricole S.A. Group and UNI Global Union. This agreement applies to all employees of the subsidiaries irrespective of the nature of their employment contract. It establishes a common reference base for the Group.

[27] https://uniglobalunion.org/news/uni-reinforces-global-agreement-with-carrefour/ date visited 14 September 2025.

[28] The IFA signed by Skanska and the International Federation of Building and Woodworkers (IFBWW) provides that the employment conditions offered to the employees of Skanska shall meet the minimum requirements of national legislation. Relevant ILO conventions and recommendations concerning the company's business activities shall be respected. See https://www.ilo.org/wcmsp5/groups/public/%2D%2D-dgreports/%2D%2D-dcomm/%2D%2D-publ/documents/publication/wcms_093423.pdf date visited 14 September 2025.

that trade unions have negotiated with MNEs. These procedures make it easier to identify any non-compliance issues and take appropriate action.

It is submitted that IFAs serve as a crucial tool to safeguard the rights of all employees, including those working for the supplier and sub-contractors of MNEs. However, it is important to keep in mind that establishing standards for third parties can be a contentious issue in law. Krause warns that it is a well-established principle that two parties cannot enter into a legally binding contract on behalf of a third party. Hence, it must be kept in mind that suppliers are not obligated to abide by the terms and conditions of the IFA.[29] It follows that independent subsidiaries and suppliers are not automatically bound by an agreement which has been signed solely by the MNE and GUF.

To effectively address these challenges, it is suggested that drafters of IFAs should explicitly state that leading suppliers and sub-contractors of MNEs are under obligation to implement them. This can be accomplished by clearly identifying the main suppliers and allowing them to express their opinions during the negotiation of the IFA, if feasible.

6.3 Monitoring and Enforcement Mechanisms of IFAs

6.3.1 Monitoring of the Implementation of IFAs

Bourguignon recommends that, for the successful implementation of IFAs, it is necessary to monitor compliance at two main levels.[30] The first level comprises tacking and monitoring by external agencies, followed by the active participation of trade union representatives.[31] The second level requires MNEs to establish robust systems that ensure compliance with human and labour rights standards across their entire supply chains.[32] This involves external and internal audits to demonstrate their level of compliance.

As previously discussed, it is within the purview of MNEs to terminate or temporarily halt supplier contracts in case of non-compliance with the prescribed standards under the IFA or any other relevant instrument.[33] However, self-monitoring and third-party auditing, which are commonly used to monitor and enforce compliance, often suffer from capacity issues due to the impracticality of having auditors in every supplier worldwide.[34]

[29] Krause (2012), p. 755.

[30] Bourguignon (2019), p. 521.

[31] Bourguignon (2019), p. 521.

[32] Bourguignon (2019), p. 521.

[33] See Chap. 5 para 5.2.

[34] See Chap. 5 para 5.2.

Certain IFAs have established complaint mechanisms that allow trade unions to raise non-compliance issues throughout the supply chain.[35] However, the success of such an exercise is dependent on MNEs providing a list of its lead suppliers.[36] This information may be commercially sensitive and therefore not open for trade union scrutiny. Consequently, IFAs rarely contain such information. It is recommended that provisions be made for such information to be made available to ensure effective monitoring.[37]

Drouin highlights that the right to freedom of association and collective bargaining is a complex issue in the national frameworks.[38] He argues that, although MNEs may commit to complying to international human rights and labour standards in the IFAs, this is not always adequately enforced by competent authorities in developing countries.[39] Consequently, implementing and monitoring IFAs become voluntary and the sole responsibility of MNEs who are not legally accountable for any failure to do so.

Similarly, Helfer has pointed out that local trade unions are often uninformed of their factory's obligations under IFAs.[40] In cases where MNEs have suppliers located across different countries, monitoring and enforcement of these agreements are left to local stakeholders such as trade unions, subsidiaries, and suppliers. It is submitted that the approach undermines the effectiveness of such agreements, particularly in highly decentralised and fragmented supply chains.[41]

6.3.2 Enforcement Mechanisms of the IFAs

The ability to impose penalties or to sanction MNEs, sub-contractors or suppliers in case of infringements of human and labour standards set out in the IFA is a very important task. Hernstradt argues that even if IFAs are well drafted to include proper coverage and implementation procedures, they are essentially meaningless in the absence of effective dispute resolution and enforcement procedures. He submits that the IFA should be able to assist employees in asserting their rights as agreed between parties to the agreement.[42] However, it seems that MNEs are unwilling to conclude IFAs with binding dispute resolution processes such as arbitration.[43] It is

[35] Coleman (2010), p. 609.

[36] Hadwiger (2015), p. 84.

[37] See Chap. 7 para 7.2 of Directive of the EU Parliament and the Council on Corporate Sustainability Due Diligence Directive require certain companies to disclose a list of its main suppliers.

[38] Drouin (2010), p. 604.

[39] As above.

[40] Helfer et al. (2016), p. 635. See also Chap. 1 para 1.3.

[41] Helfer et al. (2016), p. 635.

[42] Hernstradt (2007), p. 201.

[43] Coleman (2010), p. 609.

not surprising that most IFAs do not include detailed provisions on dispute resolution procedures over alleged breaches of standards.

Hadwiger's critique of certain IFAs that delegate dispute resolution to national laws of respective countries is supported by this study.[44] This study argues that national regulations already failed to hold MNEs responsible for working conditions in their entire supply chain, leading to the necessity of IFAs. Therefore, requesting employers and employees at national levels to resolve challenges which originate from international level is absurd. Marzo echoes these sentiments, suggesting that independent dispute resolution procedures would be a more effective solution.[45]

Hadwiger recommends the inclusion of mediation and arbitration in IFAs to mitigate these issues.[46] However, it seems that parties are not yet willing to adopt binding dispute resolution procedures that carry penalties for violations. However, this study submits that parties should begin to explore such avenues.

6.4 South African Experience

To the best of my knowledge, there are currently three IFAs that have been concluded by South African-based MNEs with international trade unions. The first IFA was negotiated and concluded by Anglo Gold Ashanti Ltd. (Anglo Gold) and the International Federation of Chemical, Energy, Mine, and General Workers' Unions (the ICEM) and the National Union of Mineworkers (NUM). The second agreement was established by Shoprite International Ltd. and Union Network International (UNI), and the third one was signed by Nampak Ltd. and UNI. The efficacy of IFAs can be evaluated based on their potential and actual impact. Niforou submits that the potential impact considers the content and the motives behind their adoption. On the other hand, the actual impact examines the implementation of existing IFAs.[47]

In the parts that follow; this study will assess the efficacy of IFAs mentioned above by first evaluating their scope of coverage, including whether the rights they aim to achieve go beyond fundamental working rights to encompass decent work. Furthermore, the study will scrutinise the monitoring and enforcement mechanisms that are in place to ensure that MNEs and their factories/suppliers provide better working conditions for their employees.

---

[44] Hadwiger (2015), p. 83.

[45] Marzo (2011), p. 480.

[46] As above.

[47] Niforou (2012), p. 3.

6.4.1 The IFA Between Anglo Gold Ashanti Ltd and the International Federation of Chemical, Energy, Mine, and General Workers' Unions and the National Union of Mineworkers (the Anglo Gold IFA)

Anglo Gold is a South African-based gold mining company with business operations in several countries around the world.[48] The ICEM represents trade unions that organise workers in the mining industry world-wide. The National Union of Mine Workers (NUM) is a South African trade union with most members in the mining industry.[49]

6.4.1.1 Standard Setting

The Anglo Gold IFA was signed in 2002 and was the first IFA in the mining industry and by a developing country.[50] The agreement outlines a set of labour standards, namely, freedom of association and the right to collective bargaining, the abolition of forced labour, the elimination of child labour, the elimination of discrimination of any kind and the promotion of occupational health and safety of workers.[51]

It is imperative to acknowledge that the agreement while recognising fundamental rights, falls short of expectations. As previously discussed, but worth reiterating that merely committing to follow these rights is merely meeting the bare minimum.[52] The Anglo Gold IFA does not include important issues such as fair compensation and hours of work. It is argued that such issues can impede progress towards the attainment of decent work for employees working for MNEs or their suppliers. Moreover, the agreement does not mandate suppliers and sub-contractors to comply with the specified standards. This overlooks the sustainability and safety of workers and undermines the agreement's credibility as most employees are based in factories.

Kweku argues that there is a limited spread of information on the Anglo Gold IFA to its subsidiaries as the agreement is unknown.[53] It is not surprising that the NUM perceived the agreement as a tool for Anglo Gold to appeal to international and other global institutions that prioritise social responsibility in their investment

[48] Para 1 of the Anglo IFA.

[49] As above.

[50] Kweku (2016), p. 87 states that AngloGold Ashanti (AGA) has always been positioned as the only mining company in Africa which is an International Framework Agreement (IFA) signatory when it comes to any scholarly discussion of IFAs at the global level.

[51] As above.

[52] See Chap. 1 para 1.1. Para 2 of the IFA states that the parties agree that 'no additional processes or rights other than those specified in this agreement will be imposed by the application of the agreement by ICEM affiliates'.

[53] Kweku (2023), p. 10.

decisions.[54] This study supports the sentiment and argues that in its current form, the IFA left out employees who are employed by suppliers and, independent contractors working at the Mine. This omission has the potential to hinder efforts to promote fair and just working conditions for all workers involved in the production process.

6.4.1.2 Monitoring and Enforcement Procedures

The Anglo gold IFA committed to establishing a sub-committee to address complaints about breaches of labour standards.[55] The agreement provides for an annual meeting to review the terms of agreement and share information. Further, it provides that local parties will first resolve alleged breaches at national level.[56] If case remains unresolved, it will be placed on the international agenda to be considered by the sub-committee. This is a positive step towards recognising the MNE's responsibility for improving working conditions in its entire supply chain.

The Anglo Gold IFA's dispute resolution procedures have shown promising outcomes in resolving conflicts. Recently, IndustriAll Global Union filed a complaint against Geita Gold Mining Ltd, claiming that it breached the IFA by declining to negotiate with Tanzania Mines, Energy, Construction and Allied Workers Union (TAMICO) and coercing its officials to resign. Moreover, the company dismissed the trade union's secretary and chairperson.

However, Anglo Gold took a positive step by appointing Ernst and Young to conduct a membership audit. The audit concluded that over 50% of employees were members of TAMICO, thereby satisfying the requirements to negotiate with management over salaries and working conditions. It is a positive sign that such agreements can be effective in resolving disputes at the international level. The dismissed trade union officials were also reinstated.[57]

6.4.2 The IFA Between Shoprite International Ltd and Shoprite Checkers (Pty) Limited ('Shoprite Checkers') and UNI Global Union ('UNI') (the Shoprite IFA)

Shoprite Checkers is a South African multinational retail MNE, and Union Network International (UNI) is a global trade union representing workers in the commerce (Wholesale & Retail) and services sectors, incorporating over 900 different trade

[54] Papadakis (2011), p. 72.

[55] Para 4 of the Anglo Gold IFA. See also Papadakis (2011), p. 72.

[56] Para 4 of the Anglo IFA.

[57] https://www.industriall-union.org/membership-audit-at-anglogold-vindicates-tanzanian-union date visited 14 September 2025.

unions representing over 20 million workers.[58] The Shoprite IFA was concluded in 2010.

6.4.2.1 Standard Setting

The Shoprite IFA is an initiative that covers all Shoprite operations and its subsidiaries worldwide.[59] However, it is unfortunate that the scope of the agreement excludes suppliers and sub-contractors. Niforou argues that an IFA that fails to include this feature is considered less effective.[60] It is submitted that if these suppliers were included, it could have far-reaching benefits, especially in the agricultural and food production companies. By adhering to the standards set out in the agreement, working conditions in that sector could be greatly improved. Therefore, it is suggested that the agreement should be revised to include suppliers and sub-contractors to make it more effective and impactful.

In terms of the agreement, the parties strive to uphold basic employment rights in the workplace as outlined in the ILO's Declaration on Fundamental Principles and Rights at Work.[61] Moreover, Shoprite is dedicated to adhering to the employment conditions and terms of each country in which it operates. This includes minimum wage, working hours, health and safety, training, and holidays benefits.[62] The agreement is a commendable effort towards regulating aspects beyond basic worker rights and it has the potential to significantly contribute to the attainment of decent work.

However, the parties agreed that local trade unions and employers would handle issues for collective bargaining in accordance with relevant local laws.[63] Despite the existence of the IFA, this study highlights a critical gap that remains unaddressed. To create a safer and more supportive global workplace, the parties to the Shoprite IFA must consider including suppliers in the agreement and increase the number of standards beyond the fundamental rights.

6.4.2.2 Monitoring of the IFA

The Shoprite IFA has established a platform for discussions between both parties, with a shared commitment to effectively implementing fair labour standards and resolving any disagreements that may arise.[64] The forum is dedicated to addressing

[58] Para 2 of the Shoprite IFA.

[59] Para 2 of the Shoprite IFA.

[60] Niforou (2012), p. 2.

[61] Item 3 of the Shoprite IFA. namely: freedom of association, the elimination of forced and child labour, the elimination of unfair discrimination in employment practices.

[62] Para 2 of the Shoprite IFA.

[63] Para 2 of the Shoprite IFA.

[64] Para 5 of the Shoprite IFA.

a range of issues, including the state of labour relations and health and safety standards of workers in all countries where Shoprite operates. Furthermore, the parties have expressed their intention to amicably resolve disputes that may results in industrial action. In the event of any unprotected industrial action, the trade union will take active steps to normalise the situation.[65]

It is submitted that the Shoprite IFA monitoring mechanism is undoubtedly a step in the right direction towards resolving disputes related to breaches of worker rights standards in all its workplaces. It is, however, submitted that the voluntary implementation of the agreement by the company is concerning. Therefore, it is necessary to introduce the enforcement section to ensure that these commitments are taken seriously.

6.4.3 The IFA Between Nampak Ltd and Union Network International (the Nampak IFA)

Nampak is Africa's leading diversified packaging manufacturer and has been listed on the JSE Limited (Johannesburg Stock Exchange) since 1969. Nampak operates from 19 sites in South Africa, contributing approximately 68% to group revenue, and 14 sites in the rest of Africa, contributing 32% to group revenue.[66]The Union Network International is a global trade union representing more than 20 million workers in the services sectors in over 150 countries.[67]

6.4.3.1 Standard Setting

The Nampak IFA extends to all its subsidiaries under its umbrella. As previously submitted, this scope unfortunately restricts the company's capacity to promote better working conditions throughout its entire supply chain.[68] It is worth noting that both the company and the trade union have committed to informing all trade union members about the agreement.[69] It is argued that it would be better if the agreement is shared with the management of all subsidiaries. The management of each subsidiary should also be required to implement the agreement.

It is submitted that the Nampak IFA sets itself apart from the two South African-based IFAs that were previously discussed by pledging to uphold all fundamental rights, while also promising to enhance worker compensation, prioritise health and

[65] Clause 6 of the IFA.

[66] www.nampak.com/About/Overview# date visited 14 September 2025.

[67] https://uniglobalunion.org date visited 14 September 2025.

[68] Para 2 of the Nampak IFA. See Niforou (2012), p. 2.

[69] Para 6 of the Nampak IFA.

safety measures, and provide better educational and training opportunities.[70] By committing to these important initiatives, the IFA demonstrates a strong dedication to the well-being and advancement of workers and serves as an exemplary model for other agreements.[71]

6.4.3.2 Monitoring and Enforcement

The parties have committed to maintaining an open and continuous dialogue, by scheduling meetings to exchange pertinent information regarding their respective businesses and strategies.[72] Additionally, they have agreed to convene upon request to resolve any disagreements that might arise in implementing the IFA.[73] However, this study argues that the monitoring mechanisms were designed solely to address critical business-related issues, with no provision for addressing worker-related concerns regularly. Furthermore, the agreement does not contain any formal dispute resolution procedure to deal with employee complaints. It is submitted that the agreement should endeavour to provide clear dispute resolution procedures.

In the section that follows, the Daimler IFA is discussed.

6.5 International Experience: The IFA Between Daimler Chrysler and IndustriALL Global Union (the Daimler IFA)

In 2002, the Daimler IFA was signed, becoming the second agreement in the automotive industry after Volkswagen's agreement earlier in the same year.[74] Daimler is a German passenger car, truck, and commercial vehicle manufacturer with a strong presence on all continents.[75] The Daimler IFA is widely recognised by the ILO as the most comprehensive and successful in monitoring compliance and implementing standards, according to the ILO and some experts.[76] The Daimler IFA was updated on 1 September 2022, making it one of the most up-to-date IFAs. It is of utmost importance to conduct a thorough evaluation of this agreement to identify the key factors that make it unique. These findings will prove to be invaluable for

[70] Para 4 of the Nampak IFA.

[71] Para 3 of the Nampak IFA.

[72] Para 5 of the Nampak IFA.

[73] As above.

[74] Stevis (2009), p. 9.

[75] As above.

[76] https://www.ilo.org/global/about-the-ilo/newsroom/news/WCMS_080723/lang%2D%2Den/index.htm date visited 14 September 2025. See also Stevis (2009), p. 26.

those involved in drafting future IFAs, facilitating their ability to take these crucial elements into account.

6.5.1 Standard Setting

The scope of the Daimler IFA encompasses the entire supply chain of the company, regardless of the country where business partners are based.[77] To maintain a positive commercial relationship with Daimler, suppliers and sub-contractors must implement comparable standards in their respective workplaces.[78]This requirement serves as the foundation for commercial dealings with Daimler, with suppliers expected to pledge their adherence to the terms of the IFA. This implies that suppliers that commit to comply with the Daimler IFA may receive preference in procurement processes over the suppliers without such approach. This agreement is a commendable step towards enhancing working conditions on a larger scale.

One of the Daimler IFA's key provisions is to uphold fundamental worker rights, even in countries where such standards are not recognised.[79] Additionally, the company has pledged to integrate ILO Convention 190 on violence and harassment into its policy on equal opportunities and non-discrimination.[80] This commitment is praiseworthy and has the potential to create a positive impact on a larger scale.

6.5.2 Monitoring and Enforcement

The Daimler IFA is a significant step towards ensuring fair treatment of employees across the global supply chain. One of its key strengths is the creation of a Global Employee Committee (GEC) that addresses issues related to breaches of the agreement.[81] This committee comprises 15 members, and it provides an opportunity for employees to voice their concerns, and its annual meetings offer a platform for discussing issues and finding solutions.[82] The signatories to the Daimler IFA meet regularly and exchange views on working conditions.[83]

---

[77] Page 4 of the Daimler IFA. Also see Stevis (2009) *ILR* 12.

[78] As above.

[79] As above.

[80] As above.

[81] Stevis (2009), p. 9. The WEC was formed in 2002 together with IFA. It comprises of WEC agreement allows for a maximum of 15 members, but the organisation has largely consisted of 13 members. The original members were 6 from Germany, 3 from the USA, and one each from Canada, Brazil, South Africa, and Spain.

[82] Stevis (2009), p. 8.

[83] Hadwiger (2015), p. 40.

In addition to the above, any employee who has experienced a violation of their labour rights by Daimler as their employer or by their suppliers can file a complaint with the WEC. The WEC will gather pertinent details and forward them to the company's labour law division that will investigate the matter. From there, the company's top officials will be informed and urged to take corrective action.[84] An example of a case resolved under this agreement involves Ditas, a Turkish supplier to Daimler. In this case, Ditas workers embarked on an industrial action because the employer refused to respect trade union rights at the workplace and to bargain with the union.[85]

This action was a direct breach of the provisions of the Daimler IFA. A letter from the WEC to the management about the breach played a significant role in reaching a negotiated settlement.[86] For instance, in a Brazilian case, the trade union shut down machines at Daimler to compel the MNE to exert pressure on the supplier. Eventually, the supplier agreed to re-employ the dismissed union representative.[87] Unfortunately, the names of the parties have not been reported.

It is submitted that the Daimler IFA is one of the few strict agreements at the international level. Failure to comply with this agreement may result in termination of the supplier contract by Daimler. For instance, in Brazil, a trade union pressured Daimler to enforce the IFA, resulting in eight suppliers being replaced.[88]

6.6 Positive Aspects of IFAs

According to Hernstradt, even though collective bargaining is recognised at national level, trade unions and employers have the right to affiliate with international organisations and negotiate and conclude IFAs.[89] In fact, IFAs can provide a constructive framework for national negotiation and establish a minimum standard.[90] Du Preez and Smit suggest that negotiated IFAs can supplement the current social regulation instruments that are insufficient to address globalisation's challenges.[91] Therefore, formalising IFAs is a crucial step as it recognises trade unions globally. This move

---

[84] Stevis (2009), p. 135.

[85] Stevis (2009), p. 24.

[86] As above.

[87] As above.

[88] IMF background paper prepared for the IFA World Conference Frankfurt am main, Germany (2006) 13.

[89] Article 5 of the C087 - Freedom of Association and Protection of the Right to Organise Convention, 1948 (No. 87).

[90] https://www.ilo.org/global/about-the-ilo/newsroom/news/WCMS_080723/lang%2D%2Den/index.htm date visited 14 September 2025.

[91] Du Preez and Smit (2017), p. 71.

may pave the way for international labour law and bridge the regulatory gap in the global labour system, Coleman suggests.[92]

IFAs can be a valuable tool in promoting social partnerships across national borders.[93] By signing IFAs, MNEs commit to respecting core labour rights in all countries where they operate, and they recognise the GUF as the voice of workers in their supply chains. This IFAs' strategy represents a very ambitious attempt to intervene in the governance of global supply chains by agreeing to international human and labour rights standards, establishing dispute resolution procedures for conflict resolution by MNEs and GUFs.[94] This helps to reduce concerns about a race to the bottom, as MNEs may not have a strong motive to relocate to countries with lower labour standards.[95]

Furthermore, IFAs can replicate relationships and cultural norms of social dialogue and industrial relations from national affiliates to a global level.[96] This is particularly important when the MNE operates in a home country with higher unionisation. For instance, the IFA between ICEM and Anglo Gold provides communication channels and improves relations between employees and management at all levels. However, it is important to note that IFAs may also export negative practices such as trade union militancy and uncooperative behaviour, which can disrupt peaceful workplaces.[97] Overall, IFAs can be a powerful tool for promoting fair labour standards globally.

It is submitted that IFAs are not an afterthought to a company's corporate social responsibility program. They represent an opportunity to prevent potential abuses by MNEs seeking to win contracts without ensuring fair working conditions for employees. It is argued that the primary objective of an IFA is to improve working conditions and promote equitable employment practices, and MNEs must embrace them as a constructive step towards a more sustainable future.

It is argued that IFAs can drive progress towards better working conditions and workers' rights. By laying the groundwork for improved conditions, MNEs can negotiate even better terms, demonstrating their commitment to fair employment practices.[98] Additionally, IFAs promote international comparisons of terms of employment conditions, leading to a general improvement in working conditions throughout the entire supply chain.

The contrast between codes of conduct and IFAs primarily lies in their enforcement mechanisms.[99] While codes of conduct may not have any impact, IFAs can be

---

[92] Coleman (2010), p. 602.

[93] ILO (2018) International Framework Agreements in the food, retail, garment, and chemicals sectors Lessons learned from three case studies 15.

[94] Helfen and Fichter (2011), p. 2.

[95] Coleman (2010), p, 602.

[96] Myant (2020), p. 20.

[97] Stevis (2011), p. 18.

[98] Stevis (2011), p. 16.

[99] Marzo (2011), p. 470.

enforced through various specified procedures. Legal expert, Burkett suggests that integrating IFAs into other binding norms could give them the necessary legal effect.[100] The first means of giving legal effect to IFAs is by integrating them into other legally binding norms. This can be done through referring to the IFA in collective agreements made in each country or in a subsidiary, which could reinforce local actors' incentive ownership. It is submitted that the implantation of IFAs lends greater credibility to MNEs' sense of responsibility and their non-unilateral nature adds legitimacy. Furthermore, in some IFAs it is agreed that the lead MNE undertakes additional monitoring measures to ensure compliance along the supply chain.

6.7 Negative Aspects of IFAs

One of the major drawbacks of using IFAs to regulate human and labour rights is that MNEs have no obligation to negotiate with GUFs, and they may only choose to do so at their discretion. Additionally, there is no direct legal framework governing the formulation, implementation, or enforcement of IFAs at the international or regional level. It must be indicated that there is no common definition of the 'mandatory features of IFAs'.[101] As a result, MNEs may only prioritise issues that are important to them, often disregarding necessary working conditions that are critical for their employees. For instance, the International Textile, Garment, and Leather Workers' Federation made efforts to improve labour standards with six major MNEs in the global garment, textile, and footwear industry, but unfortunately, all six campaigns failed for various reasons, such as employer hostility.[102]

Further, the content of the IFAs varies greatly in their content. Some agreements may not fully cover supplier and sub-contractor involvement, which can limit their ability to improve working conditions in factories. Additionally, certain IFAs may lack crucial follow-up mechanisms, making it challenging to track progress in their implementation. For this reason, it is crucial to establish guidelines from the ILO to ensure that all agreements incorporate the necessary elements that safeguard workers' rights.

The analysis of IFAs revealed an area of concern: the lack of a clear set of penalties or sanctions for MNEs, and their sub-contractors or suppliers who breach the internally recognised human and labour rights. This lack of consequences allows MNEs to avoid accountability when they fail to set standards. Consequently, trade unions must rely on MNEs' willingness to uphold their commitments under these agreements.

A prime example is the IFA between the Bosch Group and the International Metalworkers Federation (IMF). The principles of the said agreement are based on

[100] Burkett (2011), p. 93.
[101] Hadwiger (2018), p. 23.
[102] Miller (2004), p. 14.

the ILO's core labour standards.[103] Several complaints were raised about Bosch World and some of which were alleged breaches of the IFA provisions on freedom of association. One complaint was about the Bosch-owned Doboy plant in the US. When workers embarked on strike, management threatened to dismiss them from work if they refused to return to work, a practice permitted under US laws but not under the agreement.[104]

Despite these concerns, the Bosch management chose not to address them, asserting that such issues should be resolved by local trade unions and management, rather than at the international level. The failure to intervene in this regard renders the agreement ineffective. It is not surprising that trade unions may view the IFAs as an instrument for the MNE to attract investors and to win procurement contracts. According to the NUM, the investors, global finance institutions and tender committees increasingly link access to loans and funding with compliance with human and labour rights.[105] These cases illustrate the difficulty of enforcing the provisions of an IFA in the absence of any global industrial relations regulatory framework.

Further, there are financial cost implications on the side of MNEs in that they may be required to finance trade union officials' exchange programmes at the company's expenses and finance and support global committees of trade union leaders. Marzan suggests that signatory parties and other stakeholders should consider having a non-binding arbitration process in line with the ILO norms. However, this study argues that it is unlikely that parties are ready to harden their agreements by making them judicially enforceable. It is submitted that the non-binding arbitration could help to incrementally harden IFAs and resolve interpretation disputes.[106]

This legitimacy in representing employees is not easily achieved, because of the geographical and cultural distance of GUFs from the grassroots level.[107]

6.8 Conclusion

This Chapter delved into the reasons why MNEs and GUFs engage in negotiations and ultimately sign IFAs. Additionally, it scrutinised the contents of the said agreements, as well as the procedures for their implementation, monitoring, and enforcement. The detailed analysis yielded significant findings on the impact of IFAs on working conditions within the supply chain of MNEs. It is argued that the existing legislative framework regulates collective bargaining between employers and employees at national level. This process includes negotiation for improvement of

---

[103] https://www.industriall-union.org/archive/imf/imf-signs-framework-agreement-with-bosch date visited 14 September 2025.

[104] As above.

[105] Stevis (2011), p. 16.

[106] Marzan (2024), p. 1751.

[107] Barreau et al. (2020), p. 42.

working conditions by local trade unions, factories, and suppliers in their capacity as employers. However, it does not extend to MNEs that own products being manufactured.

It is argued that MNEs and GUFs believe in the potential of the IFAs' initiative as a groundbreaking addition to the existing collective bargaining landscape. This initiative is poised to create a new avenue for social dialogue, enhance the scope for collective bargaining, and foster a more just and equitable world. This chapter demonstrated that the IFAs are the only system that attempt to fill the gap by creating platform for dialogue between trade unions and MNEs. The IFAs have emerged as a more comprehensive and inclusive approach to regulating labour standards.

Unlike their predecessors—private regulation instruments—these agreements involve trade unions in their formulation and monitoring. This makes them more effective in addressing the limitations of the previous approaches and ensuring fair and safe working conditions for workers in the global supply chain. The system also addresses the need for supranational structures and the regulation of labour standards and industrial relations at the transnational level.

This Chapter further demonstrated that the IFA system underwent serious development since 35 years ago when the first IFA was concluded. Today, these agreements are no longer just useful for creating a platform for social dialogue at the international level, but they regulate important matters which include a systematic increase of the labour standards in the entire supply chain of MNEs. This is useful especially in countries with lower labour standards and have no standards at all.

However, this Chapter presents compelling evidence that demonstrates the significant limitations of IFAs. One major drawback is their voluntary nature, as they are created by MNEs and GUFs without a legal framework. As a result, there are many unanswered questions surrounding them. Specifically, the legitimacy of the actors involved in adopting them and the scope of their application in terms of companies, as well as coverage of workers who are employed by suppliers and subsidiaries, need further research.

Finally, it is worth noting that IFAs have contributed to improving standard-setting roles. However, there are still limitations regarding monitoring and enforcement provisions of the said agreements. The monitoring procedures are not as effective as they should be, and the complaints-handling mechanisms are not robust enough to provide solutions to workers. Nonetheless, the IFAs system has the potential to create internationally acceptable labour standards that protect employees working in the global supply chain. To achieve this, it is suggested that the guidelines should be issued at ILO for model IFA. Further, the MNE office of the ILO should be responsible for registering the concluded IFAs.

References

Barreau J, Havard C, and Bah A (2020) Global union federations and international framework agreements: Knowledge exchange and creation. European Journal of Industrial Relations

Bourguignon R (2019) Global framework agreements and trade unions as monitoring agents in transnational corporations. J Bus Ethics

Burkett B (2011) International framework agreements: an emerging international regulatory approach or passing European phenomenon. Can Labour Employ Law J

Coleman S (2010) Enforcing international framework agreements in U.S. courts: a contract analysis. Columbia Hum Rights Law Rev

De Koster P, Van den Eynde P (2009) International framework agreements on corporate social responsibility: conflict of laws and enforcement. Bus Law Int

Drouin R (2010) Promoting fundamental labour rights through international framework agreements: practical outcomes and present challenges. Comp Labour Law Policy J

Du Preez H, Smit P (2017) The role of international framework agreements in transnational labour regulation. South Afr J Labour Relat

Hadwiger F (2015) Global framework agreements: Achieving decent work in global supply chains? International journal of labour research

Hadwiger F (2018) Global framework agreements: achieving decent work in global supply chains? Int J Labour Res

Helfer R, Wuerth B (2016) Customary International Law: An Instrument Choice Perspective. Michigan Journal of International Law

Helfen M, Fichter M (2011) Global production networks and global union federations: Re-assembling transnational union networks by International Framework Agreements? University of Johannesburg

Hennebert M, Roberge-Maltais I, Coiquaud U (2023) The effectiveness of international framework agreements as a tool for the protection of workers' rights: a metasynthesis. Ind Relat J

Hernstradt O (2007) Are international framework agreements path to corporate social responsibility? J Bus Employ Law

Holdcroft J (2018) Transforming supply chain industrial relations. Int J Labour Res

Krause R (2012) International framework agreements as instrument for the legal enforcement of freedom of association and collective bargaining the German case. Comp Labor Law Policy J

Kweku R (2016) Corporate social responsibility policies and labour practices in Ghana: a case study of AngloGold Ashanti and the International Framework Agreement (PHD Thesis). University of Leicester 2016

Kweku R (2023) How Effective Are International Framework Agreements in Subsidiary Companies of Multinational Enterprises? A Case Study of the International Framework Agreement of AngloGold Ashanti, Ghana. International Journal of Research in the Humanities

Marzan C (2024) Labour's soft means and hard challenges: fundamental discrepancies and the promise of non-binding arbitration for international framework agreements. Minn Law Rev

Marzo C (2011) From codes of conduct to international framework agreements: contractualising the protection of human rights. North Ireland Leg Q

Miller D (2004) Negotiating International Framework Agreements in the Global Textile, Garment and Footwear Sector. Journal of Social Philosophy

Myant M (2020) European Multinational Companies and Trade Unions in Eastern and East-Central Europe. Social Science Research Network

Niforou C (2012) International framework agreements and industrial relations governance: rhetoric versus local realities. Br J Ind Relat

Papadakis K (2011) Shaping global industrial relations. Palgrave Macmillan

Rub S (2006) Guidelines for implementing and monitoring an international framework agreement. IG Metall

Stevis D (2009) International framework agreement and global social dialogue: lessons from the Daimler Case. Int Labour Rev

Stevis D (2011) The Impacts of International Framework Agreements: Lessons from the Daimler Case. In: Papadakis, K. (eds) Shaping Global Industrial Relations. The International Labour Organization. Palgrave Macmillan

Stevis D, Fichter M (2012) International framework agreements in the United States: escaping, projecting, or globalizing social dialogues. Comp Labor Law Policy J

Thomas M (2011) Global industrial relations: framework agreements and the regulation of international labour standards. Labour Stud J
Van Leur A (2018) International framework agreements in the food retail, garment and chemicals sectors. ILO Geneva
Zimmer R (2020) International framework agreements. Int Organ Law Rev

Chapter 7
Directive of the European Parliament and the Council on Corporate Sustainability Due Diligence

7.1 Introduction

The preceding chapters comprehensively scrutinised the strategies implemented by numerous international institutions, MNEs, and NGOs to address challenges posed by globalisation. These entities adopted soft law regulatory mechanisms, such as the OECD Guidelines, ILO MNE Declaration and various codes of conduct, to define human and labour rights standards for MNEs throughout their global supply chain. While these instruments hold the potential to enhance the working conditions of employees within MNEs' supply chains, they share a common deficiency, notably the absence of penalties for human and labour rights violations by MNEs and redress for affected employees.

To enhance working conditions in global supply chains, some EU countries, like France, have enacted mandatory due diligence legislation. However, national efforts have limitations and there is a need for a more comprehensive approach. To bridge the gap, the EU adopted the Corporate Sustainability Due Diligence Directive (the Directive) which is a significant step towards providing legal certainty for MNEs and those impacted by their operations.[1]

The Directive mandates MNEs to conduct human rights due diligence to ensure that their operations, subsidiaries, and suppliers do not adversely impact human and labour rights. Its adoption follows the advocacy of civil society movements pushing for increased accountability for preventable human and labour rights violations within MNEs' supply chains.[2] This shift signals a recognition of the inadequacy of

[1] Bueno et al. (2024), p. 1.

[2] Otteburn and Marx (2003), p. 3.

F. Maluleke, *Compliance with Decent Work Standards by Multinational Enterprises*, European Yearbook of International Economic Law 48,
https://doi.org/10.1007/978-3-032-21261-0_7

soft law instruments in deterring MNEs from engaging in practices that undermine human and labour rights.[3]

It is essential to analyse the Directive in detail for several reasons. Firstly, it stands as the sole hard law instrument adopted by an international organisation to oversee and enforce human and labour rights by MNEs. Secondly, it introduces penalties for none-compliance and seeks to provide remedies for affected employees. Thirdly, the Directive carries implications for both EU and non-EU MNEs, requiring them to identify, mitigate, and address adverse human rights and sustainability impacts regardless of location, with potential sanctions and civil liability in the EU.[4] Moreover, the Directive sets itself apart by not only imposing obligations on MNEs but also introducing responsibilities for directors to oversee this process and ensure its effectiveness.[5] Holding directors accountable for their company's actions promotes corporate responsibility and fosters trust among stakeholders.

7.2 Application of the Directive

The Directive applies to both EU and non-EU registered MNEs that meet specific thresholds with regard to turnover and number of employees.[6] It is important to note that the Directive applies to large EU MNEs employing more than 500 employees and generating a net worldwide annual turnover of EUR 150 million, regardless of the sector in which they operate.[7] It is also applicable to MNEs that have 250 employees and generate a net worldwide annual turnover of EUR 40 million if they are involved in high-risk sectors which include the manufacture of textiles, extraction of minerals and agriculture.[8] The Directive specifies that the due diligence obligations of MNEs regarding their supply chains are confined to third-party companies that have established business relationships with the MNE.[9] For the purpose of this Directive, established business relationships mean:

> such direct and indirect business relationships which are, or which are expected to be lasting, in view of their intensity and duration and which do not represent a negligible or ancillary part of the value chain.

However, scholars such as Zonta and Schall have expressed concerns regarding the broad scope of the Directive and its potential ineffectiveness. Zonta argues that the current scope places significant expectations on large MNEs to ensure compliance

---

[3] Clause 1 of the explanatory memorandum. See also Otteburn and Marx (2003), p. 5, who argued that the voluntary due diligence approach has several shortcomings that may dampen its contribution toward reducing corporate abuse of human rights and the environment.

[4] Zonta (2024), p. 95.

[5] Article 25 of the Directive.

[6] Article 2 of the Directive.

[7] Bueno et al. (2024), p. 2. See also Chap. 1 Para 1.1.

[8] Article 2 of the Directive.

[9] Article 3 of the Directive.

with human and labour rights across their extensive supply chains.[10] Schall points out that the administrative burdens associated with meeting due diligence requirements will be substantial.[11] Additionally, the applicable MNEs may face challenges related to insufficient personnel and financial resources to effectively monitor all suppliers.[12]

In addition to administrative challenges, Trombin submits that the imposition of the Directive to none-EU countries is a form of disguised coercion, whereby the EU leverages on its internal market and indirectly influences the global business environment.[13] The trigger of jurisdiction for non-EU companies is their economic presence as a proxy for effects in the EU, making the Directive a measure of territorial extension, as the economic presence consists of a link to the EU territory.[14]

On the contrary, scholars such as Lennarts argue that the Directive's scope of application in its current form is narrow and ignores a number of important third parties.[15] He argues that the limitation of due diligence obligations to third party companies with whom the MNE has 'established business relationships' is not appropriate.[16] Lennarts criticises such limitation and argues that the more severe risks may be present in the lower tiers of the value chain.[17] He submits that the severity of the risk and the likelihood of the risk materialising should be decisive in determining whether the Directive should be applicable to the MNE.[18]

In response to the concerns raised, it is important to find a balanced approach. The limitation of due diligence obligations to any long-standing business relationship is reasonable, as MNEs should be able to detect non-compliance with international human and labour rights in their long-standing business partners. However, there is also merit to the argument that severe risks may be present in the lower tiers of the value chain. Balancing these considerations are key to ensuring effective and fair implementation of the Directive. It is agreed that the concerns raised by Schall and Lennarts are both valid and important to consider. It is crucial to find a balanced approach that addresses the practical challenges faced by MNEs while ensuring compliance with international human and labour rights standards.

In respect of Lannart's view, this study argues that the risk assessment approach ignores the practicality of a large MNE being expected to ensure compliance with standards by small suppliers. The MNE concerned may not have systems, resources, and personnel to monitor and enforce compliance with all small third parties everywhere on the world especially those that supply, or may not supply, the MNE

[10] Zonta (2024), p. 114.

[11] Schall (2024), p. 56.

[12] Schall (2024), p. 56.

[13] Trombin (2023), p. 22.

[14] Zonta (2024), p. 122.

[15] Lennarts (2023), p. 259.

[16] Article 3 of the CSDDD.

[17] Lennarts (2023), p. 259.

[18] As above.

directly. This study supports the Directive to the extent that it seeks to hold MNEs accountable for human and labour rights violations by easily traceable third-party companies. It is argued that an expanded scope beyond the companies with established business relationships with the MNE may impose unfair obligations to the MNE.

The concerns raised by Zonta and Trombin's regarding the EU's jurisdiction to set binding laws that impose obligations on companies registered in other countries outside the EU are valid. However, it is argued that such measures are justifiable. Patrin argues that companies engaged in international trade naturally tend to adhere to the most rigorous standards to avoid customising their production for different markets.[19] This study concurs with Patrin's assertion and maintains that the obligations outlined in the Directive hold significant potential to ensure compliance with the human and labour rights standards from a social justice point of view.

7.3 Monitoring and Enforcement

The Directive mandates EU member states to ensure that relevant MNEs conduct human rights due diligence.[20] Due diligence should be understood in the same way with respect of the UNGPs and the OECD Guidelines.[21] A key obligation introduced by the Directive is the mandatory integration of due diligence into corporate policies, requiring MNEs to identify, prevent, mitigate, end and minimise potential and actual adverse human and labour rights within their operations, and those of their subsidiaries.[22]

One primary challenge facing workers with claims against MNEs is the lack of a binding legal obligations holding MNEs accountable for violating internationally recognised human and labour rights standards.[23] As a result, employees encounter difficulties in pursuing claims, including time limitations, stringent procedures, and limited access to supporting documents.[24] In addition to the above, soft law instruments have also been ineffective in assisting workers, as they often lack remedies and necessitate resorting to civil actions, which are complex and costly.[25]

Kilimciolu and Ann-Charlotte assert that the obligations in the Directive are legally enforceable, holding MNEs accountable liable for damages resulting from adverse impacts that could have been identified, prevented, terminated or

[19] Patrin (2021), p. 380.

[20] Bueno et al. (2024), p. 3.

[21] Hasselblatt (2023), p. 14.

[22] Pantazi (2022), p. 3.

[23] Farah et al. (2022), p. 511.

[24] Villiers (2018), p. 14.

[25] Farah et al. (2022), p. 512.

minimised.[26] The crux of the Directive lies in establishing clear rights and obligations, and mechanism for filing complaints regarding potential human and labour rights violations, as well as providing remedies.[27] In this respect, the Directive will be enforced at two levels: Firstly, EU member states are required to designate an authority for supervision and enforcement. Secondly, EU would set up a European Network of Supervisory Authorities to streamline cross-national company supervision.[28]

Under the Directive, complainants can bring civil claims before national courts to seek compensation for damages resulting from adverse human and labour rights impacts, whether in the MNE's operations, subsidiaries, or direct or indirect business partners in the supply chain.[29] Pacces submits that if the MNE fails to comply with human and labour rights obligations, it may be liable for the damages even if the violation was made by third parties.[30] For example, the EU based MNEs will be liable for human and labour rights violation committed by their established business partners in other continents such as Africa or Asia.

The national authorities and the European Network of Supervisory Authorities will possess extensive powers to verify compliance, collaborate with similar authorities in other EU countries, conduct investigations, and impose sanctions.[31] When transposing the Directive into national law, EU member states must establish regulations outlining penalties for MNEs failing to meet human rights obligations, along with clear remedies for employees whose rights are violated. These regulations may take the form of cease-and-desist orders and fines, based on the company's revenue or temporary measures. It is submitted that the regulations should contain clear remedies which will accrue to employees whose' human and labour rights are violated by MNEs.[32] Such remedies may amongst others include compensation and reinstatement in the event of unfair dismissals.

It must be indicated that the Directive does not require MNEs to ensure the absence of infringements of human and labour rights in all circumstances. It acknowledges that in certain scenarios, such as state intervention, complete prevention may not be possible. Instead, it expects MNEs to take reasonable measures to minimise infringements of human and labour rights based on the specifics of each case. For instance, the MNE may not be able to prevent human and labour rights violations where the state is responsible for such infringements.[33] Therefore, the main obligations of the Directive should be 'obligations of means' which implies that the MNE should take the appropriate measures which can reasonably be

---

[26] Kilimciolu and Ann-Charlotte (2023), p. 3. Also see Articles 7 and 8 of the Directive.

[27] As above.

[28] Schmidt and José (2023), p. 12.

[29] Pacces (2023), p. 3.

[30] Pacces (2023), p. 4.

[31] Article 20 of the Directive.

[32] Clause 56 of the Directive.

[33] Article 7 of the Directive.

expected to result in prevention or minimisation of the adverse impact under the circumstances of the specific case.[34]

The Directive strikes a balance by imposing obligations on MNEs while also considering the efforts to counter negative impacts when assessing civil liability. It aims to ensure that MNEs take appropriate measures to uphold human and labour rights, providing a framework for accountability and redress while considering the complexities of global business operations. Efforts made by a company to counter negative impacts must be considered when assessing the existence and extent of civil liability.[35] It is argued that the Directive is balanced as it imposes obligations on MNEs and at the same time it reduces liability of the MNE where the adverse impact results from conduct which the MNE could not prevent.

7.4 Positive Aspects of the Directive

Firstly, it is submitted that the Directive is a crucial instrument, being the sole law adopted by a legally recognised international institution to enforce mandatory due diligence duties for MNEs. Further, recent studies have demonstrated the potency of mandatory due diligence in incentivising MNEs to adopt due diligence. For instance, Lafarre and Rombouts' 2022 study revealed significant improvements in human and labour rights scores among French MNEs after implementing due diligence, emphasising its role in promoting sustainable business practices and safeguarding human and labour rights.[36]This indicates that mandatory due diligence can be an effective instrument in promoting sustainable business practices and safeguarding human and labour rights.[37]

Moreover, the Directive offers employees an additional platform to address human and labour rights violations by MNEs and allows for public law supervision, enforcement mechanisms such as civil liability for damages.[38] Enforcement of human and labour rights standards at the supranational level, such as EU, is preferred over national regulations due to weak institutions in developing countries, making international statutory dispute resolution vital for delivering a public good. The ability to take legal action in Europe against companies violating human rights standards in the global south is a powerful tool.

More significantly, it provides for public law supervision, enforcement, and provision of sanctions by national authorities of EU member states.[39] This does not take away the private enforcement mechanisms such as civil liability for damages.

[34] Clause 15 of the explanatory memorandum.

[35] Kilimciolu and Ann-Charlotte (2023), p. 3.

[36] Lafarre and Rombouts (2022), p. 12.

[37] Lafarre and Rombouts (2022), p. 12.

[38] Jäger et al. (2023), p. 6.

[39] Jäger et al. (2023), p. 6.

Further, it is submitted that the enforcement of compliance of human and labour rights standards at supranational level such as the EU are preferred over regulations at the national scale.[40]

De Jager contends that if the Directive is implemented in its current form, MNEs not adhering to human and labour rights standards have three options: Firstly, comply with the standards and continue their business. Secondly, server ties with potentially problematic companies, or cease non-compliant activities. Thirdly, they can shut down the restrictive business activities.[41] This could lead to reduced economic activity for non-compliant companies and an increase for compliant suppliers, ultimately enhancing working conditions in the global supply chain.[42] It is submitted that such action favour the promotion of improvement of working conditions of workers in the global supply chain.

The Directive is poised to increase the bargaining power of workers in developing countries, as EU based MNEs will be compelled to address human and labour rights violations, ultimately respecting labour rights as part of human rights.[43] It is also submitted that states and investors stand to benefit from early mitigation and prevention of investment disputes, as the timely consideration of human rights standards by investors may reduce state interference such as license cancellation.[44]

Furthermore, the Directive's extraterritorial effect and the implementation of new mandatory standards in the EU are set to create a level playing field among MNEs in terms of responsible business conduct compliance.[45]

7.5 Negative Aspects of the Directive

The successful implementation of the Directive may be hindered by several challenges. One of the likely primary obstacles concerns the monitoring and enforcement of compliance with international human and labour rights standards by MNEs.[46] It is estimated that around 13,000 EU MNEs and 4000 non-EU MNEs would fall under the scope of the Directive, and therefore would have to comply with its obligations concerning their operations, subsidiaries, and value chain, regardless of where they are located.[47] It is submitted that enforcing compliance with due diligence obligations, particularly with non-EU MNEs, poses a

[40] Jäger et al. (2023), p. 10.

[41] Jäger et al. (2023), p. 19.

[42] Jäger et al. (2023), p. 20.

[43] Jäger et al. (2023), p. 21.

[44] Levashova (2024) research paper no 381 *Joint Center for Columbia Law School* 2.

[45] Villiers (2018), p. 14.

[46] Zonta (2024), p. 98.

[47] Zonta (2024), p. 98.

considerable challenge, and the practicality and reasonableness of the expectations may be brought into question.[48]

The second challenge relates to the costs associated with the implementation of the Directive. Such costs include screening human and labour rights activities, setting up standards to avoid violations at third-party workplaces, and performing human rights due diligence regarding business partners.[49] Thirdly, the requirements for MNEs to perform due diligence in respect of their business partners is limited to the businesses with whom the MNE has established business relationships. The term 'established business relationship' remains open for interpretation, which may lead to MNEs exploiting the ambiguity by opting for shorter, less intensified relationships to evade their due diligence responsibilities. Starver warns that MNEs may opt to move towards shorter, less intensified relationships to evade performing the due diligence duty as described in the directive.[50]

Fourthly, contractual assurances are also seen as a challenge, as MNEs may use them to evade liability in the event of violations at their workplaces and third-party companies.[51] This may lead to passing the risk to third-party auditing firms, promoting a mere tick box approach to demonstrate compliance with contractual agreements.[52] Fifthly, the EU registered MNEs may face competitive pressures from companies not obliged to comply with human rights mandatory due diligence, potentially leading to market share loss in sectors like mining, textiles, and agriculture, as well as the construction sector.[53]

Sixthly, it is submitted that the national public authorities may face limitations in investigating human and labour rights violations beyond the EU's territory and imposing sanctions and remedies on MNEs based in non-EU countries.[54] For instance, the network may not be in position to investigate the US or Chinese based MNEs and impose sanctions and remedies to employees. Although such is the intention of the Directive, it is questionable how a member state would sanction a MNE abroad and enforce a penalty in practice.

7.6 Conclusion

This chapter examined the Directive to assess its potential impact in its current form. At the heart of the Directive, lies a recognition by EU that business does not only have significance for its own residents, but it is of global importance which is

[48] See Apple case in Chap. 1 para 1.3.

[49] Jäger et al. (2023), p. 19.

[50] Straver (2024), p. 27.

[51] Straver (2024), p. 28.

[52] Saloranta and Hurmerinta-Haanpää (2022), p. 225.

[53] Jäger et al. (2023), p. 28.

[54] Bueno et al. (2024), p. 5.

commendable.[55] The Directive seeks to address longstanding challenge of holding MNEs accountable for human and labour rights violations across their entire supply chain. The analysis of the Directive revealed that its adoption represents a significant shift from voluntary to mandatory corporate human rights due diligence. The move addresses the shortcomings of voluntary initiatives which was perceived as biased in favour of MNEs due to the lack of penalties and inadequate remedies for affected employees.[56]

The analysis of the Directive yielded insights into the potential impact of the Directive on its scope, monitoring, enforcement procedures, as well as its positive and negative effects. The chapter established that the Directive extends to MNE's operations and business partners, including subsidiaries and suppliers. To prevent undue burden on MNEs, the Directive introduces the concept of established business relationships, limiting application to well-known business partners. While there is potential for manipulation, the limitation is deemed reasonable and justifiable, considering the impracticality of enforcing due diligence on every supplier. It is submitted that it would not be practical for the MNE to enforce due diligence requirements to every supplier as such would need extensive financial and human resources.

The Directive introduces mechanisms for monitoring compliance at both national and EU levels, aiming to ensure consistent standards across EU member countries and prevent a race to the bottom approach. The EU member countries would set up institutions to handle labour relations disputes against MNEs. Such disputes may emanate from any country on the world where there are MNEs doing significant business at the EU. This has the potential of rendering the EU registered MNEs to be less competitive against MNEs from other countries where human rights due diligence is not existing or not mandatory. However, this study concludes that the EU market is huge, and the mandatory human rights due diligence will have a positive impact on working conditions of the employees in many countries.

While the Directive provides a procedure for finding MNEs guilty of violations, it also includes limitations on MNE liability in certain situations, such as adverse impacts caused by indirect partners with established business relationships and contractual assurances backed by verification processes. Farah et al. argue that such limitation reduces the efficacy in achieving improved outcomes for workers and insufficient to prevent and address human rights impacts.

There are however several benefits of the Directive in that employees will in addition to their national remedies also have international platform for dispute resolution. Overall, the Directive represents a significant step towards stronger accountability and working conditions, albeit with some limitations that warrant consideration.

It is submitted that the international organisations, particularly the ILO, which has been in the process of adopting a similar instrument for over five decades, may

---

[55] Cernic (2022), p. 22.

[56] Rusinova and Korotkov (2021), p. 67.

draw important lessons from the Directive. Similarly, the NGOs which handle labour disputes against MNEs on a voluntary basis may also take some lessons from the Directive.

References

Bueno N, Bernaz N, Holly G, Ortega M (2024) The EU Directive on Corporate Sustainability Due Diligence (CSDDD): the final political compromise. Bus Hum Rights J

Cernic J (2022) The Human Rights Due Diligence Standard-Setting in the European Union: Bridging the Gap Between Ambition and Reality. Global Business Law Review

Farah Y, Kunuji V, Kent A (2022) Civil liability under sustainability due diligence legislation: a quiet revolution? Kings Law J

Hasselblatt M (2023) Unravelling corporate civil liability in the proposal for a Corporate Sustainability Due Diligence Directive through value chain governance and the concept of sustainability due diligence (Master thesis). Lund University

Jäger J, Durán G, Schmidt L (2023) Expected economic effects of the EU Corporate Sustainability Due Diligence Directive (CSDDD). Verlag Arbeiterkammer Wien

Kilimciolu B, Ann-Charlotte N (2023) Taking a closer look at the prevention and remediation mechanisms of the Corporate Sustainability Due Diligence Directive and the Loi de Vigilance. The NOVA BHRE Blog 3

Lafarre A, Rombouts B (2022) Towards mandatory human rights due diligence: assessing its impact on fundamental labour standards in global value chains. Social Science Research Network

Lennarts L (2023) Civil liability of companies for failure to conduct corporate sustainability due diligence throughout their value chains - Is Art. 22 CSDDD fit for purpose? Ondernemingsrecht

Levashova Y (2024) Mandatory human rights due diligence: what does it mean for foreign investors and why should it be in IIAs? Working paper No. 381. Columbia Center on Sustainable Investment

Otteburn K, Marx A (2003) Seeking corporate accountability: progress and pitfalls of mandatory due diligence. University of Leuven

Pacces A (2023) Law Working Paper NO 691/2023 University of Amsterdam

Pantazi T (2022) The proposed Corporate Sustainability Due Diligence Directive and its provisions on civil liability and private international law in particular. Adjuris

Patrin M (2021) The Brussels effect: how the European union rules the world. Eur J Leg Stud

Rusinova V, Korotkov S (2021) Mandatory human rights due diligence models: shooting blanks? Russian Law J

Saloranta J & Hurmerinta-Haanpää A (2022) Proactive contract theory in the context of corporate sustainability due diligence. Journal of Strategic Contracting and Negotiation

Schall A (2024) The CSDDD: good law or bad law? Eur Company Law J

Schmidt K, José M (2023) Assessing the impact of mandatory corporate sustainability due diligence for the greening of EU competition law. Social Science Research Network

Straver H (2024) Navigating the CSDD directive proposal: implications and strategic planning for procurement in financial organisations (PHD Thesis). University of Twente

Trombin E (2023) Measuring the Brussels effect of the due diligence directive (PHD Thesis). Free International University of Social Studies

Villiers C (2018) Collective responsibility and the limits of disclosure in regulating global supply chains. Deakin Law Rev

Zonta E (2024) The EU's CSDDD: lawful extraterritoriality or jurisdictional overreach? Trento Student Law Rev

Chapter 8
Conclusion

8.1 Introduction

The responsibility of MNEs for the prevention of human and labour rights violations across their global operations remains a contentious topic among scholars and human rights professionals. One issue that arises is whether MNEs should be legally required to utilise their influence to ensure that their suppliers, business partners, and sub-contractors comply with established international human and labour rights standards. This is a difficult undertaking as MNEs operate at an international level where binding ILO conventions are not enforceable, leading to a regulatory gap. As a result, their compliance with labour standards is primarily governed by voluntary soft law instruments. Despite considerable academic research on the effectiveness of these voluntary measures, significant gaps and unanswered questions persist regarding their regulatory efficacy.[1] This study aims to address these challenges by providing answers to four key research questions.

The first research question asked in Chap. 1 is whether labour rights should be classified as human rights.[2] This enquiry was approached by considering two different viewpoints. The first view unconditionally acknowledges labour rights as human rights, while the second viewpoint argues that human rights should be restricted to a modest list.[3] It is crucial to determine the answer to this question because recognising labour rights as human rights would prohibit MNEs from disregarding these rights for their own convenience. This would require a thorough investigation in the event of any violations. This inquiry also sets the goal of determining whether the

[1] See Chap. 1 para 1.3.

[2] See Chap. 1 para 1.2.

[3] See Chap. 2 para 2.3.

F. Maluleke, *Compliance with Decent Work Standards by Multinational Enterprises*, European Yearbook of International Economic Law 48,
https://doi.org/10.1007/978-3-032-21261-0_8

current regulatory instruments ensure that MNEs work towards eliminating human and labour rights violations and seek to promote decent work standards.

The second research question delved into the effectiveness of the dispute resolution mechanisms provided by the ILO and the Organisation for Economic Co-operation and Development (OECD) related to complaints of human and labour rights violations against MNEs.[4] Three public institutions have adopted legal instruments specially intended to regulate MNEs. These instruments include the ILO MNE Declaration, OECD Guidelines, and CSDDD. While the ILO MNE Declaration and OECD Guidelines are considered soft law instruments, the CSDDD is a hard law instrument. Although the CSDDD is yet to be implemented, the EU parliament voted in its favour. Both the OECD Guidelines and the ILO MNE Declaration aim to prevent and protect employees from business human and labour rights abuses. In cases where abuse has occurred, these instruments strive to ensure that employees have access to remedies in accordance with UNGPs.

In the third research question, this study examined the effectiveness of the dispute resolution mechanisms provided by NGOs related to complaints of human and labour rights violations against MNEs.[5] The main aim of these NGOs is to establish and enforce the human and labour rights standards by MNEs.[6] Furthermore, NGOs also strive to protect employees from human and labour rights abuses and provide access to remedies to employees where violations occurred.[7] By analysing the strengths and weaknesses of NGOs as regulatory institutions, this study can pinpoint areas for improvement and gain a better understanding on how to encourage compliance with labour standards.[8]

Moving on to the fourth research question, this study explored the role of International Framework Agreements (IFAs) in holding MNEs accountable for human rights and labour rights violations within their global supply chains. As MNEs continue to globalise, negotiations between trade unions and companies are mostly limited to national levels, leaving employees in the global supply chain without a voice.[9] By improving collective bargaining at the international level, this study submits that it can ensure that MNEs are held responsible for the working conditions of their employees worldwide.[10] This would contribute to creating a more equitable and just global labour system, where decent working conditions are reflected in the profits of MNEs.[11]

The following sections articulate the outcomes in a positive and constructive light, along with specific recommendations for improvement. In the final instance,

---

[4] See Chap. 1 para 1.2.

[5] See Chap. 1 para 1.2.

[6] See Chap. 5 para 5.3.

[7] See Chap. 5 para 5.2.

[8] See Chap. 5 para 5.2.

[9] See Chap. 6 para 6.1.

[10] See Chap. 6 para 6.2.

[11] See Chap. 6 para 6.2.

this study proposes the addition of an addendum to the ILO MNE Declaration. It is suggested that the proposed addendum could be a crucial step towards strengthening the ILO MNE Declaration. It is submitted that the addendum could have a positive impact on the regulation of MNEs regarding human and labour rights.

8.2 Conclusions with Respect to Question 1

8.2.1 Are Labour Rights Human Rights?

In addressing the inquiry on whether labour rights are human rights, this study adopted three tests: the positivist approach, instrumental approach and normative approach.[12] The applied tests conclusively demonstrated that labour rights are indeed human rights.[13] It is contended that the right to decent work is an indispensable element in the realisation of human rights. Even in situations where the proposition is uncertain, it is argued that ignoring labour rights is incompatible with the fulfilment of human rights.

It is further argued that work plays a crucial role in the lives of many individuals worldwide as it serves as a primary means of earning an income to meet essential needs such as food, clothing, shelter, education, and healthcare.[14] As such, the realisation of labour rights is a critical vehicle for achieving traditional human rights.[15] For instance, the right to life cannot be fully attained without a job that provides a fair wage, offers a leave of absence, eliminates hazardous labour, and prohibits forced labour and excessive overtime.[16]

It is crucial to acknowledge the potential dangers of limiting the regulation of labour rights outside human rights principles.[17] It is submitted that such an approach could risk commodifying labour and exploiting workers' rights. The ILO firmly believes that labour is not a commodity.[18] Given the recognition that labour rights are a fundamental aspect of human rights, it becomes imperative to establish robust legal frameworks that prevent the violation of such rights, even by MNEs. These frameworks should offer effective remedies to workers who suffer such violations.

---

[12] See Chap. 2 para 2.4.

[13] See Chap. 2 para 2.4.

[14] Frey and MacNaughton (2016), p. 1.

[15] See Chap. 2 para 2.4.

[16] As above.

[17] See Chap. 2 para 2.3.

[18] As above.

8.2.2 *Implications for Classifying Labour Rights as Human Rights*

The concept of human rights encompasses a set of fundamental rights and freedoms that every individual possesses simply by virtue of being human.[19] The Universal Declaration of Human Rights states in its preamble that recognising the inherent dignity and equal, inalienable rights of all members of the human family is the foundation for freedom, justice, and peace in the world.[20] It is argued that classifying labour rights as human rights would elevate them to the same status as the rights to life, liberty, and security, as well as protections against torture, discrimination, and arbitrary detention.

The implementation and protection of human rights typically occur through various entities and procedures at domestic, regional, and international levels.[21] Different enforcement mechanisms, such as monitoring mechanisms, have been established to oversee the implementation of human rights obligations.[22]These mechanisms include individual complaint procedures, treaty bodies, and courts, which are discussed in more detail below:

8.2.3 *Individual Complaint Mechanisms*

A human rights treaty is a formal document negotiated by States that imposes binding obligations on State parties to protect and promote rights and freedoms, provided they have officially ratified the treaty.[23] Classifying labour rights as human rights would be a significant step toward enforcing these rights, as some human rights treaties include provisions for individual complaint mechanisms. These mechanisms allow individuals to bring allegations of human rights violations before international bodies.[24] For example, the International Covenant on Civil and Political Rights (ICCPR) permits individuals to submit complaints to the Human Rights Committee.[25] The complaints are handled by quasi-judicial processes designed to be simple and accessible to the public.[26] This approach could help bridge the governance

---

[19] Dargad (2017), p. 904.

[20] Mantu (2019), p. 5.

[21] Dargad (2017), p. 904.

[22] Atta (2024), p. 53.

[23] https://www.ohchr.org/en/treaty-bodies/human-rights-bodies-complaints-procedures/complaints-procedures-under-human-rights-treaties#:~:text=This%20part%20of%20the%20Fact%20Sheet%20explains%20the,Elimination%20of%20All%20Forms%20of%20Discrimination%20against%20Women. Date visited 23 September 2025.

[24] Atta (2024), p. 55.

[25] As above.

[26] As above.

gap, providing workers who are victims of severe human and labour rights violations with a platform to lodge complaints and seek remedies.

8.2.4 International and Regional Courts International

States have an obligation to investigate gross violations of human rights and, if sufficient evidence is found, to prosecute the individuals allegedly responsible and punish them if they are found guilty.[27] Additionally, states must provide adequate, effective, and prompt reparations for the harm suffered. This can include restitution, compensation, rehabilitation, satisfaction, and guarantees of non-repetition. It is argued that categorising labour rights could reshape how courts address human rights violations.

A landmark judgment from the Gauteng South Division of the High Court of South Africa demonstrated that violations of human and labour rights can result in severe penalties for both individuals and businesses. In this case, seven Chinese nationals and one business entity, Beautiful Life (Pty) Ltd, were found guilty of various labour law violations, including child labour, forced labour, and non-compliance with the national minimum wage.[28] The accused received guilty verdicts on 160 counts, leading to direct imprisonment for 20 years each and a fine of R300,000 for the business entity.[29]

Cases of human rights violations that cannot be addressed through national courts should be elevated to international courts. These courts function as instruments of justice that operate beyond national borders, holding states and individuals accountable for serious violations of human dignity and freedoms.[30] Their establishment reflects a global consensus that certain rights are so fundamental that their protection should not be left solely to the discretion of individual governments.

Elevating labour rights to human rights would make it possible for workers who are victims of human rights violations to approach the courts, such as the International Court of Justice (ICJ) and the European Court of Human Rights (ECHR). In this context, the role of international courts is multifaceted, involving adjudication, interpretation, enforcement, and norm-setting in the realm of human rights.[31] Judgments from these courts often draw global condemnation and can lead to diplomatic, economic, or political repercussions.[32]

---

[27] Ratner et al. (2009), p. 114.

[28] https://www.gov.za/news/media-statements/employment-and-labour-sentencing-seven-chinese-nationals-160-counts-human. Date visited 20 September 2025.

[29] As above.

[30] https://lawvs.com/articles/the-role-of-international-courts-in-enforcing-human-rights date visited 23 September 2025.

[31] As above.

[32] As above.

It is submitted that characterisation of labour rights as human rights would promote compliance with core labour rights and contribute significantly to the attainment of decent work.

8.3 Conclusions in Respect of Question 2

The evaluation of the effectiveness of the OECD and the ILO's complaints-handling mechanisms regarding violations of human and labour rights by MNEs.

Three prominent public institutions prioritise monitoring and enforcement of international labour standards in global supply chains, namely, the ILO, OECD, and EU. The ILO has implemented the ILO MNE Declaration, while the OECD has adopted the OECD Guidelines, and the EU has embraced the CSDDD which is yet to be implemented but approved by the EU parliament. Below I discuss the findings in respect of both instruments (ILO MNE Declaration and OECD Guidelines).

8.3.1 The ILO MNE Declaration

The ILO was established in 1919, and it has been responsible for setting decent work standards in the form of conventions. The ILO encourages its member countries to ratify these conventions and enforce compliance through national legislation.[33] However, the emergence of powerful MNEs in the labour market due to rapid globalisation has fundamentally changed the situation.[34] It is acknowledged that MNEs conduct business in a complex network across many countries, and employees involved in producing goods and products for these companies are mostly subcontractors and suppliers.[35]

The current approach of the ILO has left a significant gap, enabling MNEs to operate without any labour laws or regulations.[36] As a result, competition has been based on conditions of work among ILO member states, leading to a race to the bottom. This has resulted in MNEs showing an increasing interest in setting up factories in countries with lower labour standards, while governments of poor ILO member states have lowered their standards to attract MNEs.[37] Unfortunately, this approach has purposefully weakened the position of workers and their trade unions.

[33] See Chap. 3 para 3.1.

[34] See Chap. 3 para 3.1.

[35] See Chap. 1 para 1.2.

[36] See Chap. 3 para 3.1.

[37] As above.

The ILO member states have been very slow to conclude a convention which can regulate MNEs at the international level.[38] Instead, to counter this challenge and to level the playing field, the ILO adopted the ILO MNE Declaration to specifically regulate MNEs. The ILO MNE Declaration sets out the human and labour rights standards that MNEs are expected to follow.[39] Such standards include the promotion of employment; social security; elimination of forced or compulsory labour; effective abolition of child labour: minimum age and worst forms, equality of opportunities, employment, and training.[40]

The ILO MNE Declaration places great emphasis on the responsibility of governments to safeguard the rights of workers and provide them with effective remedies in case of any abuse within their jurisdiction.[41] MNEs, on the other hand, are expected to leverage their influence to encourage business partners to provide similar remedies for the infringement of labour standards.[42] Despite these efforts, evidence shows that employees whose rights have been violated by MNEs still struggle to obtain the necessary remedies.[43]

Instead, there is overwhelming evidence that labour rights and decent work standards are being violated in global supply chains. As a result, employees are unable to find remedies from MNEs through national and international laws.[44] It is argued that this is due in part to the absence of an international institution or mechanism capable of handling claims against MNEs, which presents a major challenge for employees.[45] In some cases, employees must resort to costly civil action to find relief against these companies.[46]

It is concerning that MNEs continue to bypass national laws as they operate at the international level, and they are only regarded as buyers of goods produced in their supply chains.[47] As such, they do not incur any legal liability when labour rights are being violated in such workplaces because they are not employers. There is therefore an urgent need for the ILO and its member states to introduce effective dispute resolution procedures in this area. Even though the adoption of the ILO MNE Declaration was a step in the right direction, but there is still work to be done to strengthen its monitoring and enforcement procedures.

The ILO MNE Declaration outlines a process for addressing disputes relating to its application, specifically, through an interpretation procedure.[48] However, this

---

[38] See Chap. 3 para 3.4.

[39] See Chap. 2 para 2.1.

[40] See Chap. 2 para 2.1.

[41] See Chap. 2 para 2.4.

[42] See Chap. 2 para 2.4.

[43] As above.

[44] See Chap. 2 para 2.2.

[45] See Chap. 2 para 2.2.

[46] *Bongani Nkala and Others v Harmony Gold Mining Company Ltd and 31 Others.*

[47] See Chap. 3 para 3.1.

[48] See Chap. 3 para 3.2.

procedure has limitations, as it only pertains to disputes regarding the meaning of the ILO MNE Declaration arising from the actual situation and among the involved parties.[49]

This study argues that the most practical approach to address the current gap is by establishing a partnership between the ILO and NGOs that currently handle the resolution of labour disputes between MNEs and employees.[50] This can be achieved by adding an addendum to the ILO MNE Declaration that will outline the specific terms of cooperation between the ILO and NGOs. To ensure compliance with decent work standards, the addendum should include provisions for NGO accreditation.

It is suggested that these NGOs would be tasked with handling complaints against their member MNEs, and the ILO would be responsible for reviewing their reports. It is expected that MNEs and NGOs will accept the proposed amendments, as similar procedures already exist through the adoption of codes of conduct. Weiss argues that incorporating NGOs into the ILO poses challenges regarding legitimacy and representation, but at the same time, he emphasises that it is worth exploring this possibility and address any concerns that may arise.[51]

8.3.2 OECD Guidelines

The OECD Guidelines prescribe labour standards that MNEs are expected to follow, which align with the ILO conventions and often exceed them in quality.[52] However, the OECD Guidelines lack legally binding mechanisms and depend on voluntary compliance.[53] The OECD Guidelines also establish focal points (NCPs) responsible for handling cases of non-compliance. It is submitted that the dispute resolution under NCPs is relatively hassle-free, flexible, does not require legal expertise, and involves no financial risk.[54]

The NCPs have successfully resolved numerous disputes through mediation processes. However, the cooperation of the parties involved is crucial to the success of such proceedings.[55] It is concerning that if the MNE refuses to cooperate with the mediator, the mediation process is bound to fail, regardless of the strength of the employees' case or the gravity of the allegations against the MNE.[56] In such

[49] See Chap. 3 para 3.4.

[50] See Article 12 of the ILO Constitution.

[51] Weiss (2013), p. 13.

[52] See Chap. 4 para 4.3.

[53] As above.

[54] See Chap. 4 para 4.5.

[55] Sanchez (2015), p. 89.

[56] As above.

situations, the NCPs can only issue a statement detailing the reasons why an agreement could not be reached.[57]

It is worrisome that a significant number of cases are being rejected by NCPs without providing detailed reasons for the denials.[58] This leaves complainants without a proper appeal or review mechanisms to challenge the decisions.[59] It is suggested that NCP offices should focus on educating employees within their jurisdiction to reduce the number of rejected cases. Furthermore, it is suggested that clarifying the NCPs' limitations and outlining disputes that fall outside of their jurisdiction will reduce the percentage of complaints wrongly referred to NCPs. In cases where disputes are referred, NCPs should provide a thorough explanation for rejection, which will also serve as a valuable learning tool for OECD users.

While NCPs possess the authority to intervene in disputes, they unfortunately do not have the power to deliver a verdict, even in cases where substantial violations of the OECD Guidelines are evident.[60] It is argued that granting these powers to NCPs would earn them credibility, even in the absence of a penalty clause. It would also encourage MNEs to invest genuine effort in resolving cases, thereby avoiding a verdict that declares that they have flouted the OECD Guidelines. It is submitted that the lack of such power dilutes the effectiveness of the OECD Guidelines.

The fact that NCPs are increasingly making findings that MNEs blatantly breach the OECD Guidelines is not surprising.[61] This is an indication that the OECD Guidelines are not effective and need to be revised to grant NCPs the power to make findings that are reasonably necessary in cases that cannot be resolved through mediation. Lastly, the major concern is that complainants in cases where mediation fails have no other way of obtaining remedies.[62] This is against the UNGPs which mandates that the employees who suffer human rights violations should have access to effective remedies. It is worrying that despite the recent update to the OECD Guidelines, this area has remained unchanged.

It is argued that the OECD Guidelines are outdated and need urgent revision. The NCPs have the potential to be the ideal state-based non-judicial grievance mechanism, as called for in the UNGP. To ensure that the OECD Guidelines have a wider reach, cooperation with the ILO is necessary since the OECD Guidelines are applicable mainly to EU Countries and exclude many countries.

---

[57] See Chap. 3 para 3.3.

[58] See Chap. 3 para 3.3.

[59] See Chap. 3 para 3.3.

[60] Chapter 4 para 4.3.

[61] Chapter 4 para 4.3. See the case of *Canada Tibet Committee v China Gold International Resources Corp.*

[62] Chapter 4 para 4.3.

8.4 Conclusions with Respect to Question 3

The effectiveness of the dispute resolution mechanisms provided by NGOs.

In the early 1990s, a series of activist and media campaigns brought to light the violations of human and labour rights in global garment supply chains.[63] These violations included child labour, sexual harassment, forced overtime, violations of minimum and overtime wages, and union avoidance. The publicised concerns led to an increase in pressure to have effective government-enforced mechanisms to hold MNEs accountable for the human and labour rights violations committed in their supply chains.[64] Responding to such pressures, many prominent MNEs collaborated with NGOs, which in turn adopted voluntary codes of conduct with a view of improving working conditions throughout their supply chains, to prevent possible regulation by government authorities.[65]

These NGOs defined labour standards, which the member MNEs are obliged to adhere to.[66] The continued membership of MNEs is contingent upon their commitment to upholding the established labour standards, not just within their operation but also throughout their supply chain.[67] Under international law, MNEs are typically not held responsible for the working conditions of employees in their supply chains if those employees are employed by independent factories.[68]

Nonetheless, there are specific scenarios where MNEs may be held responsible for labour rights violations committed by third parties. This often occurs when the MNEs' subsidiaries employ workers in a country other than the home state of the MNE.[69] In such situations, employees may pursue civil actions in the courts of the home country where the MNE is registered. However, these legal proceedings are frequently deemed unsuitable for labour disputes due to their complexity and the high costs involved.[70]

It is submitted that it is challenging to hold MNEs accountable for any human and labour rights violations committed by independent third parties, such as their factories or suppliers.[71] This is because MNEs are not employers of these workers and therefore cannot be held liable for any violations of labour rights. Even though MNEs have the power to influence compliance with labour standards and own the products produced by these factories, legally speaking, attempting to hold them

---

[63] See Chap. 5 para 5.1.

[64] See Chap. 5 para 5.1.

[65] See Chap. 5 para 5.1.

[66] See Chap. 5 para 5.1.

[67] See Chap. 5 para 5.1.

[68] See Chap. 1 para 1.1.

[69] The case of *Lubbe v Cape plc* 1545 (2000) is a good example. In the said case, the court had to answer the question whether a parent company was liable for failure to ensure the observance of proper health and safety standards by its overseas subsidiaries.

[70] See Chap. 1 para 1.3.

[71] See Chap. 1 para 1.3.

liable for the actions of independent third parties is not a viable option under the current laws.[72]

It is submitted that NGOs play a vital role in monitoring and enforcing compliance with internationally recognised human and labour rights standards by MNEs. It is argued that the system is uniquely positioned to deliver such results, leveraging various mechanisms such as requiring MNEs to conduct auditing in their entire supply chain and to ensure compliance with labour standards. It also establishes grievance and dispute resolution mechanisms that are accessible to employees whose rights have been violated by these companies.[73]

The use of NGOs in regulating MNEs have shown promising results.[74] This regulatory regime offers a viable alternative to statutory dispute resolutions, which are often hampered by technical and jurisdictional challenges.[75] Such a system is capable of achieving results by bypassing the technical and jurisdictional challenges faced by employees in statutory dispute resolutions.[76] The regime is able to hold MNEs accountable for a wide range of workplace issues including those committed by their suppliers/sub-contractors.[77] Another benefit of this system is that when multiple MNEs source products from the same factory, they can work together to ensure compliance with labour standards and protect the rights of employees.[78] In cases where MNEs fail to use their leverage to secure compliance, they may be held jointly liable.

However, there are still weaknesses that need to be addressed to meet the regulatory challenges. For instance, despite the number of MNEs collaborating with NGOs, thereby committing to the implementation of codes of conduct in factories, sub-contractors, and suppliers, these measures have failed to reduce labour violations significantly.[79] Currently, the only method to penalise MNEs for such violations is through public shaming, which threatens their reputation. Unfortunately,

---

[72] See Chap. 1 para 1.3.

[73] See Chap. 1 para 1.2.

[74] See the case of PT Hansoll Hyun (a factory that was in Indonesia) the factory closed without securing money for payment of severance pay. Through many months of engagement, the WRC was able to ensure that Abercrombie & Fitch and Hansoll Textile, which sourced at Hansoll Hyun on Abercrombie & Fitch's behalf, was able to secure an additional $2.52 million contribution from Hansoll Textile to compensate the workers. Kesehatan (healthcare) https://www.workersrights.org/wp-content/uploads/2022/01/WRC-re-Hansoll-Hyun-Indonesia-01202022.pdf date visited 24 September 2025.

[75] In PT Hansoll Hyun (a factory that was in Indonesia) the factory closed without securing money for payment of severance pay. Through many months of engagement, the WRC was able to ensure that Abercrombie & Fitch and Hansoll Textile, which sourced at Hansoll Hyun on Abercrombie & Fitch's behalf, was able to secure an additional $2.52 million contribution from Hansoll Textile to compensate the workers. Kesehatan (healthcare) https://www.workersrights.org/wp-content/uploads/2022/01/WRC-re-Hansoll-Hyun-Indonesia-01202022.pdf date visited 24 September 2025.

[76] See Chap. 5 para 5.1.

[77] See Chap. 5 para 5.1.

[78] See Chap. 5 para 5.6.

[79] Bair and Palpacuer (2015) *JTA* 184.

this reliance on reputation alone has proven to be insufficient in incentivising adherence to established standards.

Additionally, even if international standards exist that could potentially prevent or decrease labour violations, MNEs cannot be held liable for violations that occur within the host country's regulations. It is submitted that the lack of accountability is a significant obstacle to the success of codes of conduct in eradicating labour violations.[80]

Further, it is important to mention that not all MNEs rely on their reputation to secure projects, tenders, and contracts. As a result, the potential negative impact on their brand may not affect them. Moreover, NGOs have been hesitant to publicly identify and shame non-compliant MNEs. This is primarily because these NGOs are funded by MNEs and exposing non-compliance may impact their revenue.[81] As a result, instances of non-compliance are kept confidential and the effectiveness of codes of conduct is significantly limited.

It is submitted that the implementation of an efficient and transparent accreditation process of NGOs is crucial to establish a rigorous system for evaluating, monitoring, and verifying MNEs' performance against a set of pre-defined international standards. In this respect, the ILO would supervise its effectiveness. It is submitted that a transparent system of evaluating and monitoring MNEs' performance against international standards, with a clear system of penalties when standards are breached, is urgently needed.

Such can be achieved by cooperation between the ILO and NGOs that are currently responsible for monitoring labour standards by MNEs. This should take place by incorporating the role of NGOs into ILO functions. However, for such an approach to be successful, the ILO should add the fourth category in addition to its current three accreditation lists of NGOs.[82] The fourth category of accredited NGOs should ideally focus on the establishment, monitoring, and enforcement of internationally recognised labour standards by MNEs. In terms of the recommended procedure, the ILO should set requirements for accreditation in respect of the list of accredited NGOs. This will include requirements to remain accredited and the power of the ILO to suspend or cancel the accreditation.

8.5 Conclusions in Respect of Question 4

The role of International Framework Agreements (IFAs) in holding MNEs accountable for human rights and labour rights violations within their global supply chains.

[80] Moghaddam and Zare (2017), p. 79.

[81] See Chap. 5 para 5.2.

[82] See Chap. 5 para 5.2.

The modern MNEs are structured in a way that grants a separate legal personality to the companies in their supply chain.[83] This means that MNEs are not held accountable for the working conditions in their suppliers' factories, even though the products produced by these factories are ultimately sold by MNEs. Unfortunately, poor working conditions in the supply chains of MNEs continue to persist, as these companies can generate significant profits without incurring the corresponding labour relations costs.[84] The lack of effective collective bargaining at the international level to regulate these matters is a challenge, as labour relations is mostly regulated at the national level.

It is submitted that MNEs generate considerable profits, which are more than enough to guarantee decent wages for all their employees including those in their supply chains. However, the problem lies with the fact that the employees in their supply chains are not directly employed by MNEs but are hired by third party companies instead.[85] The existing laws do not provide a framework for employees or trade unions to negotiate directly with MNEs to improve working conditions. Instead, they must negotiate with third-party companies.

It is argued that the IFAs system is unique in its ability to bridge the gap between global trade unions and MNEs. By providing a platform for direct negotiation, trade unions can participate in setting standards, which is crucial for achieving fair working conditions.[86] It is the responsibility of trade unions to advocate for their employees and ensure that their interests are represented in the standard-setting process, including items such as wage and working conditions.

However, there are currently no laws in place governing the issues that can be negotiated between global trade unions and MNEs. As a result, MNEs are typically only willing to negotiate on issues related to standards they have committed to comply with, such as those laid out in the ILO conventions.[87] This study found that the IFAs system focuses on six key points, including global agreement, reference to ILO conventions, clauses requiring MNEs to influence suppliers, involvement of global trade unions in the implementation process, and the right to bring complaints.[88]

It is worrisome that some IFAs lack the above basic terms, and it is argued that such IFAs are ineffective.[89] At times, such IFAs do not have important clauses such as extension to suppliers, sub-contractors, and subsidiaries. As such, they may be of no value to the employees responsible for producing the products. The most crucial one is that they also do not have clauses on how complaints must be addressed. In

[83] See Chap. 6 para 6.1.

[84] See Chap. 6 para 6.1.

[85] See Chap. 6 para 6.1.

[86] See Chap. 6 para 6.1.

[87] See Chap. 6 para 6.3.

[88] See Chap. 6 para 6.8.

[89] See Chap. 6 para 6.3.

the absence of efforts to ensure that suppliers are expected to comply with the IFAs, their impact will be insignificant.

The further challenge of the IFA system lies in its implementation.[90] The non-compliance with terms of IFAs is often committed in factories and sub-contractors which enjoy separate legal personalities from MNEs. Even in the situation where the IFA refers to suppliers and sub-contractors, the latter are not bound by the terms of IFAs. The reference to sub-contractors, suppliers, and (or) factories does not create a legal obligation on them. The agreement concluded by the GUFs and MNEs does not bind third parties even if the latter are mentioned in the IFAs.

Most of the times, IFAs refer to all suppliers while not all of them are known to MNEs. As a result, suppliers are not always aware that they must comply with IFAs. Neither are the employees aware that their factories are under an obligation to comply with IFAs. At times, the workplace of third parties may not be highly unionised making it difficult for the employees to follow up on the existing IFAs. Further, under existing law it is impermissible for two parties to conclude a binding agreement to third parties who are not a party to the negotiation process.[91]

It is submitted that to ensure the effectiveness of IFAs, it is crucial to clearly define essential focal points. Developing and issuing guidelines for IFAs at the ILO level is highly recommended. It should also be mandatory for IFAs to be registered at the ILO MNE office, which will serve as a hub for IFAs. These guidelines should include a clause stating that the MNE agrees to incorporate compliance with IFAs in its contracts with suppliers and sub-contractors. This will overcome the legal challenge that suppliers and sub-contractors are not bound by IFAs.

This proposal would align well with the proposed registration of NGOs by the ILO. As such, the ILO may require NGOs seeking accreditation to prescribe a requirement that their member MNEs conclude IFAs.

8.6 Overall Conclusions

The governments of the ILO member states cannot possibly inspect every workplace and catch every violator of human and labour rights. Globalisation has made it increasingly difficult for trade unions to effectively organise employees, particularly in sweatshop industries. It is submitted that private labour regulation systems aimed at MNEs offer viable options to supplement existing mechanisms. It is submitted that such a system creates requirements for MNEs to leverage their purchasing decisions to influence suppliers, sub-contractors, and subsidiaries to promote compliance with labour rights and decent work standards.

However, MNEs currently lack the legal power to enforce compliance by third parties. This is due to the absence of laws empowering them to do so, as well as the

---

[90] See Chap. 6 para 6.3.

[91] See Chap. 6 para 6.3.

challenges of monitoring compliance with human and labour rights across their global supply chains due to manpower shortages. Furthermore, the private regulatory system lacks credibility, as MNEs cannot be trusted to police themselves. Even in cases where MNEs utilise the services of auditing firms, they are still viewed as lacking credibility due to their main funding coming from MNEs themselves.

In response to the adverse effects of globalisation, a system of MNE regulation of a public nature was established. This resulted in the adoption of OECD Guidelines and the ILO MNE Declaration by the ILO. These guidelines are considered excellent standards-setting documents and promote negotiation and mediation as the preferred methods to ensure MNE compliance with decent work standards. However, like private regulatory institutions, the OECD Guidelines and the ILO MNE Declaration suffer from a lack of penalties or sanctions for non-compliance by MNEs. Therefore, their ability to promote compliance with set work standards is limited.

When compared to the ILO, the OECD has made noticeable progress with NPCs, even though the OECD Guidelines do not expressly provide for NCPs with the power to grant remedies. It is submitted that the findings made by NCPs constitute recommendations, and the penalty for non-compliance is name and shame or receiving bad publicity, rather than legal liability.[92] It is argued that the compliance mechanisms put in place by the ILO, the OECD, and private NGOs have failed to address violations of human and labour rights in global supply chains effectively. Furthermore, the limited presence of these private NGOs in certain parts of the world has made it difficult to monitor compliance globally. It is therefore submitted that the ILO has become the most important institution in this regard, since it is embraced by many countries and can reach most countries.

However, it would not be practical or reasonable for the ILO to establish complaint resolution institutions globally. Therefore, it is crucial to establish cooperation between NGOs responsible for monitoring decent work standards compliance by MNEs, and the ILO should encourage the establishment of such NGOs worldwide. Currently, these NGOs have only been established in certain parts of the world, like the FLA and SA8000 in the US, and the ETI and CCC from the UK and Netherlands. It is submitted that these NGOs could be supervised by the ILO through an accreditation procedure, which is allowed under article 12 of the ILO Constitution.[93]

---

[92] Castermans and Van Woensel (2017), p. 98.

[93] Article 12 of the ILO Constitution states that:

1. The ILO shall cooperate within the terms of this Constitution with any general international organisation entrusted with the coordination of the activities of public international organisations having specialised responsibilities and with public international organisations having specialised responsibilities in related fields.

2. The ILO may make appropriate arrangements for the representatives of public international organisations to participate without vote in its deliberations.

The ILO has a history of collaborating with NGOs since 1956. The ILO has several NGOs with general consultative status and a special list of more than 150 international NGOs.[94] To join the special list, an NGO must demonstrate its interest in the ILOs' programme of meetings and provide addresses of its officers.[95] It is submitted that the said NGOs should comply with the above criteria. There are however concerns from members of ILO tripartite structure especially trade unions that view NGOs as being not representative of workers.[96]

It is submitted that despite these concerns, NGOs are significant global players in civil society. They are voluntary, independent, non-profit, and not self-serving.[97] In order to alleviate the identified concerns, it is recommended that NGOs responsible for setting decent work standards and handling of complaints against MNEs should be administered by the ILO MNE office, which already exists within the structures of the ILO. The ILO GB is to set the expected standards, and the NGOs seeking accreditation and registration by the ILO should comply with such requirements. The ILO's senior structures will reserve the right to revoke the accreditation of NGOs failing to meet the standards of the ILO. In short, the NGOs will be subordinate to senior structures of the ILO, such as the ILC.

8.7 Recommendation: Addendum to the ILO MNE Declaration: Supervisory and Accreditation Procedure

Currently, the ILO accredits NGOs under three categories, namely, General Consultation status, Specialist and Roster status.[98] This study proposes an addition of the fourth category which will be reserved for NGOs that have expertise in handling labour and human rights complaints against MNEs.[99] Currently, such NGOs amongst others include, FLA, FWF, WRC and CCC.[100] To be accredited in this category, interested NGOs should in addition to commitment to the ILO

3. The ILO may make suitable arrangements for such consultation as it may think desirable with recognised non-governmental international organisations, including international organisations of employers, workers, agriculturists and co-operators.

[94] Amnesty International, the International Center for Human Rights and democratic development, the Consultative Council of Jewish Organizations, the European Disability Forum, the International Association for Mutual Assistance, the International Federation of Human Rights, the World Union of Professions, etc. https://www.ilo.org/pardev/partnerships/civil-society/ngos/ilo-special-list-of-ngos/lang%2D%2Den/index.htm date visited 12 September 2025.

[95] See Chap. 5 para 5.1.

[96] See Chap. 5 Para 5.1.

[97] Spooner (2004), p. 19.

[98] See Chap. 5 para 5.2.

[99] See Chap. 5 para 5.8.

[100] See Chap. 5 para 5.3.

constitution, also have an excellent track record on dispute resolution for complaints against MNEs at international level.

As part of this procedure, it is suggested that the accredited NGOs would be required to adopt complaint-handling procedures which would be in line with the UNGPs. Furthermore, the complaints procedure should have various stages of dispute resolution which comprise of determination of admissibility, followed by investigations and thereafter remediation if the violation is established. It is suggested that the said NGOs should also provide annual statistical reports to the ILO MNE office.

In response to the identified regulatory gap, this study suggests the implementation of an accreditation procedure to be regulated and supervised by the ILO. It is submitted that the adoption of such a procedure will enhance compliance with decent work standards as contained in the ILO MNE Declaration and consequently contribute to the attainment of decent work in global supply chains.

8.8 Contents of the Suggested Addendum

8.8.1 Introduction

The subsequent section discusses the fundamental components of the proposed addendum. This encompass examining the aims and objectives of the addendum, delineating the accreditation requirements, specifying the types and nature of complaints to be addressed by NGOs, outlining the eligible complainants, proposing dispute resolution mechanisms to be undertaken by NGOs, elucidating ILO procedures and formalities, defining the powers of accredited NGOs, and laying out the process for withdrawal of accreditation by the ILO.

8.8.2 Aims and Objectives of the Accreditation Procedure

The suggested addendum aims to fulfil several objectives. Firstly, it seeks to give effect to Article 12 of the ILO constitution by enabling NGOs to gain accreditation with the ILO and contribute significantly to its work. Secondly, it aims to ensure that workers within the supply chains of MNEs have access to efficient and cost-effective dispute resolution procedures and remedies in cases where their human and labour rights are infringed upon. Thirdly, it is intended to provide guidelines for investigators appointed by NGOs on how to handle complaints lodged by employees. Finally, the proposed addendum aims to promote uniformity and reliability in the resolution of disputes in global supply chains by adopting standardised complaint-handling procedures and prescribing remedies for breaches of human and labour rights standards by MNEs.

8.8.3 Requirements for Accreditation

It is submitted that NGOs seeking accreditation to handle human and labour rights complaints against MNEs should fulfil the following six requirements: Firstly, the objectives and mission of the relevant NGOs should be in harmony with the spirit, purposes, and principles outlined in the ILO constitution. Additionally, the NGO should commit to supporting the work of the ILO and promoting knowledge of its principles and activities. Secondly, the concerned NGO should demonstrate expertise and extensive experience in handling complaints against MNEs.

Thirdly, the applicable NGO should meet all legal requirements for registration of NGOs in the country where it was incorporated. Fourthly, the NGO should have a minimum number of influential MNEs that took its membership and committed to adhering to its code of conduct. The code of conduct should include an effective complaint handling procedure containing a clear list of remedies in the event of human and labour rights violations. Lastly, persons appointed by NGOs to carry out these functions must do so independently of the state, any political party, or trade union. It is submitted that the ILO should reserve the right to request further information in support of the application and may require the applicant NGO to attend one or more meetings with them.

8.8.4 Nature of Complaints to Be Handled by NGOs

It is suggested that the scope of human and labour rights issues eligible for workers' complaints be kept wide to facilitate the promotion of decent work for a greater number of employees. These issues may include payment below the legal minimum wage, immediate hazards to worker health and safety, the violations of freedom of association, unfair discrimination, child and hazardous labour, unfair dismissal, unfair labour practice and or any other labour and human rights violations. To adequately address employee challenges, it is suggested that the accredited NGO may consider broadening the scope of eligible complaints falling under its jurisdiction.

8.8.5 Who Can Lodge Complaints

This study proposes that the complaints referral procedure should be open to both employees and their legitimate representatives, such as trade unions. In the interest of inclusivity, it is recommended that the complaints procedure be easily accessible and allow non-unionised workers to submit human and labour rights complaints against MNEs. Furthermore, it should also include any other concerned parties, including the media, who are focused on the enforcement of labour standards at third-party companies involved in the supply chains of MNEs.

8.8.6 Suggested Dispute Resolution Process

First and foremost, it is suggested that the process should provide a simple method of referral of complaints. The one effective way to achieve this is by enabling online referral submissions. It is suggested that the process should include a declaration that the complainants will not face any form of retaliation. Furthermore, there should be an option for anonymous reporting to ensure that individuals feel comfortable coming forward.

To address concerns about ILO member countries and trade unions, this study suggests that the complaints procedure should explicitly provide that the system is not designed to supersede or undermine existing functional mechanisms. Rather, it should emphasise its purpose of reinforcing local systems, empowering trade unions, and cultivating an environment conducive to constructive social dialogue. Furthermore, transparency is paramount in the complaints' procedure. It is imperative that the process and outcomes are as transparent as possible to address public interest concerns. One way to achieve this is by publishing the list of complaints and the results of the investigation process.

Furthermore, a clearly defined set of criteria for the admissibility of complaints should be outlined to prevent the rejection of valid cases and to ensure consistency and predictability in addressing complaints. Once a complaint is deemed admissible, the relevant NGO should commence the investigation. It is suggested that investigators possess the necessary qualifications and ideally have received training from the ILO. Furthermore, the investigators should be empowered to determine the culpability of the involved MNE and to propose a cause of action.

In cases where a complaint is substantiated, the investigation's conclusion should outline the comprehensive remedial actions required. The NGO should commit to providing regular updates to the ILO, including detailed information on the status and resolution of each complaint, which should be included in its public annual reports.

8.8.7 ILO Formalities

If the application of accreditation is successful, the ILO should record the accredited NGOs in its register, issue a certificate of accreditation in the NGO's name specifying the duration and terms of the accreditation and forward the certificate to the NGO. The ILO should also communicate its decision in writing to the unsuccessful NGO. In addition to the above, the ILO should annually publish a list of accredited NGOs on its official website.

8.8.8 Powers of Accredited NGOs

Upon accreditation, the NGO should be authorised to levy annual fees on its member MNEs to cover administration expenses. Additionally, accredited NGOs should be empowered to address any complaints lodged against their member MNEs and issue findings of their investigations. It is suggested that the accredited NGO should be obligated to submit reports on all referred complaints, along with comprehensive details, to the ILO on an annual basis.

8.8.9 Withdrawal of Accreditation

This study suggests that the ILO should be empowered to suspend the accreditation status of NGOs for a period of up to three years or withdraw it under the following circumstances: Firstly, if the NGO, directly or through its affiliates or representatives, engages in a pattern of acts that are contrary to the purposes and principles of the ILO constitution. This includes engaging in politically motivated acts that are incompatible with the purpose and principles of the ILO. Secondly, if there is verifiable evidence of influence from proceeds resulting from criminal activities such as money-laundering, the illicit drugs trade or the illegal arms trade. Thirdly, if in the preceding three years, the NGO did not make any positive contribution to the ILO's work. Fourthly, if the NGO fails to comply to a material extent with the terms of its accreditation.

It is submitted that the ILO may withdraw its accreditation of NGO after providing reasonable notice of the withdrawal. In instances where the ILO intends to suspend or withdraw the NGO's accreditation, the concerned NGO should be provided with written reasons for the decision and be granted an opportunity to present its response for consideration by the ILO promptly. If the NGO's accreditation status is withdrawn, it may not be eligible to reapply for membership status for three years after the date of withdrawal.

The part that follows shows the step-by-step flow chart of the recommended dispute resolution procedure (see Fig. 8.1).

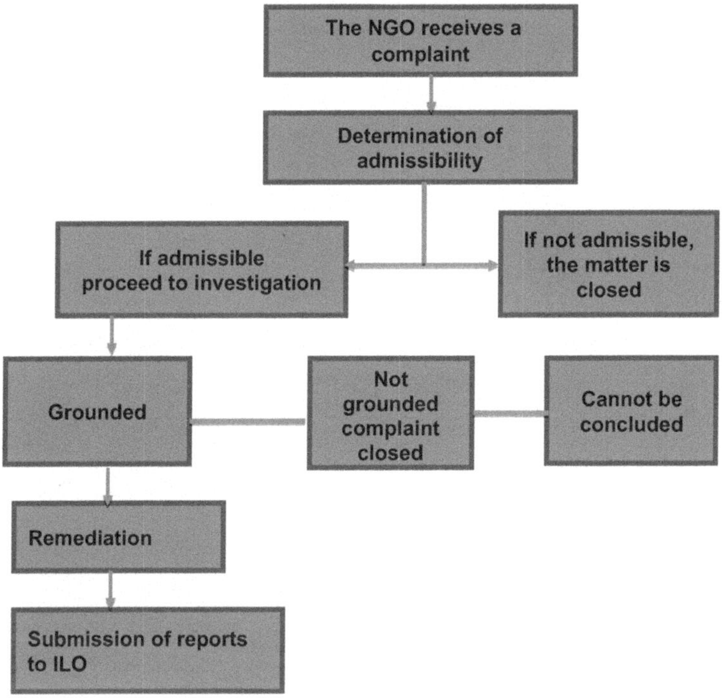

Fig. 8.1 The flow chart dispute resolution procedure

References

Atta S (2024) Effectiveness of international human rights treaties: enforcement mechanisms and compliance challenges in global governance. Int J Creat Res Thoughts

Bair J, Palpacuer F (2015) CSR beyond the corporation: contested governance in global value chains. J Transnatl Aff

Castermans A, van Woensel L (2017) CSR for young business lawyers. Eleven International Publishing

Dargad B (2017) The International Court of Justice and its role in safeguarding human rights. J Emerg Technol Innov Res

Frey D, MacNaughton G (2016) A human rights lens on full employment and decent work in the 2030 Sustainable Development Agenda. J Workplace Rights

Mantu J (2019) International institutions and the protection of human rights regionally and internationally. Social Science Research Network

Moghaddam M, Zare A (2017) Responsibilities of multinational corporations on environmental issues. Canadian Center of Science and Education

Ratner R, Abrams S, Bischoff L (2009) Accountability for human rights atrocities in international law: beyond the Nuremberg legacy. Oxford University Press

Sanchez J (2015) The roles and powers of the OECD National Contact Points regarding complaints on an alleged breach of the OECD guidelines for multinational enterprises. Nord J Int Law

Spooner D (2004) Trade unions and NGOs: the need for cooperation. Taylor & Francis, Ltd

Weiss M (2013) International labour standards: a complex public-private policy mix. Int J Comp Labour Law Ind Relat

The manufacturer's authorised representative in the EU is Springer Nature Customer Service Centre GmbH, Europaplatz 3, 69115 Heidelberg, Germany. If you have any concerns regarding our products, please contact ProductSafety@springernature.com

Printed and bound by CPI Group (UK) Ltd, Croydon, CR0 4YY
05/10/2026
02228046-0004